Pashena

the dirt field

SHINGI MAVIMA

HOUSE CAPACITY PUBLISHING

House Capacity Publishing
housecapacity@gmail.com
www.housecapacity.com

Ordering Information:
Quantity sales. Special discounts are available on quantity purchases by corporations, associations, and others. For details, contact the publisher at the address above.
Orders by U.S. trade bookstores and wholesalers. Please contact House Capacity Publishing: Tel: (586) 209-3924

Printed in the United States of America

ISBN-13: 978-0-9998863-2-8

for Gogo and Kulu—your book is here

Shingi Mavima

Acknowledgments

Ndotangira poyi? Where do I begin?

As in all things, I want to acknowledge my Creator, for in Him all things good manifest. *Pashena* has been years in the making, and I am eternally grateful for all who have helped bring this dream to light. I want to thank Amai Shingi a.k.a. "the Good Doctor," not only for loving me like only mother can, but for her unwavering commitment to seeing *Pashena* come alive. She has encouraged, edited, taken pictures, sought out publishers, edited again, and encouraged some more. Indeed, she has believed in this project—and me—more than I have many a time.

I would like to thank the slew of friends and family who read lines, revised for historical accuracy (where necessary) and plot holes, and laughed at the better parts of the story. Thanks to Takunda Mavima, Ruvimbo Gwatirisa, Tafadzwa Mudhokwani, Kudzai Tabaziba, Godwin Jabangwe, Angelee Santillo, and Innocent Bangani. Your work on the book is priceless, yet you gave it freely— and for that I am forever indebted. Special thanks to munin'ina Tinashe Nondo for the cover picture.

To the Dangamvura community at large, and to Sheni Primary School and MaOwnership in particularly, ndoite wekudini ko? I am the man I am today because of you—ndini mukorore wenyu. To my Pashena crew—Ta, Nigel, Nanu, Brighton, Trust, Blessing, Innocent, Farai, Kosi, Faru, Tinashe, Donny, Anthony nevamwe vese—this is your story; thank you for allowing me to tell it.

Thank you to everyone who has asked about the book, bought it, and helped spread the word.

Finally, I want to thank the good people at House Capacity Publishing for taking these rustic pages filled with puerile anecdotes and turning them into something readable. You have made my dream come true, and we are forever bound by this one immortal moment.

◁▷◁▷◁▷

Introduction

"Ta!" I yelled through the holes of the wire fence that separated our yard from his. "Ta! They are here! The team is here, ready to play! Ta!"

Takura, or Ta for short, was my next-door neighbor. He was the first person outside of our household that I had ever known. Our relationship had meandered through the rocky infant years, but we had since grown to be best friends.

On this day, Ta was his vintage fickle self. We had challenged a group of local boys to a game of football at our local pitch, the infamous Pashena. *Now* that they were here, Ta did not seem keen on playing. He would not even leave the house.

"Kuziwa!" I screamed his sister's name, "Kuziwa, is Takura there?"

He emerged looking like he had just woken up. "Hey Shingi, what's going on?" He asked, feigning ignorance while avoiding eye contact.

"Hurry up and get ready!" I commanded, "We are late. Richie and his boys are at the field. Everyone is already waiting!"

Reluctantly, almost apologetically, he gathered his wits and finally replied, "I am not going to be able to play today."

"What!?" I protested, "We already agreed on this yesterday. You have to play!"

"I am sorry, *sha*[1], but there is no way I am playing against those boys! I-i-it's all trouble, and I am honestly surprised that you, of all people, don't see it. Wasn't Richie just suspended from school? They are not good people, and the game just wouldn't be fun. I am sorry," he said uncompromisingly, before slamming the door behind him and shuffling back inside.

As I turned and took the seventy to eighty-meter solemn walk towards Pashena, I mumbled displeased musings to myself.

"Some friend and team player, that Ta. You just can never count on him!" There was a part of me that was genuinely disappointed that we may not have enough people to play against Richie and his friends. The sensible part of me knew that Ta was right.

Those boys were no good. People from outside our neighborhood were usually no good, and Richie and his friend were especially notorious around Dangamvura.

It was the likes of them that had led to the creation of *Pashena* in the first place.

---

1 Term of endearment; short for shamwari (friend)

1

To the unfamiliar eye, Pashena is a 60 by 8-meter patch of dirt in the unremarkable Home Ownership neighborhood of the Dangamvura area in Mutare, Zimbabwe. To the same eye, the story of Pashena probably starts and ends with a group of primary school-age rokesheni[2] boys whose ignorantly blissful lives revolved around football, watching cartoons and action movies by day, and catching flying ants or locusts (depending on season) under a streetlight by night.

The unfamiliar eye would have been right.

To the boys, the neighborhood's residents and others who had been privy to the legend of Pashena, the dirt field was sacred. It represented the unrelenting passion that is almost always evident in the hearts of children, and almost never in the hearts of adults. It stood for the constancy of time and her passage, only to return and repeat the cycle. It stood for an understanding of said cycle. To them, the story of Pashena was the story of the timeless war between children and their parents; the story of true wealth and happiness; the story of losing it all in one turn of fate. Most importantly,

---

2 Localized version of "location", the colloquial term for high-density, low income neighborhoods

the story of Pashena is born of a realization that, as long as the hearts of people and the soul of the world can still carry memories of beauty, beauty will surely manifest itself again– even when unexpected.

They would be right, too.

***

The Home Ownership neighborhood, or MaOwnership, as it is commonly known, was a unique community in Dangamvura. It was one of the several low-to-middle income, high-density urban communities developed across the country by the government after independence in 1980. As the rather uncreative name implies, MaOwnership residents initially owned their houses, while those in the handful other Dangamvura neighborhoods rented or leased theirs. What this meant, then, was that MaOwnership residents were still poor, but they were slightly better off than those from surrounding areas. The houses and yards were big; at least by Dangamvura standards. The semi-detached three-bedroomed houses typically boasted a verandah, driveway, a vegetable garden, and front lawn. Each household came with a geyser, guaranteeing warm water in the mornings—a luxury largely unknown across Dangamvura. In the early days, the roads had been well paved in tar, and we would get the newspaper, milk, and bread delivered right to our doorsteps. The call of the plain yet beautiful house sparrows that were a staple of the neighborhood punctuated the day as if to give this imperfect paradise an appropriate theme song.

The people of MaOwnership represented a mixture of the peaceful finesse that comes with the acquisition of moderate wealth and the grounded humility of still being of limited means. Everyone had an interesting story. Some people had been in the *Chimurenga,* the war that led to independence in 1980. Others worked for high government offices. My grandparents were nurses which, for an upstart *rokesheni* community, meant as much as doctors to the people. Our neighbors, Ta's parents, owned one of the more popular beer-halls in

Dangamvura. As it would happen, our houses were behind a house that belonged to the African Church of God, and thus was inhabited by a succession of pastors. These differences meant little to anyone. People were easy-going and hospitable.

When all was considered, MaOwnership was a utopia to its residents.

As the years passed, however, the original essence of MaOwnership had been compromised, as several of the original residents moved to the more plush Eastern suburbs and rented their homes out. At the same time, a few other Dangamvura communities also introduced home ownership schemes. Nevertheless, MaOwnership people still carry themselves with an air of elitism that had its roots in the early days. That feeling was not lost on the children of the original denizens (and eventually their children too), who inherited the slightly smug yet pleasant demeanor, albeit without understanding its origins.

Ta and I were four when we first met. For reasons unknown to me then, my grandmother, who we lovingly called Gogo, was fiercely protective of my cousins and me and was wary not to let us play in the streets with the neighborhood children until we were old enough to go to school. From what I could understand, it had something to do with the other children being naughty and the danger of getting run over by cars.

Both Gogo and Kulu[3] were nurses, and thus particularly paranoid due to the horrible injuries they dealt with daily at work. Although I mulled at this injustice now and then, I did not complain much about it: the cousins and my toys sufficed for me.

At any given moment during my childhood, there were more than ten people living at 1043, our MaOwnership address. Of course, there was Gogo and Kulu. Then, at times, there was my aunt Mai Nigel[4'] and her two sons, my cousins Nigel and Anesu. Their dad, my

---

3 Grandpa

4 Mai = Mother, thus 'Mai ....' (The mother of ...) Is the common respectful way in

uncle Baba Nigel[5], worked at a school out of town, and would often be back for the weekends. There was also my uncle, Sekuru Gerry, and Aunt Pepe and Paula, who, together with Nigel's father, were my mother's siblings. My mother lived in Harare where she worked and attended university and would come back to visit every month or two. Most of the time, we would also have a housemaid to help with the children and household chores. One could never be short of company.

On this warm Saturday morning, I stepped out onto our concrete-paved front yard to play with some toy soldiers that my mother had recently brought from Harare. Gogo had finally allowed me to leave the house to play and chat with the other neighborhood children, as long as I did so over the fence and did not leave the yard. Through the diamond-shaped holes of the fence, I saw a little boy, slightly shorter and probably not more than a year removed from me.

"Hello," I called out to him, excited to make my first non-family acquaintance.

"My name is Shingi, what is yours?"

"I am Takura! What do you have over there?"

"Oh, these?" I replied with the intuitive pride that stems from rousing the envy of your peers, "These are just some toy soldiers that mom brought me from Harare!"

Takura's interest in the toys shot up as soon as I said that, childish curiosity now mixed with the foreign fascination. The mere thought of Harare, the significantly larger and fancier capital city, always excited the residents of Dangamvura, especially the children.

"Can I see?" He asked, slipping his tiny hand through one of the fence holes.

---

which mothers are referred to, with the name of the eldest child being used to complete the title.
5 Baba= Father, 'Baba ....' (The father of ...) Is the common respectful way in which fathers are referred to, with the name of the eldest child being used to complete the title.

"Sure!" I said as I handed him what I considered to be the best of the troop. This soldier came complete with a huge gun on his back and bullet belt on the front, just like the soldiers on *Tour of Duty* did.

As soon as Takura grabbed it, however, he screamed, "Good! Now I'll never give it back!"

I stood there in utter confusion. No one in my family had ever been that inexplicably mean, and the idea that someone could set out to do something that upset another purely for their enjoyment was a novelty to me.

True to his word, Ta never returned my toy. I went back into the house and tearfully told my Gogo what had happened. Never the one to seek conflict, she simply said "It's okay, *mwanangu*[6], let him play with it! You still have all these other toys, and maybe he does not have as many." For all of Gogo's magnanimous rationale, it would be years before I forgave Ta.

As time went by, Ta and I began attending the same crèche[7]. It was at my grandparents' church, and most of the local children went there. Because our housemaids took turns to take us there, we had to walk together. Soon, the transgressions of our first encounter were forgotten, and we warmed up to each other.

I hated crèche. The early mornings were painful, and I always felt that the teachers were mean. Most importantly, and possibly the reason I made up those other reasons, I missed Gogo when I had to go. Also, having lived a rather sheltered existence up until then, I was socially awkward, making me a prime target for bullies. The worst of my assailants were three boys from the notorious MaTwo Rooms neighborhood. Two of them, Lazarus and Barnabas, were twins, and the other was a short, chubby and bow-legged boy with a foul mouth and unmistakable meanness. Their teasing was unceasing and brutal, and soon I disliked crèche. I also knew that, if I told Gogo about it,

6 A term of endearment which means "my child"
7 Early kindergarten, pre-school

she would storm right up to the school and give the teachers and the boys a piece of her larger-than-life mind. I was not willing to risk facing the wrath of the "Terrible Three" or the humiliated looks of my shamed teachers, so I never told her.

As bad as the bullying had been, the boys had never touched me. Then one day, during break-time, I broke out my yellow lunchbox to reveal the egg and bacon sandwiches that my Aunt Paula had made that morning. I also had a piece of cake left over from a family friend's birthday party we had attended in the city over the weekend. I could not have been more excited!

No sooner had I opened my lunchbox did I see three dreaded shadows towering over me from under the small tree under which I had sat for shade.

"Lazzie! It seems we will be having cake today!" yelled the chubby bully whose name I cannot remember, while the twins grinned and drooled over my Aunt's labor of love like starved hyenas. I sat still, in a mixture of fear and seething anger.

"Can we have it?" Lazarus asked, with the assurance of someone who had asked that question a thousand times and not once heard no. I did not respond.

"*Mfana*[8], don't you hear us?" Barnabas chimed in as menacingly as his brother had. Again, I remained silent, futilely fighting back tears.

Annoyed and hungry, the chubbier boy dove for my lunchbox and grabbed the piece of cake before I could do anything. In doing so, however, he failed to get a strong enough hold on it, and it fell onto the dirt. For a second, the three boys exclaimed with the hollow disappointment of losing something that meant little to them. Then, as if nothing had happened, they turned to walk away amidst condescending snickers and talk of finding another victim.

---

8 "Little Brother" used, in context, either as a term of condescension or endearment

I lost it. With tears furiously trickling down my cheeks, I felt the weight of everything I hated pushing me onto my feet. I charged at the three boys, who were now at least ten meters away from me. Because he walked slower, I reached the chubby one first and, with my sealed lunchbox, hit him as hard as I could on his head. He had not seen it coming, neither literally nor figuratively, so it took him a moment to realize what had happened. When the pain and shame sank in, he started wailing and running in place: a sight that instantly betrayed his tough-guy image, especially since it caught the attention of the rest of the playground. For a few seconds, I was in a daze. I was as shocked as anyone when I realized what had happened, let alone that I had been the aggressor. I was also afraid of the inevitable, imminent retribution. Most importantly, however, I was in heaven. Regardless of what would now happen, I had done what nobody had ever dared to do.

My moment of glee was cut almost instantly, as the twins began stomping the ground towards me. What chance did I have against two, bigger, meaner and angry kids? Putting my hands over my head, I cowered in resignation and waited for my penance...

Then the weirdest thing happened. In the distance, I heard a familiar stutter; "Le-e-leave him alone! Or else!"

It was Ta. As it turned out, he had watched the whole thing from a distance and decided to step in just as things were looking bleak for me. Although he was the same size as I was, he had been playing with other children in MaOwnership and other neighborhoods for much longer, so he commanded a little more respect and knew more people than I did. The bullies must have known it too because they just walked away with a timidity none of us had ever seen from them, and I never had any trouble with them again.

In that instance, Ta and I became the best of friends. We were an odd pair. Ta had a short-temper and was notoriously unreliable. He also stuttered when he spoke, and many people said that contributed to his temper. He must have thought I was a spoilt, self-centered kid who thought himself better than his peers. Despite these unfavorable, albeit justifiable, perceptions of each other, we got along famously.

We grew even closer when we began first grade at Sheni Primary School. The school was two kilometers away, so it took us a while to get used to the trip. We could not complain though, as some of our classmates walked more than twice that distance. I had to be up at the crack of dawn to catch an early bath, especially since my grandparents, uncles, aunts, and cousins had to bathe and get to their day-to-days as well. I would meet up with Ta an hour before school to start walking. His sister, Kuziwa, was in the grade above us, and she would often join us. The company, added to the comfort of our classmates who had to walk much further, made the trip bearable. We made lots of other friends too.

Now and then, we would get a ride in Kulu's light green Datsun on his way to work. On those days, we would feel extra special since almost no one else, except maybe some of the teachers' children, came to school by car. Once or twice, we even rode in the back of a huge truck that Ta's father used to drive for the tobacco company. The wheels alone were bigger than us! If we felt cool when we came in Kulu's small Datsun, we definitely felt superhuman when we got out of the truck.

That was Ta. That was Ta and me.

In the third grade, Ta's father passed away. He had been ill for a while, and my grandparents spent many evenings at the hospital with Ta's mother and other people from the neighborhood. Ta's uncle had moved in to help with work around their house, as their mother was hardly ever home now, tending to their father. One morning, Ta and I were playing in his front yard when we saw his cousin coming down the street. When he got closer, we could tell he was teary-eyed. He greeted us and asked Ta if uncle was there, and then proceeded into the house. I turned to Ta and, with the stoicism typical of children that age, asked him if he thought something had happened to his father. The rumor-mill had been hard at work that week, and it fell on my infant ears that his time was nigh. Ta seemed to know too, as he turned and ran towards his house without answering.

His cousin had, indeed, come to deliver the news from the hospital to uncle and the children.

The funeral was the most spectacular thing I had ever seen. People came in their hundreds to mourn and stayed at Ta's homestead for three whole days until the burial took place. Ta and Kuziwa moved in with us until after the burial. All the people from their church, everyone from the neighborhood, and all who used to frequent their beer-hall, among others came to pay their respects. People would wail, dance and sing until dawn and then some would leave to bathe and feed the children, before coming right back, and the funeral festivities would continue again around noon. After the funeral, a few people from the neighborhood, Mai Ta's church group and their extended family stayed for two or three more days to help the family with the clean-up and getting life back to some semblance of normal.

In the aftermath of his father's passing away, Ta's mother got a new job just outside the city and, with that, Ta transferred to a different school closer to her workplace. We figured it was a better school because he now wore a blazer; a privilege only known to people from the richer primary schools. I only recall two or three other boys in MaOwnership who wore blazers to primary school: and by then, I knew everyone in the neighborhood.

That was just it. MaOwnership was the type of neighborhood where, by the time you were ten, you could name the ten families living in either direction of you, complete with the names of everyone who lived there and their actual address.

2

Our house was not initially supposed to be at the corner. By some fate, the corner house was never built, and thus half of what would have been that yard space became part of ours. This stroke of luck more than doubled our yard size, which just delighted my green-thumbed grandparents. Through the seasons, my grandfather would have a variety of crops growing. Usually, we would have onions, tomatoes, peppers, and greens; but now and then he would experiment with strawberries, carrots, or some other exotic crop. That, added to the fruit trees that majestically governed our backyard, made for a well-fed household. The barbed fence on the far-side of the house was adorned with a granadilla vine; a tall and luscious avocado tree stood dead center of the yard, lemon and orange and tangerine trees galore filled the front lawn, while we also had a pomegranate tree and grapevine just outside. When they were not at work, my grandparents would spend hours at length tending to the plants: my grandfather with the vegetables and my grandma with the flowers, often switching roles.

We also had a wooden shed immediately outside our front door, in which Kulu raised chickens for food, eggs, and sale. Some seasons, he would also raise rabbits, and guinea pigs in a smaller cage kept in the shed. While I could never stand the damp, vile smell and loud clucking of the chickens, I was obsessed with the guinea pigs.

We also had two dogs, Spot, and her son, Chips. They fit neither the traditional roles of pets nor guard dogs but fell delicately in between. They were beloved members of the household but spent almost all their time lingering in the backyard, watching for local hoodlums. Legend has it that Spot had been a prized hunter back in her day. People were afraid of her. By now, she was a shell of her vicious self, fallen victim to old age and domestication. It was Kulu's sole responsibility to feed the dogs, so none of us were as close to them as he was. I did, however, carry a unique sense of kinship with Chips. He was a puppy when I first knew of him, so we grew up together. He was mostly peaceful but would stay up all night howling like the wolf he resembled.

In some ways, my grandparents' household was the envy of the others in MaOwnership. The self-sustaining values of community and emphasis on family that we enjoyed under Kulu's roof were, however, pretty standard among our neighbors.

After Ta, Antony was my second friend. He had a few older siblings who were friends with my cousins and aunts, so our friendship was fated. Although he was a couple of years older than Ta and me, we were already as tall as he was. That, and being soft-spoken and reserved, made him the ideal 'older' friend. While the three of us would play altogether from time to time, Antony was often the friend that either Ta or I would run to when we were sick of each other. As my temperament would have it, I found myself running to him much more than Ta ever did and, soon, we were spending almost all our playtime away from school together. When his parents were not home, we would often sneak in and run havoc on anything we could get our hands on.

My absolute favorite thing about Antony's house was the big vintage radio in his parents' bedroom. If there was any debate on whether we were allowed to play in the house or not, playing in the parents' bedroom was a resounding no-no. That, however, just made the adventure more exciting for us. Tucked away in the far-left corner next to the giant windows was the ancient machine; cleverly put together with knobs and buttons that would rival a small plane. We spent hours and hours on it. Antony and I would take turns to play "DJ" on the radio. When we got bored with that, we would pretend it was a switchboard at ZESA[9], or helicopter; anything that our puerile minds figured had a lot of buttons on it. Aside from cooking over an open fire with my Gogo, playing with Antony's radio was quite possibly the highlight of my crèche days.

Then one day, Antony left. No goodbye, no messages, nothing.

I came back from school one day, and was getting ready to run down the street when my aunt Paula announced, "Oh, Antony's family left for Masvingo[10] this morning." I could not understand. No one had ever moved away. My cousins from Harare would often visit during school holidays, but I knew they would be back soon or I would be visiting them. My first question, then, was when they would be back.

"Oh, they live there now. They are not coming back," my aunt explained.

"Can I still play with Antony then?"

"He is gone, Shingi. You will just have to play with your other friends."

I was dumbfounded. I did not know how to feel. For days on end, I would walk into the street after school hoping to see him walking down as he always did. After a week or two, I realized he was

---

9 Zimbabwe Electricity Supply Authority
10 Another of Zimbabwe's cities.

not coming back. Another family moved into their house. To make matters worse, the two children there were girls and therefore impossible to play with.

Up until then, I thought furniture and household items came with the house, and when people left, they just took their clothes. Although Antony had left, I could at least still play with the radio, I figured. Right then, I made it my life's mission to get my hands back on that beautiful old machine. I watched the house for days, often under the guise of playing in the street with Ta and the other boys I had now met in Antony's absence. I soon got to know how many people lived there and what their leaving patterns were.

Then, one day, I made my move. Without telling anyone and with stealth that surprised even me, I sneaked up to the back door, all the while hoping that it would be unlocked. Although MaOwnership was a relatively safe and docile neighborhood, the residents still abided by the cautionary habits of any other low-income, high-density suburb, so the door would have most likely been locked. On stretched tiptoes to reach the doorknob, I turned it and, much to my excitement, it was not locked!

Once inside I was somewhat put off by all the new things and unfamiliar order, but who cared? I had a job to do, and that is all that mattered. I headed straight to the main bedroom and just stood there in shocked disappointment. The radio, the majestic cornerstone of my childhood, no longer stood where it had! With my heart beating for nerves and tears trickling for sadness, my knees weakened, and I fell to the floor. While I was down there, I looked under the bed and frantically around the room—in the faltering hope that someone had moved it. It wasn't there.

My t-shirt now soaked in nervous sweat and the onslaught of disappointed tears, and my heart disillusioned, I gathered my little self up and started to head back home. Then the door creaked open...

It was the stuff of childhood nightmares. I had meticulously planned my adventure and taken extra caution only to go in when nobody was home. As fate would have it, the old man who lived there now—we never got to know his name; to us, they were always the family that moved into Antony's house—had forgotten some papers he needed for work. With nerves rattled, I had a simple decision to make: I could either stand there and try to explain myself to this strange man who was almost certain to see me as a neighborhood scoundrel as opposed to the curious kid I was, or I could hide behind the TV cabinet and scratch my nose[11] that I would remain unseen until he left.

I went with the latter. Thinking with the slick cunning that, to this day, has never grown on me, I dove behind the cabinet and made sure not to bump into anything. I was back there for what seemed like the whole morning. I prayed repeatedly, as much as I understood prayer then. I cursed my decision to go after the radio. I cursed the radio itself. Most of all, I cursed Antony. It was his fault that I found myself in this predicament. Everyone knew that, if there was one game I could not stand, it was Hide and Seek; and yet here I was, playing the most intense game that I had ever played! Would the old man leave already?

In reality, he must have only stayed for a minute or two; enough to grab his papers and some fruit from the basket that garnished the living room table. What sweet relief it was to hear him open the door and make his way to the bus stop across the street! When I finally emerged from behind the cabinet, I told myself that this would be the last time I would go to that house. Even if Gogo sent me with onions or other gestures of goodwill that she was fond of doing in the neighborhood, I would tell her to send someone else! That would be the last time I mentioned or even thought about Antony too.

And it was...

There were several other characters on our street. Opposite our house lived Strive, who we nicknamed Fox, after a villain from a

---

11 Invocation of luck, similar to "cross your fingers"

Kung Fu movie, and his brother Wellington. And their guava tree. Oh, The Guava Tree.

Next to where Anthony used to live was Norman. Although we never saw much of him, we were always at his house because of the old shell of what had been an army truck in his driveway, even in his absence. Since no one was ever there to explain to us, none of us knew how it had gotten there. The body was battered from bullet scars and rust, but the steering wheel, seats and bulletproof windows were still intact. We would play war for hours, taking the utmost delight in hurling rocks at the impenetrable glass screen.

Next to Norman lived Tinashe and his brother who never left the house. Although Tinashe was younger, Ta had taken a liking to him and developed a mutually beneficial acquaintance: Ta filled the void created by Tinashe's own brother never leaving the house, and Tinashe's reverence sat well with Ta's youthful insecurities. Tinashe's father owned a farm on the outskirts of the town and would often have local children over to help him shell peanuts or peel potatoes for a small payment in the form of sweets. Across the street from them was a tuck shop[12] that belonged to the ever-so charismatic and witty Old Man Chimutondo. A true MaOwnership staple, Old Man Chimutondo's was both popular with the children for the cheap sweets and soft drinks, and with the mothers and grandmothers for the convenience and reasonable prices.

Several hobbies made our childhood delightful. On some days, we would just sit around a small mound of rocks next to our house, in the other half of the space where the house had never been built, that all the boys affectionately called The Mountain. As an alternative to Norman's army truck, The Mountain was a free and nearby source of never-ending adventure. Sometimes we would play a version of "King of the Hill" that we had fashioned, albeit innocently, to reflect the pride we took in being from our particular street. The game was simple:

---

12 Neighborhood Kiosks that sold basic groceries and sweets

the boys from our street would have to ward off attacks from the ones from the backstreet in a play war, and what team could get all its members to the top of the hill before the other would have captured The Mountain for the day. We had no way of knowing it then, but the game we played on The Mountain then would resurface to haunt our childhoods.

The backstreet was peculiarly different from ours, despite the fact that the two combined to make the majority of, and thus what people typically referred to as, MaOwnership. Starting with the Church of God pastors who lived directly behind us, the residents from yonder street tended to be ostentatious, even by MaOwnership standards. They often extended[13] their houses and drove fancier cars. The children went to the city council schools in Dangamvura as opposed to the government ones that Fox, myself, and the other children on our street attended. For the supposed status they represented, I still could not tell you what there was to choose between the council schools and ours. They were all far and always cost about the same. They also followed the same pattern of morning and afternoon sessions. Because there were not enough rooms at the schools, half the students had to come in early in the morning to use the rooms, and be out by 11:30 and spend the next one and a half hours learning under a tree. The other half would have arrived at school at ten o'clock, spend the next one and a half hours under a tree before going into the classrooms when the others got out. All Dangamvura schools were this way. The only recognizable difference seemed to be the two council schools wore slightly more dignified khaki and grey uniforms, while our two wore brown and blue strips that were synonymous with *Rokesheni* schools across the country.

The odd cast of characters from the backstreet included Tiberius and Fungai, two brothers who played tennis and had a mother

---

13 Renovated to increase the size of the house from the blueprint three bedroomed Ownership style houses.

who taught at one of the council schools. Fungai was our age, and Tiberius was a couple of years younger. We knew them because they went to the same Methodist Church that Ta attended. Their father had been a key figure in the post-independence government, but there seemed to be an unspoken agreement to not talk about him anymore. There were Rutendo and her older brothers. Their dad drove a Hyundai—a most fashionable car in its day—and the brothers played tennis in national tournaments. There were, over the years, a succession of pastors' daughters and sons from The African Church of God who we most likely detested or, at best, never got to know.

It was, indeed, inexplicable, how two streets in the same neighborhood could have such distinct personalities. They would always be into a new game fad, the boys from the street behind us would; from cricket to ping pong and tennis. We, on the other hand, reveled in little games that made use of our immediate environment. When we were not in Norman's truck or by The Mountain, we were making toy cars and house sparrow traps out of wire. I was never crafty and found any activity that involved the transformation of one physical form into another particularly daunting, so I opted to watch my friends assert their dominance over little pieces of metal and wood instead. Fox was especially good and would often take up dares to make "Kitt" from the popular TV show "Knight Rider," and other fancy cars we saw on television. Once, he made a house sparrow trap and gave it to me but, as soon as I caught my first one, I received a harsh talking to about 'kindness to all of God's creatures' from a granduncle that was visiting at the time. I decided that also was not for me.

My pastime of choice was locust catching. At the end of the rainy season, green locusts would descend upon the land and flock around the streetlights and other lit up grassy patches. When dusk set in, we would all go out with plastic bags and catch as many as we could. They were naturally oily, so we would fry them over an open fire for a most delightful snack. Most of the Ownership kids did it only as a hobby, so we would only walk around to the four or five streetlights in the neighborhood: besides, our parents would not have allowed us to go too far. People from other neighborhoods saw the locusts as an important and cheap source of food, so they were willing to travel all around Dangamvura to catch bucket loads. Often, even the parents would come too! Sometimes, there would be too many people under one light and fights would break out. Because it was never that serious for us, we would quickly back down and go back home if it ever came to that.

Then came the guinea pigs. Having typically avoided any yard work and domestic duties, often delegating such to my cousin Nigel or sweet-talking Gogo out of it, my obsession with guinea pigs was unforeseen. When I was about eight, I found myself volunteering to help Kulu feed old cabbages and pellets from the store to the rabbits and, when he had them, guinea pigs too. Excited to see me interested in a homestead chore for once, Kulu did not hesitate to give me a small section of the wooden shed to raise my guinea pigs when I finally asked him. I started with five: two males and three females. Wellington from across the street shared this fascination with me, but only had two females at the time. I offered to sell him one of my males to mate with his ladies for a few dollars, but he did not have money then. I ended up giving him one anyway in exchange for two babies from his litter when they were finally born. It worked out well for both of us. Soon, Wellington had connected me with some of his friends from surrounding neighborhoods, and I was selling my stock all across the land and trading it for books and toys. At any given time, I maintained a kraal of between 12 and 15 animals—an impressive record for anyone our age.

My guinea pig empire lasted for two years before, as all empires do, it succumbed to neglect and external elements. In my case, I visited my cousins in Harare for a month over the Christmas holidays and came back to a most horrific fate that had befallen my pride and joys. Despite his best attempts, Kulu had been busy and could not watch over the guinea pigs like I did. In my absence, rats had sneaked into the guinea pig section of the shed and left them diseased. I returned to find close to a dozen carcasses and three starved, miserly ones nibbling on what little was left of their food and the remains of their fallen comrades. It was an ugly sight. My heart heavy, I decided to close the once-mighty empire's doors for good. I sold the rest to Wellington, who was only thrilled to grow his own kraal and, more importantly, become the sole overlord of MaOwnership's guinea pig industry.

I raised guinea pigs. Others were masters of the wire car. Others still knew everyone from the neighborhood and beyond. We were a diverse and pretty divided group—until we discovered football.

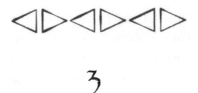

3

None of us could point, with any certainty, to the very moment when we fell in love with the beautiful game. I gathered from the nicknames of some of the older boys that our community's infatuation with football was nothing new. There was one boy down the street who everyone called "Diego" after Argentine legend Diego Maradona. Another young football star, Chris, was known better by his nickname "Wadho"; it wasn't until my teens that I realized he was named after former English superstar Chris Waddle. In Dangamvura, everyone had a nickname. If you did not have one, it meant you did not have any friends or just never left the house. As long as you played with the other kids, you had to have a nickname. The most common ones were just funny or shorter versions of your name, such as "Ta" for Takura, "Dahwa" for Tawanda, and "Bruno" for Brian. Fox, a recurrent villain in many a farcical Kung-fu film of the time, seemed an apt moniker for the action-movie obsessed Strive, so that is who he became to us. I had a second cousin who everyone called "Gandanga," meaning guerrilla because his father had been prominent in the Chimurenga War and was now a revered soldier in the Zimbabwean army. Other names were just absurd. For example, we had a classmate named Abel who, during a fight, had been called "Abigail," and it stuck. Still, the football-themed nicknames were the Holy Grail. They were the highest honor your peers could bestow upon you.

For me, Ta, and other boys our age, our first acquaintance with the game came during the reign of the Zimbabwean Warriors *Dream Team*[14]. The year was 1993, and we had just started first grade. The Dream Team was all the buzz. Every news broadcast, half-drunken adult conversation, and playground argument involved the Warriors. There was not a single person in Zimbabwe who did not know the national team's German coach, Reinhardt Fabisch, and his marauding troops that included Bruce Grobelaar, Henry McKop, Francis Shonhai, and the Ndlovu brothers Madhinda, Adam and Peter. The team was playing to qualify for the 1994 African Cup of Nations, which would have been the first time in Zimbabwe's history.

The Dream Team moniker was well earned. That unheralded bunch of players had gone on a thirteen-game unbeaten streak, defeating Africa's heavyweights such as Cameroon, Angola, and Egypt along the way. Oh, what fortune it was to be introduced to the game at its arguable peak in our country's history! As far as we knew, Zimbabwe was the best team in the world, and football was the most delightful game. We had just stumbled upon the finest pastime ever created.

Zimbabwe's last qualifying game was against Zambia. If we won that game, the Dream Team would have been twice immortalized. As wicked fate would have it, the Zambian national team had more to

---

[14] The endearing moniker for the Zimbabwean National Football Team of the early 1990s

prove to themselves and their fans than we did. In April of 1993, at the height of qualification, a plane carrying them had crashed over Gabon and killed everyone on board: players, coaches, pilots—everyone. It was a sad day for everyone, but especially for Zambia. A few of their players who had not been on the plane vowed to fight on. Their captain, Kalusha 'King Kalu' Bwalya, had been supposed to come in from the Netherlands to meet the team in Gabon when the crash happened and ended up being the backbone of a hastily constructed team that would finish the qualifying campaign.

Hence, when that final qualifying game was played, the neighboring countries had everything at stake, and they played as they did. Zimbabwe, eager to live up to their hype, took an early lead through imposing defender Henry "Bully" McKop's goal. We were ecstatic. I remember my uncles running outside to join in the chorus of street celebrations that had erupted. We were well on our way now! As the game neared the end, however, there was a moment of inspiration by Bwalya, and I saw our goalkeeper Bruce Grobbelaar outstretched to make the save; he couldn't make it. Zambia had scored. They had done it. The makeshift team which, a year back, would have never realistically represented their country, let alone face the mighty Dream Team, and win, had given the Zambian people the miracle they needed.

This time, my uncles just sat there. Then they started crying: grown stolid men whom I had never seen shed a tear up to this point were sobbing. I was baffled. Less than an hour ago, we had all been in the streets in celebration, and now all of that was gone? Besides, the score was only 1-1.

"*Sekuru*[15], why are you crying? We didn't even lose? It's a draw!" I asked with a mixture of curiosity and attempt at comfort. "No!" he snarled into the unforgiving air, "We lost! That's it!"

I looked around the room, and everyone seemed to share his sentiment. As I later understood, it is possible for teams to draw and, in some cases, lose, yet end up on top of total points. Despite their gallant efforts, the Dream Team had failed to reach the Promised Land. In the eyes of a neutral, Zambia qualifying was one of the most inspiring stories to ever come out of football. For us, our Dream Team had fallen short, and we were condemned to live with that pain forever.

If the Dream Team's African adventure had planted a seed in us, it was the 1994 World Cup that allowed the flower to blossom. A month before the games, my mother had bought me a beautiful t-shirt that had Striker, the official mascot of the 1994 World Cup, on the front. Admittedly, the relevance was initially lost on me. Once the games started, however, I was the envy of all my friends. Most of all, we just enjoyed the games. We all marveled as 42-year-old Roger Milla of Cameroon dribbled his way past much younger players; boasted at memorizing the entire line-ups of different teams; and who can ever forget the moment when Baggio of Italy missed his penalty in the final shoot-out against Brazil? Up until then, we had had TV shows such as McGyver, the A-Team, and the Monday night local dramas as common interests. The World Cup, however, was the first real event that leaped from the television screen into the classrooms, the streets, and the playgrounds of Dangamvura. The games would be televised at night, and the morning couldn't come soon enough for us to discuss what had happened. Any gap we had between classes was spent in an argument about the games and, when school was done for the day, it was time to show off your latest "Bebeto" move on the field. By the

---

[15] General term for all male maternal relatives; "Uncle" in this case

summer of 1994, the game's takeover among my group of friends was well in motion. We were in love.

No one in my MaOwnership circle of friends was particularly good at football. We were all sort of fast, all sort of big, all almost good; but not quite there. The boys from surrounding neighborhoods were excellent; it is as if they had been born playing the game! To an extent, they had. As I mentioned earlier, our neighborhood was slightly more sheltered than the others so, by the time the 1994 World Cup rolled into town and brought football to our doorsteps, we were already in first and second grade. On the other hand, children from Areas B, C, and MaTwo Rooms neighborhoods had been allowed to play in the streets as soon as they could walk. Indeed, we had Diego and his brothers who played as well as anyone in Dangamvura; but for the most part, MaOwnership boys were synonymous with being more reserved and studious than athletic. What we lacked in talent, however, we soon made up for in passion.

Across the Rokesheni, there was—and still is—a game of football being played on any available, somewhat flat piece of land. Almost always, the field was set up with two pairs of stones on either side of the 'pitch' serving as goals. The ball was ingeniously crafted out of old newspapers and plastic bags on the inside and covered with a tougher plastic bag such as those used for maize-meal or sugar, then bound with a rubber band. We called this type of ball *hweshe*, a crude translation of "plastic". It did not bounce much and would often only last a few games, but it was what we had. Even if we could have afforded real football balls, it would not have made much sense to play with them barefoot on the tarmac or concrete surface—as we often did—or on the small pieces of backyard lawn that were near windows and barbed wire. The softer, cheaper *hweshe* was perfect for our means and purpose, except during the drought and subsequent maize-meal shortage of 1993, where we were forced to make our balls with substandard, easily-torn grocery store plastic bags. Trying times.

Not just anyone could make *hweshe* though. Anyone could try, and most of us did; but as with most things in life, it was an art form best left for those who had mastered it. The ball had to be the right mix of newspaper and other material, the right tightness to give it a little bounce, and nicely molded to ensure that it was close to round as possible. In MaOwnership, we had one undisputed master of *hweshe*-making; Wellington from across the street. Having already established a name for his birdcages and wire cars, it only made sense.

Wellington was one or two years younger than us, but we got to know him through his brother Fox, who was one year our senior. Before they came to MaOwnership to live with their uncle and cousins, they had lived in Birchenough, one of the rural areas near Mutare. Their uncle had been good friends with both my uncles and their aunt was particularly close with my aunt, Mai Nigel. Our families were so close that their son would come over to our house every Saturday for Gogo's renowned farmhouse breakfast. I, together with Ta and the others, used to go to their house all the time because they had a large guava tree in their front yard, and when they were in season, they were the best you could find anywhere in the area. When they were not, the tree was still pretty fun to climb. At the time, Fox and Wellington would only come to MaOwnership to visit during school holidays.

With time, Wellington's uncle did not look so well. He was losing a lot of weight and did not go out with the other men as much as he used to. From what the adults would say, he was gravely ill. They would often talk about him being 'taken by the same creature that took Fox's parents", and neither the other children nor I could see beyond that cryptic message. Before we knew what was going on, he had died. It was yet another sad day.

After the funeral, Fox, and Wellington moved in with their aunt. Fox was intelligent and even funnier. He hunched over a little when he walked, and always had a smile on his face. Whenever you saw him, he would either tease you light-heartedly or have a funny story about someone in the neighborhood. For the most part, the story was made up and ludicrous, but he spoke slowly and with such attention to detail, perfectly placing his punchlines that, even though we knew better, we found ourselves wishing the stories were real. Despite his confident mischief and somewhat abrasive nature, we soon became friends. He and I bonded because there was a side to him that enjoyed geeky things like crossword puzzles and ghost stories like I did, a rare quality of intrigue to me in MaOwnership. Fox was one of those people who had more friends than anyone, and yet none of us can ever say we were remarkably close to him. One could say he had a 'best friend' for different seasons and reasons.

Wellington was similar to his older brother in that he also told a great story, and their rural upbringing made him a different type of mischievous to the other MaOwnership children. The similarities, as far as I could tell, ended there. Although he lacked Fox's charisma, Wellington was a lot more playful and had a much larger range of talents. He was more athletic, craftier and good at board games, while Fox was better in school and with crossword puzzles and charming people. When he told stories, they often carried a much meaner undertone than Fox's. A natural hothead who had been further disillusioned by the passing of his parents, he was much more temperamental than Fox was, and would often get into fights. They spoke little about their rural life before they came to MaOwnership, only giving us glimpses through humorous tales from their herding and hunting escapades when we would convene under The Guava Tree. The adult rumor mill had since made it known that their parents had died—carried away by the same creature that took their uncle and others. A year after they had moved in with their aunt, she moved to another part of Mutare, leaving the house and the brothers under the custody of their 16-year-old sister, Sincere. She became their mother.

Although we were young, we could not help but notice that a lot of people were dying. Ta's uncle who had moved in with them just before their father died also fell deathly ill. He lost so much weight that he had to cut off the back parts of his trousers and re-sew the front part to half their size so they could fit him. His belts no longer fit him, and he had started using pieces of string to hold up his pants. He still insisted on going to the beer hall though, and would painstakingly make his way up the street at snail's pace, in clear discomfort. Finally, it was so bad that Kuziwa and Ta sought my aunt's help in keeping him home. One day as he took off for the beer hall, she called out to him and said she had a package for him that she would pass to him over the fence. Once he was back in the yard, Kuziwa had locked the gate. As determined as he was to leave, he was too frail to climb over the gate or argue anymore, so that worked well.

He died a week later.

The people dying were not old, either. It was always people that had just started working or parents and uncles of our friends. It must have been something in the air. It was as if a hell-sent death wind was sweeping across the land. It was a sad and confusing time. For days, we would not see, and even if we did, would not know what to say to our friends who had had a death in their family.

With time, however, they would come back to the rest of the group. For as long as we had a game of football they could join in, no words needed to be said. They were home.

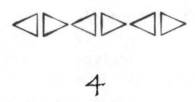

4

The most obvious place to get a small game going was in the backyards.

Although only a few people in Dangamvura had cars, most homes in MaOwnership had decently-sized driveways, usually for work cars and visitors. Ta's driveway was long and spacious, but it was paved with concrete strips, so we had to be cautious when we played there. They also had a big metal gate that we used as the goal and, if the ball was hit hard, it would rattle loudly, and his mother would get upset and chase us out.

Fox's backyard was slightly smaller than Ta's, but the ground was definitely smoother, and there was no loud rattling gate. In fact, there was no gate at all. Fox and Wellington, however, preferred that we did not play at their house. Although we hardly ever saw her, their sister Sincere, who had assumed the maternal role after both their parents had died, was usually home, and would always interrupt the game by yelling out some command for either or both of them.

"Strive! I need you to start the cooking! I told you 30 minutes ago!"

"Wellington, have you gone to see Mai Mutasa yet? Do it right now!"

She appeared tight-fisted and mean to the rest of us, but for all their protests and smirks, her brothers always obliged. They clearly shared an understanding that was lost on us.

As time passed, the backyard games were becoming harder to play. We were not in first or second grade anymore. We were getting bigger and, as more children were finally allowed to come out and play in the street and others moved in from other parts of town, we now had many more friends than before. We needed a bigger space. Somebody suggested playing on the street using Ta's gate as one goal and the gate for the house across the street as the other. We could mark off the rest of the "field" with sand spread across the street in a straight line, to show when the ball was out of bounds.

Because the two gates were a street and some lawn space apart, and the side markings were up to our discretion, playing on the street solved our space dilemma, but that was all. Ta's side of the street was more elevated than the other, so the field sloped down as it headed towards the other goal, giving the higher side an undeniable advantage. We would try to make it fair by switching sides halfway through the game, but once a team was losing, their confidence would be dented, and the game just wouldn't be the same anymore.

We also had to deal with the perils of playing barefooted on a tarmac surface. None of us had football shoes, and only a couple of us had any running shoes at all. Most of my friends only had their school shoes, some casual shoes for when they would go visiting, and a pair of slippers for when we were walking around the neighborhood, and the ground was too hot. Others had one or two more pairs, but none could afford to scuff and tear up a perfectly good shoe playing street football. Even if they could, it wouldn't be fair on the other boys who did not have the shoes. Nobody ever told us that; it was just something we knew, so nobody wore them. What that meant, however, was we would always go home with bloody feet from having stubbed our toes in the ground or falling over after a hard tackle. It came with the territory, and it never kept us away for too long.

One day we, as we often did, played for hours, right into the early evening when the street tower lights came on. There were maybe ten of us playing, five to a side. This particular game was the last one, and because of its intensity and the pending darkness, everyone's concentration was heightened. I was playing goalie on the side opposite to Ta's gate, while Fox, Ta and the rest of their team were on the other side. Ta had just kicked the ball down towards my goal, and Fox began charging after the ball with as much vigor as he could muster after a long day's work. I just stood there, gathering my nerve and preparing to stop the inevitable shot. He was free and was giving it his all, and face-to-face with him, I did not fancy my odds of catching the ball. He was going to score and win the game for his team.

Then the most remarkable thing happened. From up the street, past my house and headed down, charged Tiger, Tinashe's German Shepherd, chasing some phantom rabbit at full speed. So now you had Fox charging towards me across the street with furious intensity, and the dog running down the street as dogs do. At the very instant that Fox lifted his foot to hammer the ball towards goal, the dog was running past him: neither had noticed the other. With all the power and momentum he had gained, Fox could not stop. They collided with the force of two rams bumping heads before Fox proceeded to tumble over Tiger onto the tarmac surface, face first! Amazingly, the dog just let out a pained squeal, stayed on its feet and went about its chase. It was an incredible sight. We all stood there, not knowing whether to be concerned, to laugh, or just be still and absorb the moment. After a few seconds, we ran over to make sure Fox was okay. He had cut his lower lip wide open, bruised his chin and chipped a tooth. Once he came around to it, he jumped up and ran home, wailing so loudly that the neighborhood parents who had just returned from work came to see what had happened.

The bruises and, more importantly, the humiliation of that moment were enough to keep him away from the group for a week or two. Although the rest of us had walked away with nothing more than an amazing story to tell for years to come, the warning was well-served: the intensity that our games now generated made it potentially dangerous to play in the street. Oh, did I even mention the cars? Because our street was one of two or three that connected the rest of Dangamvura with the southern suburbs and, particularly, The Complex—Dangamvura's main market—there was occasional traffic right in the middle of our field of play. Usually, games would resume soon after the cars passed; but the parents were getting paranoid.

"One of these days, I tell you, we will have to carry one of you guys over to Shingi's grandparents after you've been run over!" Mai Ta would say, to a chorus of approval from the other mothers.

"*Imi zvenyu imi!*[16] Last week I had to wrap Tinashe's foot up in bandages for a few days after he kicked the tar! He couldn't walk for two days and had to miss school," Tinashe's mother, who lived directly across the street from where Anthony used to live, chimed in. She looked down as she spoke, worried that the other women would bring up her rampaging dog and the injuries to Fox.

"You wouldn't believe the damage they have done to the carnations that I had planted right in front of my gate! They have run all over them, and there is nothing to show for them now!" added Mai Mucha, who lived next door to Tinashe. We had, indeed, been unkind to her front lawn and what flowers she had planted there.

The message from the parents, and the gods that induce injuries and other misfortune, was clear: we had to move. So, with the

---

16 "Agreed!"

winter of 1996 pending, we found ourselves at the height of our passion and, for the first time in a while, without a pitch. We would occasionally gather ourselves and go to Beit, Dangamvura's only proper football field, which was conveniently located about a mile from MaOwnership. It was big and spacious and fell right where many of Dangamvura's neighborhoods intersected, so it was the preferred place of play for most children. There usually would be several splinter games going on, with people from different neighborhoods, different ages, and different skill levels laying claim to their little portion of the field. Often, however, there would be an actual team from an adult or youth league practicing or playing a match, and we would have to leave. Sometimes, we hung around and watched some of the games. There was an amateur "Boozer" league, which featured mainly groups of young men who either worked or drank together playing against each other. Many of the players were out of shape and drank just before the game. They were usually terrible, and therein perhaps lay our fascination with them. One of the regular players was our teacher's husband, and he was awful. We would watch him just to find reasons to snicker behind our teacher's back at school the next week. My friends and I enjoyed watching the games. We would go to the field every Saturday afternoon, buy *Freez-its* [17] and *maputi* [18] from the women at the market between the field and the aptly named Neighborhood Tavern, and just sit under a tree and enjoy the lackluster attempts of grown men at the game we loved the most. Now and then, a fight would break out but, for the most part, levity prevailed.

Often, companies based in and around Dangamvura would form semi-professional teams, some of which were decent. There was a Border Timbers team that made noise for a few years and an even

---

17 Frozen juice sold in small plastic bags, much like popsicles in other parts of the world
18 Native roasted corn snacks.

better Coca-Cola team that used to draw crowds of hundreds at Beit. People liked these teams because, not only did they approach the games more seriously than the Boozers, they often recruited promising young players from the neighborhood to play for them. Because you had to be an employee to actually play, players who were deemed good enough would receive some job training and part-time jobs. It made the townsfolk happy to watch their favorite homegrown players play for a pretty good team and get a job while they were at it. It was that type of community.

As much as we loved Beit, it just was more convenient to have our own MaOwnership field; not only for the reasons listed above but because many of us were embarrassed to be seen by the kids from the other areas, who tended to be much better. We were thus committed to finding a place to call our own.

Then one day, an option we had never previously thought about occurred to us.

Ta, Fox, my cousin Nigel, and I were sitting in the shade of our big Avocado Tree, feasting on our beloved *mauyu*[19]. Often, I would boil the seeds in water and stir in some sugar to create baobab pulp porridge, but I usually saved that for night time TV. On this day, we had cracked one big one open, and we were going to work on it.

"Shingi, why is our yard so much bigger than the others?" Nigel asked. Being a few years younger than me, he had missed out on the several times that we had had this conversation.

"Well, I'm not too sure. I think it is because our house is on the street corner. I have also heard that there was supposed to be a house built next to ours but, for some reason, it never did. Just our luck of the draw, I guess."

"Ha ha, you guys got lucky! See how much crops Kulu can produce when the season is right?" Fox said, "Like right now, your

---

19 Baobab Fruits

onions are doing great. What is that big open space over there, though?"

"That's where were we usually have the maize when the rainy season comes!" I replied

"So... so... so you're saying it is never used this time of year?" Ta stuttered

"No, not usually."

"Why, we should play there! Do you think Kulu will allow us? Can you find out? This would be perfect!"

They did not have to ask me again.

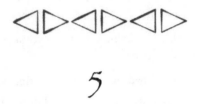

5

I was much closer to Gogo than I was to Kulu. It was like that with all the grandchildren. Kulu was always busy with work and, as a community elder, advising random people on different matters. We would speak about the rabbits and guinea pigs when he would take me to school. We would also see him when we were sick, where his wealth of medical knowledge and empathy would become ever so apparent. Outside of that, he was a man of few words, often leaving his wisdom for the big occasion. Gogo, on the other hand, lived to spend time with us. She worked at the hospital as well, and very often would work the night shift. In spite of all that, we could always count on her to have a hefty farmhouse breakfast ready when we got up, and that she would spend some time with us in the early evening watching High Schools' Quiz, her favorite game show. Now and then, Nigel and I would go too far with the running around the house and fighting, and she would be forced to yell and occasionally spank us. When that would happen, we would cry for what seems like hours for two reasons: being spanked was embarrassing, but more importantly, it hurt us that we had put our dear Gogo in a position to get that angry at us knowing very well that it hurt her to be that way. She was a darling.

So, when my friends tasked me with asking if we could use the backyard as our football field, I knew whom to ask. "She won't mind. In fact, she'll like it! She's always talking about how we should be as close to the house as possible, so this is perfect," I rationalized, trying to remain calm as I planned my attack. "Besides, it is not like that part of the backyard is being used for anything right now anyway; it won't be until the rains fall..."

I needed tact. I had to wait until the time was right: she had to be particularly pleased with us. Nigel and I decided to be consciously more pleasant around the house. Nigel and I were always close. He spent the early years in the rural area where his father taught, but they always came to see us on the weekends and holidays. Nigel was more mischievous and athletic than I was, but I always made sure to assert my big brother status; I would make sure to pick him up from school and keep him out of trouble, which was no easy task. There was always a classmate complaining to Gogo that Nigel hit them. One time, I stood on our verandah and saw a group of four neighborhood kids chasing him towards our house with sticks, clearly angered by something he had said. I wasn't too worried about it because he was a healthy distance in front of them and was faster than most boys his age and, frankly, a good number of us as well. Before I could grasp what was happening, Nigel slowed down methodically, allowing the aggressors to catch up with him. Without being any the wiser, the other boys thought he had just tired and pounced on him. What happened next was nothing short of spectacular. Nigel turned around and, like a lion amidst a pack of hyenas, beat up every last one of the neighborhood scoundrels and sent them running back home. As much as I had enjoyed watching little brother working the enemy, I had to put on my stern exterior and tell him not to do it again.

That was Nigel. That was Nigel and me.

We waited until one evening when we knew Gogo would be home from work, relaxing with us while my aunts prepared dinner and before Kulu got back from the tavern. That way, we could capitalize on her larger-than-life generosity without dealing with Kulu's fierce pragmatism or the aunts' jealousies towards Gogo's leniency towards us. It was a Thursday evening, and Nigel and I had been without blemish all week. We had been early to school, home before dark, watered the onions, fed the chickens and even resisted the relentless urge to chase each other down the tiny spaces that were our hallways.

All that said, I knew I still had to present our case with the utmost tact.

"Gogo, what month does the maize season begin again?" I asked, attempting to smooth my way to the topic. She knew me too well to fall for that gimmick, and it did not help that I had asked the one question to which I obviously knew the answer.

"What?" she replied, with a slightly confused yet sly grin, "You know very well that we start preparing the fields in October to catch the first rains in early November? Now, what is this really about? I have never known you to care much about the field!"

She was right.

"Well," I proceeded, having put myself in a position to do nothing else but "You know how you have always worried about us playing on the busy, tarred street—or how sometimes we have to go to these weird neighborhoods where no one can keep watch on us? We had thought that, seeing as we have all this space that will not be used until later this year, maybe we could have a few friends come and play there on occasion?"

"Please, Gogo?" Nigel reentered the conversation, turning on the charm that always lacked in my very practical way of seeking favors, "I hate going to the other neighborhoods; the other boys often turn violent if they lose! We would much rather play here. That way, we are always nearby, in case you need us to run errands for the home!"

"I don't know, boys" Gogo seemed to mull our plea over and over in her head. On the one hand, we made a strong case; she especially wanted us closer to home. She was also wary, however, of having too many area boys coming to play. We had said "a few friends," but she knew better. It would soon turn into flocks of little boys she had never seen before frequenting her backyard. She also had doubts about making any yard decisions without Kulu's input.

"If you boys promise to stay in the top five of your class after exams, and to help out a little bit with tilling the field when the season comes, then I guess it is okay. If there is any trouble, or if Kulu isn't happy with the arrangement, then it will have to stop immediately..."

We didn't hear anything after "if you boys"—we had the field! All that was left was to let the boys know.

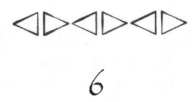

6

How fitting that we had been told we could play in the yard on a Thursday! We could break it in that Friday afternoon and spend the whole weekend familiarizing ourselves with the rugged terrain. The next morning, we made sure to tell Fox and a few other friends of Gogo's verdict. Because Ta went to the city school, I would not be able to tell him until later that afternoon. As for the rest of the boys, we could barely contain our glee as we agreed to meet at my house at two o'clock when we all got out of school.

Nigel and I got home at around one-thirty and made quick work of the little bit of Sadza[20] and Lacto[21] that his mother had prepared. As was typical, the sadza was left over from the previous night's supper. It was an economic arrangement that saved both time and money. In fact, leftover Sadza for lunch was one of the few great

---

20 Zimbabwean staple, a thickened maize-meal porridge, often served with meat and leafy vegetables or sour milk
21 Popular brand of sour milk

equalizers in the rokesheni; almost every child we knew would have that dish once or twice a week after school.

When we were done, we walked out to Fox, Wellington, and young Tinashe already waiting in the backyard. Never having been used for any purpose other than Kulu's seasonal gardening, it was going to take some leveling to bring it to some semblance of a playing field. We grabbed two small hoes that Gogo favored for her flowers, a bigger one used for the maize field, and two spades. We each found our tiny spot on the field and began clearing. It was tedious work. We were not able to play on that first day, but we were happy with the progress. Despite being exhausted and calloused, we decided to meet up the same time the following day to finish working on the small part of the field that was left.

The next day, we finished clearing the field and played until dusk, when Sincere came out and called for Fox and Wellington to come home. About then, Gogo was walking down the road from work. Nigel and I ran up to meet her as we had always done.

"*Nhai vanangu!* [22] You boys are so dirty!" She exclaimed with an annoyed chuckle.

Because the field was used for vegetables in the rainy season, there was no grass covering it the rest of the year. There were a few weeds, but after the clearing we had done, and a few hours of play, the soil had become loose and would rise and cloud the field; leaving us covered in dirt from head to toe. Gogo's nurse uniform, which was always clean and pristine white, was now tinted in dirt by our witless embrace. Much as she may have wanted to, she could not muster even an ounce of anger. After a long day at work, she was happy to see us in high spirits.

We played on that space for about two weeks before we came upon problems, one after another. Because the field was within our

---

22 My dear children!

yard, which happened to be on the street corner, its edges tended to be more rounded than straight, making for a rather awkwardly shaped football pitch. Once the games started, the ball would find its way into Kulu's gardens more than we had bargained for. Needless to say, he was distraught each time he came back from the hospital to find his vegetables ravaged by the ball and the tiny footprints that had repeatedly chased after it. Also, half a dozen boys stomping and racing on a piece of dirt field inevitably led to a daily cloud of dust covering the entire backyard where, incidentally, my aunts hung the laundry to dry. When some Gogo's uniforms returned from the washing line with a distinct shade of brown, the entire household had just about had it.

The final nail in the coffin of our short-lived affair with the tiny backyard field came when one of Kulu's hammers turned up missing. He had always been wary of the neighborhood boys and was anything but thrilled when I had started playing with them a few years earlier. He had also made no secret of his disapproval when Gogo permitted us to play in the yard. When, a few weeks later, he could not find a hammer from the toolshed, he fumed.

"I told you that this arrangement would be nothing but trouble! Why can't they play at Beit like they used to?" I overheard him say to her through their bedroom wall. I could not make out what her subdued response had been before he bellowed again,

"Well, you talk to them then! If we don't find that hammer, they can never have their friends over here again!"

The following day, Gogo came and found us by the rock under the big Avocado Tree where Fox, Nigel, Wellington and I were sun-basking. I could tell as she approached us ever so slowly with her head held low that she was both dreading having this conversation with us and still upset at Kulu for putting her in charge of finding the hammer.

"Nhai vakomana, pane akamboona nyundo yanga iri muchikwere umu (Boys, has anyone seen the hammer that was in the shed)?"

As soon as she said that, Fox and Wellington began snickering, much to my and Nigel's disgusted panic. How rude! Painfully, I watched as Gogo's jaw fell and her eyes began to water. She turned solemnly and walked towards the house, calling out to Nigel and I as she did. The moment we stepped into the house, she spoke sternly;

"Now boys, not only are your friends the rudest kids I have seen in all my time here, but I am convinced they stole Kulu's hammer. They can never come back here! As for that little field of yours, it has been nothing but trouble! From today, you can no longer play there."

Whether the brothers had stolen the hammer, I do not know. I doubt it. The reason they had burst out chuckling was because Gogo had unwittingly used a word for hammer that was uncommon in the local dialect. While it meant hammer in the Northern part of the country were Gogo had grown up, it had found its way into the local slang as a vulgar word; a hilarious moment for two of the neighborhood's most mischievous boys! Regardless of who had stolen the hammer, I felt so ashamed of what had happened and furious at my friends that I did not put up a fight against the field ban.

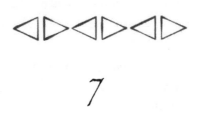

7

The following weeks in MaOwnership were uneventful. I was still dismayed with Wellington and Fox and, without the medium that was football, there was little incentive for me to meet up with everyone else. Nigel and I settled into the drab routine of getting out of school, stopping by the local market to buy some mauyu, making mauyu porridge, then watching the road for people while we sat under the Avocado Tree. Occasionally, Ta would come back from school early, get off the bus and sit with us for a short while. It was mundane, and most of our friends would have found it boring, but we enjoyed it.

We knew, however, that a life away from the game, and the friends that we so loved was never going to last long. We had no idea how we would find our way back to the old Ownership kick-about we had grown up on, but we just knew it would happen.

Then it did. One day, Nigel and I were coming back from Old Man Chimutondo's shop where Gogo had sent us to buy some drinks. As we walked past Fox's house, a most unusual sight struck us—the guavas had not been picked in a while. The tree was full of yellowing, over-ripe deliciousness. Many of them had already fallen to the ground, filling the surrounding air with the weirdly enticing stench of rot.

Nervously, we looked at each other and immediately established that age-old understanding that we had always shared. The un-harvested feast was so odd a sight that we knew something had to be wrong in their house, and we had to find out. In that brief moment, the tensions that hung over our relationship with the brothers were temporarily suspended. Admittedly, we were only partly driven by concern for our estranged friends; we just had to find a way to get to the guavas. We rushed home to drop off the drinks, turned around and ran back towards the street.

I led the way.

Although only a few meters, the walk up to their door seemed to last an eternity. At the worst, we would find something drastic had happened and, at best, we were going to have an awkward conversation with the boys we had sworn never to talk to again. It was with that heaviness of thought that I reluctantly knocked on the door.

Sincere answered with her trademark sternness that would have done little to calm our nerves.

"What do you want?"

"Oh, w-w-w-we were just walking by and thought we would come and say Hel—"

"Look, guys, your Sekuru Gerry has already been here to ask about that hammer. I swear upon my mother's grave, my brothers did not take it! Besides, I have already dealt with them for their unbecoming behavior towards Gogo," she said, struggling to maintain her overbearing tone under an obvious defensive cloud.

Having come with neither the intent to talk about the hammer nor the knowledge that Sekuru Gerry had been there, Nigel and I were caught off guard.

"Oh no! We weren't even here about that! Are Strive and Wellington here?"

Fox happened to be, and he had been listening in to the conversation from inside the house. At the mention of his name, he came towards the door and exchanged glances with Sincere as if to let her know that he would take it from there.

"So, how is it going?" he asked as he stepped outside and down from the porch, half-brandishing the awkward, mischievous smile with which he was synonymous.

"Aah, nothing sha. We were just..." I began, bringing my own share of awkwardness to the table. It was all so weird, dealing with these ideas of the bigger man, forgiveness, and reconciliation. At a loss for words, I blurted out,

"Can we have some guavas?"

Relieved that the ice was broken, Fox had never been more willing to have people over by The Guava Tree.

"Of course, boys! I haven't even been over there in a while myself; let's go see what fine crop the recent rains have brought us."

Nigel, who had watched this entire exercise in diplomacy with detached fascination, wasted no time in dashing to the tree, both in anticipation of the feast and the relief of having survived that uncomfortable encounter.

Fox and I sat on the concrete blocks that lined the tree and amidst the rotten guavas on the ground, while Nigel climbed up the tree and just tossed us any green-yellow, firm fruits he could find. Very few words were exchanged, but it was apparent there was a lot of remorse going around. Up until then, the fear of confrontation and loss of their friends had been enough to stop the brothers from indulging in The Guava Tree experience; they had just walked right past it into the house.

Nevertheless, we were here now. Nothing was forgotten, yet all was forgiven. When Ta got off the bus that afternoon, he was understandably surprised to see us breaking bread with our sworn nemesis. He decided not to dig deep for an explanation; he was just happy not to have to pick sides anymore. Wellington, the epitome of primary school angst, had a difficult time moving past the fallout. He came back home to see us sitting by the guavas, cast one resentfully guilty look at his brother and us before hastening into the house. Fox smiled wryly and said, "It's going to take some time, but I'll talk to him."

After a few days, Wellington started coming around. His pride would not let him see strangers constantly enjoy the fruits of his birthright while he locked himself in the house. First, he would stop by the tree for a few minutes, pick a few guavas and act like he was paying no mind to us, and then go inside. Then, a few days later, he would sit among us, not saying a word. We were in an awkward place in which the victims were extending a hand of truce while the aggressor still debated whether he was ready to make peace.

There were a few undeniable truths among the Ownership boys. One was a game of football was always about to happen, even if nothing foreshadowed it. Another was you could not stay angry at your friends for too long; every fight would soon boil over and simmer down like it never happened, only to exist in Fox's morbid story-telling for years to come. Finally, when someone asked you for the fruit of your tree, you never said no.

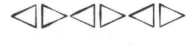

8

One unremarkable Wednesday afternoon, we convened under the old Guava Tree. Fox and I were attempting to work our way through the previous weekend's crossword puzzle. Nigel had established a base for himself at the treetop and was feasting and throwing fruit down from on high. Although Wellington was still reclusive towards me, he had since made peace with the less stubborn Nigel. He was also slightly more sociable because Ta, Tinashe, and some of the other neighborhood boys who had not earned his ire were also coming around all the time now.

Despite the fading cloud that continued to linger over The Guava Tree, there was an unspoken consensus amongst everyone that the return to calm was a much needed and pleasant turn. On this particular day, my best friend from school, Innocent, had also joined the feasting party. He lived in Area B, adjacent to the infamous MaTwo Rooms, but we had bonded at school over our love for chess and American and British children's adventure books. He carried himself with confidence and charisma that made him stick out from among us, and yet he fit in well with the rest of my MaOwnership friends: a rather rare quality amongst other alien friends of MaOwnership boys.

As we sat, we saw a new face approaching us from around the corner from the backstreet. He was a tiny boy, no bigger than Nigel and his classmates, although his face bore the wisdom of a fifth or sixth grader. He was walking with a spring in his step that, to us, was a clear sign that he was not from the neighborhood. MaOwnership boys, real MaOwnership boys, didn't walk with a spring, they dragged their feet languidly with an assumed air of importance.

"Hello, friends! My name is Blessing, and I'm..." the diminutive newcomer began to speak when he was right in front of The Guava Tree.

"Yea yea, you are that new African Church of God pastor's son, aren't you?" Fox interrupted, making little attempt to conceal his disdain.

The African Church of God people meant well, but their reputation was skewered among the Dangamvura residents for many reasons. Their brand of lively spiritual worship was at odds with the traditional, conservative Catholic, Anglican and Methodist services to which the vast majority of the people belonged. They also made it a point to identify with their church, whereas it was almost impossible to tell what church the rest of us went to except on Sundays and at funerals. Of particular annoyance to us, and as unapologetically expressed by Fox, was that they would only move in for a year at a time and then a new pastor would come into town. It was almost impossible to become good friends with the children from there. The children must have known it too, and they generally made little effort to befriend us. If him being the Pastor's son was not enough for us to view Blessing with cynicism, he also lived on the backstreet, and there was just something about those people.

This boy, however, was different.

"Yes, I am!" he continued, unfazed by the hostility. "I was just stopping by to ask if I could have a guava or two."

If somebody asked for fruit from your tree, you were obliged to give them at least one. The exceptions were if the fruits weren't fully ripe yet, or if you had due and justified reason to despise the person asking. Fox fell short on both accounts. He also understood that doing the right thing was more important than making our hate felt.

"I guess you can have a coup..." Fox started to say begrudgingly but, before he could finish, the new boy dashed towards the tree and, with the agility reserved for monkeys, climbed up to the top.

His brash confidence made him all right by us. He did not come across as thinking he was better than us like the previous pastors' children had, yet did not seem too desperate to belong. If the verdict was still out on how we felt about him, the next words out of his mouth sealed it for us.

"So, do you guys play football around here?" We looked around at each other with wry smiles that communities across creation use when they have effortlessly stumbled upon one of their own,

"Why, yes we do. What's your name again?" I asked. He yelled something as he climbed down, but Fox interrupted him. "They will be moving again before you can memorize it, these church people. We will just call him... Babylon!" He joked, grasping for the first biblical reference that came to his mind. We laughed, and the new boy laughed along.

He climbed down and sat under the shade with everyone, and we began to explain to him what had happened. What was supposed to be a simple story of why Gogo had kicked us off the yard became a well-choreographed exercise in storytelling, in which we all took turns to tell the history of MaOwnership. Between Fox's cynical humor, Ta's stuttered neighborhood gossip, Nigel's youthful regurgitation of everything he heard adults say, and my constant fact-checking made for an exciting and rich narrative equally enjoyed by the storyteller as by the listener. Although Babylon tried to keep up, he was obviously struggling to remember the names and connections being thrown at him all at once. It was almost as if his mind froze at the moment he heard that we, indeed, played football around here.

Over the next few days the new boy, now christened Babylon, joined us at The Guava Tree. For once, Nigel had someone with him high up the tree. Although he was quite talkative, he spoke little of where he had come from, with most of his conversation dedicated to sports, particularly football and cricket. He spoke about the games he had played, discussed the games he had recently watched, and argued vehemently about who was the best primary school team in the area. While his general penchant for life was apparent, there was an even brighter glimmer in his eye when he spoke about sport. As the days passed, he grew increasingly agitated at not playing football with no solution in sight.

"Ko[23], have we just given up on ever playing again? Are we just going to hope that we are chosen for our school teams to get some action?" Babylon asked from up the tree, to which Fox smirked back sarcastically,

"Yea right. I don't know about you, monkey man, but the rest of us would never stand a chance at school against the kids from MaTwo Rooms, Area 3, Area C—"

"Fox, you're missing the point!" I interjected, half trying to steer the conversation back towards the brainstorming session Babylon had initiated, and half in denial of Fox's candidly mean remarks about our abilities. "Babylon here has never played with us, and we haven't played in a while either. I think what he is trying to say is we should come up with a plan soon, right Babylon?"

"Babylon?"

---

23 Informal remark, akin to 'Say, boys...'

He didn't answer. I looked up into the tree and saw him gazing pensively across the street in the direction of our house. He was actually looking at the large unused space by The Mountain, where the house had never been built.

"Do you guys know why there is that large space over there, next to the Mountain? I know father says we will use some of it during the planting season, but does anyone know who it belongs to?"

"We-well," Ta began "I once he-e-ard Old Man Chimutondo tell another old man that there were people buried under there from during the war."

"Nxaah!" was the general reaction from everyone. Ta insisted on this story for a little while, but nobody was having it, and Babylon inevitably seized back the conversation.

"Well, seeing there won't be any building going on there any time soon, and the rainy season is some months away," our tiny ears perked up like dogs when master brings leftovers in the morning, "Do you guys think that..."

"No way man," Ta all of a sudden chimed in, "Yo-you see how bushy that area is? It would take us weeks to clear it! Besides, there really might be graves unde... ouch!"

I leaned over and mildly smacked the back of his head,

"Ta my friend, Old Man Chimutondo was clearly joking about the grave nonsense! You believed that? You are right about the clearing though; that might take a while! That place has been untouched that way since the last harvest."

Babylon was undeterred. He committed to asking his father regarding the space that night, as long as we would at least keep an open mind about clearing the field. Fox and I exchanged glances and silently agreed on a plan.

"Yes, Babylon. If you will ask your father and he agrees, we will consider clearing the field!'

We were certain that the Pastor would never agree to the field being used for football. The Church of God folk did not particularly like their children running with the non-church crowd; especially when they were still new to the neighborhood. In addition, he still planned to use it for maize in the rainy season; the ground would be rock hard from all the stomping and running by then.

9

"Who is that? Is that Babylon?"

"Yea it's him for sure! Why is he dragging that rake and hoe with him! It's not crop season yet!"

We had not seen Babylon for about a week after he decided to ask his father about the field. We figured his father had, as we had silently predicted, been furious at the very thought and assigned him a dozen church tasks to keep him away from all the mischief.

Thus, when Nigel spotted him from atop the sacred Guava Tree, slowly making his way toward us like a heroic soldier from a Van Damme or Rambo movie, we were surprised. As he drew closer still, we noticed that he carried three or four garden tools with him.

"*Ndeip*[24], boys! Ready to get clearing?"

---

24 Shortening of "ndeipi", translating to "what's up"

For a few seconds, we sat there, trying to decipher what he meant. Innocent then confirmed what everyone else was beginning to figure out.

"Wait. Your old man actually said yes?"

"Yep! As long as I promise to participate in our church youth group, keep my grades up, and help with tilling the soil when planting season comes, he says it's all good!"

We were in shock. We had apparently underestimated Babylon's charm and hastened to typecast his father. Maybe this pastor was all right after all. Who knows, we might even go visit...

"So, what are we waiting for? You promised, remember? Let's get to work!" Babylon announced, tossing a rake my way and summoning Fox to get a hoe from him.

As we walked over to honor our misguided promise, the shock began to wear off and was replaced by mounting excitement. We were finally going to be playing again.

For us, living without football was similar to when the electricity would be down for hours, which tended to happen often. At first, you are caught off-guard and do not know what to do with yourself. Because the outcome is out of your control, it is hard to plan beyond the electricity coming back. You could never be sure when that would be. You are irritable. Soon, you find the next best thing to do. You make it work with candles and matches. You roast some locusts on the open fire. After a while, you might even get used to being in the dark and begin not to miss the electricity as much. There is, however, a little being in the folds of your mind that keeps reminding you that there is something else out there; that you have tasted, seen and felt better, and this is not it. Then, with a buzz, a spark, and a flicker, the electricity comes back, and, at that moment, the drudgery of darkness becomes ever so apparent!

My mind spun. I wonder how many people we can have on the field at a time. Not only was this field bigger than the one inside our yard was. It was shaped better too. I think a five on five game would be perfect. We can even do six or seven if we have some of the smaller boys playing with us. Maybe we can have my street play against the back street and see if we can reignite the old rivalry from The Mountain. Who knows, we could even have the boys from Area C and MaTwo Rooms come play against us here! I don't know if we would be good enough though, but we'll see how we do when we start playing...

By then, we were standing at the field's edge, and it did not take us long to realize the magnitude of the task that awaited us. The grass had not been cut in years, and there were thorns reminiscent of Christ's crown every few steps. Now and then, you would come across a large rock sticking out from below the ground. That first day, we spent an entire afternoon cutting down small trees, slashing the tall grass and digging out rocks from the ground. At first, it was just Fox, Babylon and I. Nigel had gone to buy some milk at Old Man Chimutondo's but joined us as soon as he got back. A few minutes later, Ta disembarked from the bus and, upon seeing us, began to yell excitedly,

"He-e-ey! Wha-a-at's going on? You'll surely be i-in trouble with the Pastor!"

After we clued him in, he ran home, changed into some rugged clothes, and came back with a crude homemade machete that had an old rubber from bicycle bars for a handle.

Wellington did not join us then, choosing instead to watch us bitterly from across the street, high up in Nigel's usual Guava Tree spot. Although he had loosened up a little more since our falling out, and as much as he wanted to play football, his pride was still unwilling to let him spend time with us away from The Guava Tree; let alone work with us on the grueling field. I would look across to where he was and, catching his glance, would see a mixed look of resentment and jealousy seething in his eyes.

When dusk fell, we were exhausted, and our bare feet were bleeding from the thorns and rocks. More importantly, we felt accomplished. As we walked away hunched over, blood-shod and filthy, we looked back upon the labor of our hands with pride. We were less than half way there, but we had been able to clear away most of the tall grass and small trees.

The next day, Nigel and I showed up early and began work in the field. Our preferred tools were two little hoes, one rounded and the other straight at the edges that Gogo used for her flowerbeds. Ta had come home from school earlier than usual that day and joined us then. Fox was visiting one of his other friends from another neighborhood, and Babylon was helping his father with some church deliveries.

"I don't know why, but I just don't feel like doing the work as I did yesterday," Nigel said, in an unenthused tone that I unmistakably knew to mean that he was only going to do the bare minimum henceforth.

"Oh, come on, mfana! You see how much we have already done? We will be finished in no time!" I replied in a veiled attempt to convince myself as well. Despite the gains of the previous day's labor, our motivation had visibly decreased. We had anticipated that the field would take us a few hours at most, but we were now finding that we would only barely get it done in two days. We had also initially expected everyone in the neighborhood to help lighten the work, yet we were down to three men.

"Ni-Nige is right! This is si-silly. We can't be the only ones in all of MaOwnership who are excited to start playing again! Where are Fungai and Tiberius? Where are Tinashe and Faru? Wellington is still being a child, and Fox simply didn't show up today. I-I-I'm going home."

Ta began to walk away languidly as if daring me to stop him; I could not. At this point, I was just as frustrated as he was and could not, in all fairness, try and keep anyone there with me. Instead, I walked up beside him and solemnly called to Nigel to join us.

We had just walked off the field and into the street when Babylon shouted out to us. He was carrying the last basket of tomatoes that his father had sent him to gift to some church folk.

"Why are you leaving? You guys barely did anything today!" He probed, evidently bewildered at the sight of his trusted lieutenants deserting the mission at the height of battle. I relayed to him how we were slaving for hours on end, only for the fruits of our efforts to be enjoyed by everyone else. It made no sense

"Okay. How about this? If I can get a few more boys from the area to help us before dusk, will you come back? I should be back in an hour or two!" He took off before we even had the chance to agree.

Well, if he is so sure that he will be back with others to help move the work along, we might as well continue working, we decided. Ta, who had been within Babylon's earshot, still left, only now he was walking with the spring of purpose in his step. Nigel and I just looked at each other and figured that he must have remembered something he had to do back at his house. Ta had always been impulsive, and I had since given up trying to predict what he was going to do next. We would just wait and see.

True to his word, Babylon came back with reinforcements. He had gone down his street and ran into Tiberius, who was on his way back from tennis.

MaOwnership had yet another unique distinction within Dangamvura in that it produced more tennis players than any other neighborhood. This had come to be, as things often happened, by a stroke of happenstance. There were only two tennis courts in all of Dangamvura: one by Rujeko Primary School on the far side, and the one at Beit. Legend has it that a certain Mrs. Martins would bring rackets and balls to the Beit tennis court for all the children in surrounding areas that were interested in learning this new game. Most of the people who would go practice came from MaOwnership, Area B, Area C and Area P. Many boys from the MaTwo Rooms initially came as well but realized almost immediately that they would much rather play football. In football, not only did you not have to wait your turn while only two or four people played at a time, you did not need any extra hitting tools or bouncy balls! Soon, the other neighborhoods followed suit. Eventually, there were only one or two other players from other neighborhoods, but the bulk of those who stayed was from MaOwnership. Nobody mentioned it then, but it so happened because MaOwnership was the only neighborhood whose streets were paved in tar, so the interested boys could still play in the street when they got home. Also, because of the relative affluence, parents in MaOwnership were more likely to spend money on racquets, tennis balls and tennis camps in the city than the other Dangamvura neighborhoods.

Almost all the Ownership boys who had been part of Mrs. Martins' group—The Bvunzawabaya boys, The Chirembas, and Fungai and Tiberius's brothers—were all from the backstreet. They were the stuff of Dangamvura legend and were either playing professional tennis in Harare or coaching in high schools by then. They had, however, passed the tradition to their younger brothers.

On this day, Babylon had been able to smooth-talk Tiberius and Fungai into taking some time to help with what was left of the field by tapping into the age-old dormant hostilities between the backstreet and ours.

"Ndeipi guys," Babylon had called to them, "How is tennis going?"

"Good, I guess" they replied, slightly thrown off by the pleasantries, seeing as their sophisticated pastime was usually the object of envious scorn from other MaOwnership boys.

"That's cool! I wish I could play like you two do. I don't think I would be much good though. I have been trying to turn that rugged field by The Mountain into a football pitch with some of the other boys" said Babylon, slickly pandering and bringing up the field in one turn.

"Oh, yea," Fungai said, scowling, "I saw you yesterday working on it with Ta and the other boys from the front-street."

"Indeed! It's going slow, but I think it is going to be good when it's done. I think you guys should join us and help with some of the clearing."

Tiberius winced as he prepared to denounce the absurd idea, but Babylon was a step ahead.

"... and I understand you guys have not always been on good terms with the others, and that is why you should help! Look, my family will probably have to move again in a year or two. If we let only Shingi and the boys from the front street work on the field, then they will lay claim to the field and do what they will with it. And you know how hardheaded they can get; they would never let you play. I know you may not be into football right now, but I can promise you are going to want to play sooner or later. Maybe your cousins will come to visit from the rural areas or something, and they are not interested in tennis in the slightest: just football. Wouldn't it be nice to be able to play there too?"

Tiberius and Fungai hated the idea, but they also knew he made a lot of sense. Begrudgingly, they followed Babylon, who led the way to the field with the chest-out swagger of a revolutionary war hero returning home with word of the enemy's surrender. We were surprised to see them but dared not ask, lest we undo Babylon's diplomatic exploits. Setting aside all unspoken resentment, we welcomed the two new additions to the workforce with open arms and two sickles for the shrubbery. No sooner had the brothers put their back into clearing some overgrown weeds did we hear excited bird-calling and yelling coming from the direction of our street. I knew it was Ta without lifting my head; he had a distinct bird-call. It was loud and would break into three melodic syllables as if to mimic the sound made by the house sparrows. He had two other boys with him.

If Babylon's triumphant return earlier had a scent of self-importance, Ta's reeked of it. As it turned out, he had overheard Babylon talking about getting some help and figured that, if the new kid could do it, then he could too. An idea hit him. Tinashe's father had a peanut butter business, and Tinashe and his brother would spend hours on end shelling the peanuts for grinding. The work was tedious, painful and slow for the two young boys, so their father was always looking for extra help from the other boys in the neighborhood. I went there myself a few times but had since been banned because I kept eating the peanuts I shelled instead of handing them over to be ground. On this day, however, Ta figured that if he could promise Tinashe that some of the other boys would come and help shell nuts in exchange for his help at the field, he would be more than willing to.

He ran to Tinashe's house and, true to his prediction, found him, his brother, and his friend Faru buried in empty peanut shells. After a few minutes of chatter, he told them of his proposed trade-off. It was an easy sell, and Tinashe and Faru came with him.

I was pleasantly surprised by Ta's uncharacteristic enterprising. By now, Fox and Innocent had also arrived.

Excited yet wary of existing tensions, lack of motivation, and the exhaustion creeping within the group, Babylon did not relent in drumming up our workman morale. "Come on, guys. You have already done the hardest part! Let's just finish what we started."

As much as we despised him at the moment, we knew he was right. We picked our little tools up. We took to the ground lethargically at first but saw our efforts double, and then triple as the idea of actually finishing appeared within reach. We were almost done. Whenever one of us would start slacking or complaining, Ta would begin to chant the old Shona church chorus teasingly.

"Unorarirei ko? Muka! Muka iweee!"

Although referring to the story of Jesus and the sleepy disciples in the garden, it had slipped into the colloquial jukebox and was now the go-to song for anyone wishing to energize people. It was especially popular at funerals, where the crowds would sing it to the deceased. Babylon chanted it a few times before Fox took over the show with his wild and unbelievable tales about everything under the sun. He told a painfully funny story about a man he knew back in the rural area who lost his toe after sticking his foot in the spokes of a moving bicycle. He had a sad one where a dog had been slapped to death by a crazed baboon in the fields. Then he would tell us about the time he fought Paida and Mark, two neighborhood boys who were older and much bigger than him. Both times, he claimed to have won. We knew better. That was Fox; the value of his stories lay not in their truth or moral; we loved them because they were well-crafted and entertaining, even if they were only true a quarter of the times.

That evening, we looked upon the labor of our hands. It was far from perfect; but it was now passable as a football field, albeit a basic one. We still had to deal with the small rocks and thorns that were on the ground, but we also knew that none of our tools would be of any effective help. We either had to do it by hand or find another way that would allow us to pick up even the tiniest thorn. As dusk set across the land, it seemed to be setting on our dream as well. As things stood, our field would never be as good, nay, half as good as we had imagined.

"There is no way we can play here," Nigel bemoaned, putting into words what everyone was thinking.

"It is way too rocky and uneven, plus there are ground thorns all over the place. We will never be able to play without our shoes."

As he said that, Tinashe, Faru, and The Tennis Brothers were already turning around and heading back to their houses, murmuring disapprovals as they did. Fungai even had a victorious smirk on his face: this setback meant he no longer had to work with us and further emphasized how our street could never put a successful project together.

Wellington had been watching all this from The Guava Treetop with veiled interest. Each time any one of us would look in his direction, he would look away or reach for another fruit.

When he saw the four boys leaving the field, however, he climbed down and headed towards the field. His face combined both the resentment we had become accustomed to over the past few weeks and the exhilaration that comes only from stumbling upon the solution to a pressing problem.

None among us took the street divisions as seriously as Wellington did. He could not stand the sight of anybody from the backstreet. Oh, how his already loathe-filled blood must have boiled when he watched from his perch as Babylon brought Fungai and Tiberius to work with us! The only thing he hated more than the backstreet itself was being humiliated by it. Thus, the anger in him when he saw the brothers walking away from the field in utter delight at our failure trounced the pride and bitterness towards the others and me that had kept him away from working with the group.

"Of course, you guys would get stuck! I mean, you have Shingi and this new kid leading all the work, both who look like they have never dug a hole or raked a pile of leaves in their lives!"

His condescension was not without merit; I had stayed away from field work all my life, and Babylon's family probably had church folk help them each season. I was still struggling to see his point, but I held my tongue, lest I antagonize old wounds. Babylon, on the other hand, made no secret of his ire.

"Who are you to talk? You have been perched up in your tree like an aged baboon, and yet you think you can just come and speak as you want?"

Fox chuckled. Ta joined in. It had been a long day already, and the sight of Babylon's tiny built scolding Wellington combined with his colorful language made it hard not to laugh. Wellington ignored him, calling attention back to what he had to say.

"When you fools are finished messing around, I think I have an idea that could solve our thorn problem!" He announced with confidence that we had not seen in weeks.

"What is it, *blaz*[25]?" I asked, eager to know what ray of hope he had to share with us in that cold moment. I was also astounded that he had called the thorns 'our' problem. He still would not look at me, but I found myself cracking a wry smile: he was on his way back.

From where he sat, he had had an idea: What if, for the first few days, we played with our shoes on? Of course, none of us had football shoes, and most of us had no more than three pairs of shoes outside of the ones we used for school. Only a few of us had tennis shoes, and even those doubled up as visiting shoes for when we went to the city.

Wellington's ingenuity lay not in wanting to just play at any cost. He had, instead, reasoned that the little rocks and thorns would get stuck to the soles of our shoes. After a few days, the vast majority of them would have been carried off the field that way. We could then go back to playing barefoot with little threat from rocks and thorns.

If it was hard to convince the boys to play with their shoes on, it was going to be near impossible to convince the parents. None of the Ownership adults would stand to see their children's hard-earned school and church shoes scratched and battered by the rocks, thorns and the unkempt nails of their friends.

We still had to get it done.

The next day, Nigel and I made haste to get back home before Gogo came back from work. As soon as we finished the leftover Sadza that was our lunch, we changed into our tennis shoes and headed to the field where Innocent met us. We had counted on him being there

---

25 Slang for a man, usually implying familiarity

because we figured, being from another neighborhood, he and his shoes would be away from his mother's watchful eye. Due to church commitments, Babylon would not be able to join us on that day.

On my way to meet Innocent at the field, I realized that we had made the most elementary of oversights. We did not have a ball.

"*Ndeip Inno*," I yelled as I dashed in the other direction towards Fox's house, "wait for me, I'll be right back!"

Fox and Wellington, as crafty as they were, were bound to have a ball.

"Hurry up, you two! Get your playing shoes on," I said as I banged on their door, almost certain that they would both come running out. Instead, Fox peeked through the window with a look that uttered fear and disappointment. The door swung open, and I understood why.

"What do you want?" Sincere barked. She was usually not home at that time, and my obnoxious salutation had been based on that assumption. Luckily, she had not heard the part about the shoes; otherwise, she would have made sure her brothers would never leave the house. Thinking on my feet, I asked if her brothers had a ball we could use. As long as she was home, there was no chance of them coming out to play. In spite of their own circumstance, Wellington stepped outside to hand me their hweshe. I could see in his eyes a renewed sense of defiance and solidarity with me—and the others— that I knew to mean that he would be finding a way to join us before the day was done.

I tossed the ball towards the field where Nigel and Innocent were anxiously waiting. It was a celebrated ceremony to mark the beginning of game day.

10

*W*e started kicking around and playing choms, a simple game ideal for as few as three people. We would pass the ball to each other until someone missed or made a woeful pass, at which point the other two would continue passing to each other and keeping it away from the culprit while they tried to get the ball back. Once they did, whoever gave the ball away would take over in the "middle." When we grew tired of choms, we played one pagedhi, which meant that if you scored a goal, and then you got to be the goalkeeper. Two or more people would dribble and mark each other while one played in goals, and when someone scored, then they would take over as the goalkeeper. I had always enjoyed playing goalie, but the surreal feeling I had the first time I dove on the still thorny field was matched only by the wonder of the first days I watched football with my uncles. I felt a swirling in my stomach rising like September winds, slowly and increasing with each turn, until it took over my whole body and finally escaped with a vicious shaking of my upper body and an elated yelp. Nigel and innocent were too busy dueling on the field of play to notice it, which was just as well.

An hour later, I noticed Sincere leaving their house. Her hair was combed out, and she had applied so much Pond's [26] to her face that she looked pale, even from across the street. She must have been going to meet her boyfriend. Older boys must find that sort of thing attractive, I mused.

Before she left, she threw a menacing glance towards the field and then another back at their house, where Fox and Wellington were sitting on the step just outside their door. They cast an innocent one back as if to promise her they would stay put. The next one was in the direction of the field, and it bore the brothers' identical mischievous smiles that said everything we needed to hear: they were coming as soon as she was over the hill—and they did. They came in their school shoes and joined the frantic game of one pagedhi that was going on— each man playing for himself.

A few minutes later, Ta disembarked from the city *kombi*[27].

Since he had switched schools, there had been some acrimony directed towards him by almost all of us. It was a combination of the feeling of betrayal because he had left the Dangamvura schools, the jealousy of seeing him ride the bus to school and walk down the street in his shiny blue blazer and missing him. We had little to talk about these days. Now and then, he would come over and sit with us under The Guava Tree, but he would always have to leave early because he had to be up before dawn to catch the bus for the one-hour trip to school. Nevertheless, the moment we saw him walking down the street from school was always a happy one. He was our friend. "Hey, Ta! Look at you, looking better than us with the blazer and what what!"

---

26 Popular brand of vanishing cream
27 Minibus.

Wellington yelled out with hyena-like laughter. By now, Ta was used to the jabs, so he stuttered back in playful annoyance.

"Hmm hmm...Wellington thinks he's a fu-fu-funny guy huh?"

"Pay no mind to him!" I said, butting my way into the conversation, "but it would be nice of you to dress down into us normal folks' clothes and join us in a little game! We hardly ever see you anymore!"

As much as he enjoyed the envious respect that came with going to a city school, he missed the routine of playing with the rest of the boys. This particular opportunity was too appealing to resist so he, too, ran home and came back in his blue and red tennis shoes.

The game was on.

We organized into two teams. The unwritten protocol was to always separate the best players first, who would usually be chosen as captains to select the rest of the team. In this case, it was Wellington and Innocent. Then, you would separate brothers; meaning Fox joined Innocent's team Nigel did too, while Ta and I went with Wellington. There we had it; the first ever teams to take to the field in battle.

On that first day, we played for three straight hours. Just before dusk, Fox and Wellington figured they had better go wash up before Sincere came home, so they bade farewell and left. We kicked around for a few more minutes before we saw Gogo coming down the street from work with half a dozen bags of groceries in hand. Why she insisted on carrying the groceries home on the bus, I never understood, especially since she could have waited a day or two and pick them up with Kulu in his car.

Nigel and I raced up and grabbed the bags from her before we had finished greeting her.

"Oh no! You boys are playing again?" she said with the magnanimous smile that permanently garnished her face. Then, with a concerned look, she cast a glance toward the field. She must have been looking to see if Wellington and Fox were there, but because they had left already, she just smiled and waved to Ta and Innocent. While she typically held no grudges, she was always wary of any negative influences on us and, at this point, she was not ready to see us playing with the brothers yet.

After we walked Gogo and the groceries into the house, I came back outside and walked Innocent halfway home. His home was about two thirds of the way towards our school, so it was a significant amount for him to walk to my house after school. Walking him halfway back was the least I could do. I walked him to the end of the street, from which point you could see the Area B Bus station in one direction (going towards the school) and the Beit football field in the other direction.

"Thanks for coming out Inno, I'll see you in class tomorrow!"

"Sounds good blaz. Maybe we can stop by the chess club for 30 minutes or so before coming here."

"Excellent. Then we can come back and play some football with the rest of the boys. There might be a few more people tomorrow!"

"*Iri bho*[28]! See you then!"

---

28 "Sounds Good!"

11

The next day, Friday, the six of us who had been there the day before rushed to the field after school. This time, Tinashe and Faru's humble demeanors greeted us. With their heads bowed in recognition of their earlier treason, they asked if they could join in the day's game.

"Wow guys," Tinashe began, in transparent flattery, "the field looks amazing! Good job."

We were not impressed by the attempts at reconciliation. Ta, having recruited them to the job in the first place and also seeing himself as their big brother, was particular bemused and unforgiving.

"Isn't it beautiful? It's incredible what you can do when you are surrounded by committed people," He replied sarcastically. Tinashe and Faru seemed almost surprised that the most vicious hostilities were coming from their closest friend on the field. Wellington, ignoring their presence, turned to the rest of us and asked if we wanted to play on the same teams we had yesterday. Even though they were trying to shake it off, it was clear that the two boys were shattered. They looked around miserably before going to sit by The Mountain as we began to play. I could tell that Nigel, who was their classmate, was feeling guilty for playing while they sat out. It weighed on his mind for about fifteen minutes of play, before his guilt got the better of him. After a seemingly light collision with Ta, he began limping and making a public show of his apparent pain.

"I can't go on! I need a few minutes off." He whined, clearly committed to stepping out of the game. With the game picking up steam, we could neither stop nor play a man short. Nigel's 'injury' left us no choice, so I called out to the prodigal boys and asked if one of them wanted to play. Tinashe came in at once.

Although animosity bubbled in the first few minutes of him coming onto the field, all was forgiven as soon as his feet touched the ball. He was incredible! For his age, he was undoubtedly the best player in all of MaOwnership. He was chubby and short, which made his legs look like rubber when he dribbled), how he dribbled. He was so fast and nimble that even we, as the other team, stood back and marveled at how easy he made it look.

Nigel and Faru watched for a short while from The Mountain, before deciding they were too far and at an awkward angle from which to watch the game. Faru, fully aware of his continued alienation and that he did not have half of Tinashe's skills to mesmerize us and gain our favor, made his first and most meaningful contribution to the development of the new field. His uncle had recently discarded a long, flat piece of wood that used to harness the wooden shed that they had just torn down, he told Nigel. If we could find two or three smaller logs and dig them into the ground, we might be able to fashion ourselves a pitch-side bench for the substitutes and spectators. Without notice, they made their way to Faru's house, came back with the piece of wood and two logs they had found lying around in our yard, and began hammering away on the sidelines under the barren peach tree that separated the field from The Mountain. Our game was distracted for a little while until Faru explained what was happening and that they had it under control. In a matter of minutes, the substitutes' bench was in place—just in time for our break from the game. We all gathered by the bench and shared game tales and other stories.

Before we had resumed playing, Babylon came back from his chores and came straight to the field. Upon seeing it for the first time in its playable state, he was so overwhelmed with emotion that he did not know what to do. He ran across the field and screamed for the ball; Wellington obliged him with a pass, and then he juggled half the length of the field before kicking it ferociously against the fence. He then ran over and asked about the bench. I explained how that was Faru's idea, thereby rendering his next question obsolete. In his excitement, everything was a blur: he just wanted to play.

"What are we waiting for? Wellington and I will pick teams, let's go! I'll take Shingi..."

That day, we played until dusk again. There were nine of us, and Faru and Nigel were swapping after every two goals in the beginning. Then, as we all got tired or went under a harsh tackle, we would take turns to sit out on the bench. By now, we were not playing in shoes anymore—the thorns had been largely taken care of the day before. When the Pastor finally called for Babylon to come in, we decided we had played enough for that day. We came back soon after porridge[29] the next day, and again, after church on Sunday.

The field was alive. It was only about three meters wide and thirty meters long, and we figured would cap the games at five against five; maybe six against six if needed. The surface was getting smoother with each day we played.

Football was alive.

---

29 Together with another maize-meal dish, Sadza, porridge is the most popular meal in Zimbabwe (Sadza for dinner, porridge for breakfast)

We were alive.

12

Before long, word of our budding field had spread across all of Dangamvura. Although MaOwnership was a relatively small neighborhood, we had all four Dangamvura primary schools represented in our midst. That, added to Innocent being from another neighborhood and the several other school children walking through our neighborhood on their way home, made it only inevitable that everybody heard.

There were, as far as we knew, two fields similar to ours in Dangamvura. One, nicknamed Gwanzura after one of the bigger stadiums in Zimbabwe, was right next to the Beit field. It was a little bigger than ours, and I assume some MaTwo Rooms boys created it as an alternative to Beit when the adult teams would play. The problem was it was plagued with a type of evergreen thorn that would resurface almost immediately after you got rid of it. Gwanzura was also located under a giant Marula tree under which a sect of the African Apostolic church would worship. Wellington and Fox went to that church. In my unrelenting curiosity, I had attended a service with them once. It was the most fascinating thing! All the men arrived under the tree in their normal clothes and then, upon the command of the lead prophet, would pull out long white robes from their bags and wear those. The women were already dressed in white, complete with headscarves. All the men were shaved bald. As far as I could tell, they did not read from the Bible, and yet the prophet would spit out scripture after scripture from apparent memory. Then they sang and played the African drum for an hour or two at the end. When I got back home, Gogo had been furious with me that I had gone to that church; which was uncharacteristic, seeing as I would often go to my other friends' churches and she had never mentioned it. It might have been because this church was weird and no one outside it seemed to understand what they did and why they did it.

The other field was halfway towards the Complex, on the banks of the Nyamauru River. This one was a beauty. The people who had made it had even gone out and bought poles to use as goals and, due to the river water, the playing surface stayed grassy. As many times as I walked past that field, I never saw anyone playing there. A shame, I thought. If we had a field that beautiful, or a field at all for that matter, we would be there all the time.

Well, now we did. It was yet humble, not adorned with upright goalposts like the riverbank field or as celebrated as Gwanzura, but to be one of the three neighborhood fields of note in all of Dangamvura? Our pride was indeed well placed.

Word of the current state of the field finally fell upon Tiberius and Fungai's ears. Although they had known about the field's inception and probably even seen us playing on their way to tennis, it was the envy born out of hearing the rest of Dangamvura singing the glories of our field that irritated them. It was just like Babylon had predicted would happen. Because the field was located right where our streets met, the space was essentially the backstreet's birthright as it was ours.

They knew it, and we knew it. Worse still, we knew they thirsted for confrontation, and it was only a matter of time before they came. We kept watch.

They did not come during the first week. Or the one after that.

It was not until the fourth week when we had let our guard down, that they finally showed up. They came in peace, much to our surprise. They had just finished tennis practice for the day, so they strolled over to the field in their white t-shirts and shorts, racquets in hand. They were cheerful enough, went straight to the bench that Nigel and Faru had made and seemingly got lost in watching our game. They stayed for an hour and then left as inconspicuously as they had arrived. No one remarked about this, although I am tempted to believe that most of us had thought the visit strange. Two days later, they came, watched the game, and left again exactly as they had done the first time. Again, I thought it was odd. I wondered what everyone else was making of the brothers' bizarre behavior, so I finally asked.

"We-we-ell, I think they just enjoy watching a good game of football. It must be a good change for them after boring da-day of of te-te-tennis!" Ta tried to explain.

"I agree," Babylon chimed in almost joyfully, "they have been very nice about the whole affair, and here we were thinking that they would be causing trouble!"

I wasn't convinced, and Wellington made no secret that he shared my sentiments.

"You are both being silly! Those two are the worst of the backstreet bunch; there is no way they are just coming to watch some front street game for fun. They are the most devious people I know, and I am not falling for this farce!"

"Enough of this backstreet talk Wellaz," Babylon spoke up, beginning to lose his cool, "You are always so angry about things that you always see the worst in people!"

Wellington simmered. He was not used to people speaking this way and, when they did, the next step would have been to fight. Ta, Nigel, and I cringed as we saw his fists begin to clench. Babylon, being unfamiliar with Wellington's temper, did not notice how things had deteriorated.

He was ever so close to finding out when Fox jumped into the conversation and spoke sternly and softly, "Ah see, this is exactly what they want to see. I understand what Ta and Babylon are saying, but I think Wellington is right. You want to know what they are trying to do? This," he said, as he pointed at us, emphasizing Wellington and Babylon.

"They want us to fight among each other. Babylon, you have only been around for a few months, and I understand that you may not yet know how these folks work. They will have you turning your back on your friends, and then sweeping in like vultures to pick up what is left behind. You have to be very careful. Now, let's play..."

We all went back to our positions, albeit with the spring taken out of our step. I had never heard Fox speak that way. He had definitely spoken like the slightly older brother that he was. The thick tension cloud that still hung over Wellington and Babylon was transferred into some beautiful, competitive football between the two for the rest of the day.

I could live with all conflicts being resolved that way. I also knew, however, that both Wellington and Babylon were stubborn, and that we had not heard the last of the Tennis Brothers. And our field was good and popular, but it was still no riverbank field or Gwanzura.

◁▷◁▷ ◁▷

13

After the near-fight with Wellington at the field, Babylon distanced himself from the group, only showing up to the field for games. Even then, he was not his usual effervescent self. I attempted to reach out to him, a task that was made especially hard because he did not appear to be upset or quarreled with anyone. If anything, he was more pleasant than usual; just noticeably distant. The confrontation with Wellington must have left him more shaken up than he had let on.

One day, on my way back from school, I saw him sitting on the backstreet pavement with the Tennis Brothers, chatting away. It was an odd sight: Babylon had not been playing with us and had, in the past, seemed party to our backstreet bashing. A part of me, admittedly, was just jealous to see a friend we thought we had locked in as part of our group fraternizing with the foes. Maybe they just ran into each other. Besides, Babylon is technically a backstreet boy too, and he does well to at least know who his neighbors are, as manipulative as they may be. I waved to them with the diplomacy required of such awkward encounters. They waved back.

I saw them again the next day. Babylon joined the rest of us at the football field thirty minutes later and made no mention of his budding backstreet friendships. It weighed on my mind but, knowing how much more hostile everyone else on our street was when it came to The Tennis Brothers, I decided to keep it to myself and see how everything unfolded in time.

That weekend, Ta and I met up early on Saturday morning to go watch some of the Boozers play at Beit. Ever since we had started playing on our field, we rarely made the trip over there except when we had to pass by there on our way to the post office. Border Timbers was playing some city team, and a few dozen people had shown up to watch. To add some excitement to the usually drab matches, I liked to climb into trees and pretend I was the game commentator. After a while, I knew a lot of the local players' names, and that made my job more fun and easier. My friends, Ta in this instance, thought it was crazy and would have no part of that nonsense, preferring to sit under the tree and watching the game like normal people.

On our way back, Babylon and The Tennis Brothers were again sitting on the pavement. This time, Ta saw the disconcerting bedfellows as well. They waved at us. Ta didn't.

"Wha-what is that all about?" was all he was able to spit out under the weight of confused fury that now wore over him. He was further baffled by my seeming lack of concern at the unsightly scene. I explained to him that I had already seen them together before but had to reconsider before telling everyone else. I told him to do the same, even though I knew it was a losing proposition; Ta craved the attention of breaking news and lived to see the resulting drama. As soon as we parted ways, I went home for lunch and to watch the Saturday afternoon film, and he ran straight to Wellington and Fox's door. As much as the brothers disliked the backstreet and were always on the lookout for any trouble with them, they initially refused to believe Ta. Because of his dubious penchant for drama, it was not beyond him to make up such a story.

Before they could argue any further, all doubt was put to rest. Babylon ran onto the field by himself and began kicking a ball around. After a minute or two of this bizarre behavior, he stopped and began to look around to see if anyone was in sight. Ta was still at Fox's doorway, and it was impossible for Babylon to see into the yard beyond The Guava Tree from the field. Convinced no one had seen him, he whistled loudly, summoning Tiberius and Fungai to join him on the field. They came around the corner stealthily at first, and then picked up in confidence upon Babylon's 'all-clear' signal. Fox, Wellington, and Ta stood statuesque in stunned silence. As it so happened at that moment, Nigel had stepped outside to feed the dogs and, while he was also too far to see our friends across the streets beyond The Guava Tree, he clearly saw over the fence to where Babylon and the other two were. Babylon even shouted a greeting to him, but by then, he had already started running to the house to tell me. Nigel was always cognizant of his being younger than us and refused to act or feel on anything until he saw how we, and I, in particular, decided to move forward.

"You need to come to the field right now!" he screamed, explaining himself no further. He knew that was a distress call enough for me. Fortunately, that Saturday afternoon's movie was a farce about a ghost who came back for love or something, and I had no problem tearing myself away from it. I walked outside, Nigel tailing me, just in time to see Ta, Wellington, and Fox crossing the street towards the field. Just as well, I thought to myself. I had been unsure how I was going to confront the three boys already on the field, but I knew the others would have had plenty to say. Since they were bound to vent their fury, it would then move me into the diplomatic role in which I was most comfortable.

As Ta and the boys got onto the field, Babylon smiled and took a step in their direction, preparing a charm offensive for the encounter at hand. Before he got any further, Wellington motioned to The Tennis Brothers and said,

"You two... Off the field!"

with a collected yet authoritative sternness with which I had never seen his typical volatile self-handle any conflict.

Everyone stood back, caught off guard by Wellington's command. One group had been ready to argue why they were on the field, and the other had been prepared to hold Wellington back in the likely event that he would charge at the foe. His eyes bloodshot and face creased up to reveal three menacing wrinkles on his forehead, Wellington bellowed his command again, gesturing for their departure from the field with a raised index finger. This time, Babylon took two steps forward to meet Wellington halfway,

"No, I said they could be here!"

All eyes shifted towards Babylon. We had also never heard him speak like this, and even The Tennis Brothers had not expected to him to step up in their defense in that way. Fox lunged forward, intentionally placing himself in front of Wellington, now almost sure that he was going to pounce on Babylon.

"But Babylon, you know they didn't help. You saw how tough it was for all of us to bring this field to what it is now!" Fox said, almost pleading to reach Babylon's sensibilities while calming Wellington at the same time. The Tennis Brothers stood by, seemingly unperturbed.

"I know, friend; but they have apologized to me," Babylon replied, coming down from the bravado-hoisted pedestal that he had stood on earlier.

Wellington spoke again, fuming "Okay, so what? Just because they apologized to you, everything is okay? They did not apologize to everyone else, and they did not lift a single finger to help with the work. You forgot the work we put in already? We stomped all over these thorns and rocks in our good shoes! How does this even make sense?"

"Right! But look, are you now arguing that only those of us who were here for the work can play here? We have this amazing field on which only six or seven people can play? That's nonsense; if you do that, I can promise you it will get boring soon, and even the few friends you have will stop playing here" Babylon responded.

"He is ri-right," Ta said, chiming in for the first time on the field. The front-street boys, myself included, immediately turned to look at him in disappointed horror. Why would he raise his voice at this point in the argument, just to speak against the street? Even Babylon and the others were thrown off by his unexpected retort and, for that one extraordinary moment, everyone's stare was upon Ta. Not used to being the center of attention—except in the presence of the younger boys—Ta maneuvered himself to the dead middle of the ongoing debate.

"Shi-Shi-Shingi," he said, looking over the fence and bringing me into the conversation for the first time, "Wha-what do you think? He is right, no? I me-mean, how are we ever going to become the biggest, best field in all of Dangamvura if we just play among ourselves?"

He made a good point, albeit a misguided one. The problem, of course, was never that we wanted to play strictly among ourselves; we just did not want to play with the backstreet boys, especially the ones who had walked away at the height of our labors. How do we move past this though? I was not so concerned about getting The Tennis Brothers to play as I was with the point that Ta had made about creating the biggest, best field in all of Dangamvura. I had, since the first day we cleared the field, been considering different things that we could do to make the field more renowned around town. I felt the same imperial instinct that had dictated the rise of the guinea pig empire begin to kick in when, suddenly, an idea occurred to me

"Fungai, do you guys think it's fair that you get to play on the field that we slaved over while you walked away?"

"That was not okay, we agree. It is also not fair for you or anyone to stop us from using this field; it is as much property of the backstreet as it is of the front street." Fungai responded.

Wellington was livid, and Fox was reaching his wit's end as well. In addition to their initial frustrations, they were even more upset now because Ta and I had apparently failed to stand our ground in battle.

"Fair enough," I said gently to The Tennis Brothers, "we have no problem with you playing on the field—even if we have to play at different times." Fox stood upright and looked ready to throw a vicious word my way, so I raised my hand and signaled him to let me finish.

"That said, there is no way we will let you feed off our labor without your contributions. Here is what I suggest. Have you boys seen the riverbank field? The guys down there have done a good job with theirs. If you two can organize to get us wooden goalposts that we can use as actual goals instead of the rocks, we will call the labor even."

They protested, arguing that getting good strong poles was going to cost money, and none of our labor had required us to pay anything. Fox then reminded them that they had had the option to do that too, and it had been their choice to walk away. As the afternoon wasted, everyone was beginning to grow tired of the hostilities. By now, Wellington had stormed off again, uninterested in seeing any peaceful resolution. Just before dusk, The Tennis Brothers agreed to look into buying the poles. I was sure they were going to cave in right from the start. They always received substantially more pocket money than we did (which I suspect had been an important piece of bait in swaying Babylon to their side in the first place), so they would have been able to save up in no time at all. Furthermore, they would have done anything to increase their stake in the field beyond their argument about where it was located: buying the poles would undoubtedly make them invaluable to the development and reputation of the field.

14

Innocent and I were an odd pair. We met at school in the third grade and, by whatever power it is that draws people together, we became friends. Our classroom seating arrangement was designed to reflect how well the students had done in their most recent exams; the top eight students sat together on Group One, the second eight on Group Two and so forth, usually all the way down to Five as a class had between forty and fifty people. While I was always on Group One, Innocent hovered between Group Four and Three. This only made our friendship that much more of a triumph; people only played with people who either lived in the same neighborhood or were in the same group. Innocent and I had neither in common. Over the years, however, we found a series of things that kept us delighted in each other's company.

We had recently become obsessed with chess. His brother had introduced him to the game in an attempt to get him to think more creatively. Because his brother lived in the city and was only around every other weekend, he was desperate to find someone to play with during the week. He wasted no time in teaching me the basics of the game and, before long, we were spending the first part of each afternoon in heated chessboard combat. His house was on my way to school, so we would stop by there for a few games. His mother was always there and ready with the sadza and lacto for our lunch. I cannot, for the life of me, recall when we became friends. I liked that he had the street wisdom of the typical MaTwo Rooms and Area B boy- a quality notably absent in me and any of my Ownership friends. What particularly endeared him to me, however, was his discomfort with the stereotypes assigned to him based on his neighborhood. Although he played football like everyone else, he invested much of his time on learning volleyball and chess. He also read a lot, and we would spend many afternoons at the local Catholic library. Our books of choice were the Babysitters' Club and Goosebumps series. There were a lot of books we wanted, but the problem was we could only borrow two at a time. The library was far from either of our houses, and the frequent trips soon became cumbersome.

We devised a plan. What if we signed up as new members under different names? We did not have any identification; registering for a library card only cost 50 cents and the librarian's due faith that no ten-year-old bookworm would create a fraudulent account at the Catholic library. We figured out that the librarians changed shifts at three O'clock. We would create our second accounts with the later librarian, seeing as she was not too familiar with us. We did, and our plan worked flawlessly for a couple of months. We would go in soon after school and immediately check out our pair of books each. We would then hang around the library, doing homework and reading comics, until the three o'clock lady came in and then we would check out our other two books under our criminal identities. Our good run came to an end in due time though. One Wednesday afternoon, we pulled off the first heist with the clockwork precision that we had established. After three, we went back to the check-out counter, and Innocent went first. He checked his two books out and made for the door like any good fugitive should. It was my turn.

"Good afternoon, Madam!"

"Hey young man. What do you have there?

"I'd like to borrow this *Hardy Boys* book, and *Aladdin*."

"Excellent choices! What's your name?

"I am Tapiwa Dube." By now, this particular lie was second nature to me that I did not bat an eyelid when telling it.

The lady looked at me incredulously. I wasn't looking at her, but I could sense something was wrong because of how long she seemed to be taking. I would normally tell her my name, and she would get the file without hesitation. I started to shiver. I have never been a good liar, and my temperament was not built for an inquisition. Nervously, I raised my head to meet her gaze and, as soon as I looked at her, I realized where our infallible plan had gone wrong. This was not the usual afternoon librarian! They had just hired a new one, and she was none other than my second cousin and close family friend Priscilla. I was a good friend to her younger brother, Gandanga, but she had been away in college for a while and had only recently returned to town, and I failed to recognize her behind the counter.

Innocent and I got banned from the Catholic library. Priscilla was kind enough not to tell Gogo of my misdeeds, and the darling old lady never figured out why I insisted on switching from the Catholic library to the city council one

That was my first and, for a long time, last brush with the law.

That was Innocent. That was Innocent and me.

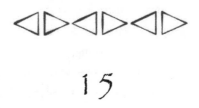

15

After the confrontation between the two streets, a relative yet superficial calm came over our field and the neighborhood as a whole. Everyone except The Tennis Brothers came back to the field in the following days, and the tension between Wellington and Babylon was impossible to miss. They would both be lively and good-humored until the other showed up or said something, then they would retreat and play without uttering a word for a few minutes. Wellington's pleasantries towards the rest of us seemed asserted. There was no way his heart would have forgiven our apparent betrayal of the front-street during the confrontation, even if his brain had understood that the compromise reached had been for the best. On the other hand, we now all harbored some suspicion towards Babylon. The situation with The Tennis Brothers had not been any more organic than Jesus' arrest at the hands of the Jewish cohort: Babylon had been the Judas and, for what I assume was a few pieces of silver from The Tennis Brothers' pocket, he had kissed away our monopoly on the field. He could feel it too, and both he and Wellington channeled their hidden feelings into the games.

The Tennis Brothers, Tiberius and Fungai, kept away from the field for the same reason they were insisting on being allowed to play there in the first place. They had not, all of a sudden, developed a passion for football or a sense of camaraderie with the rest of MaOwnership. They were, instead, only interested in a savage and prideful control in which they could do whatever they want. As long as they could lay claim to something, they would. If there was the slightest bit of debate on whether they were entitled to anything, they would be sure to let it be known. I had heard stories of Fungai punching some classmates because they had skipped his turn during a game of cards. Their family appeared to have some money, and the boys made sure that detail was never lost on us. Whether it was their brand-new racquets or novelty video games, they made sure everyone caught wind of it by walking around the entire neighborhood, drawing everyone's attention with yelled-out salutations and unsolicited bragging.

Their absence from the field was therefore not surprising; they were only going to come when they had fulfilled their end of the bargain. The only problem was, like most MaOwnership boys who had never had to build fences or anything big, they knew little about where and how to get the wooden poles. The only people I suspect may have known about any of this were Fox and Wellington, and they were obviously not interested in helping the brothers.

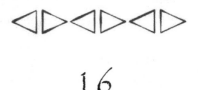

16

Innocent and I had just left school when we came upon two of
Innocent's neighbors, Richie and Mabhaudhi.

"*Ndeip* Inno! What are you up to this afternoon?

"Nothing much *sha*; Mavima and I were probably going to play
chess for a short while, before going over to MaOwnership..."

It was obvious to me that they had checked out of the
conversation by the time Innocent mentioned MaOwnership. The
typical Area B boys they were, they had no interest in either chess or
spending time in arrogant, unexciting MaOwnership.

"Man Innocent, you are never around here anymore. You
don't like your neighborhood anymore?" Richie said with a half-smile
that spoke to both the accuracy and comic value of the statement. The
truth was Innocent loved his neighborhood and the neighbors that
came with it. He also knew that, in addition to the exciting football
games and parties, he was more likely to get in trouble hanging out
with the boys from his neighborhood than he was with us. By then,

some of our classmates from his neighborhood were smoking on the weekends, skipping school, and rumors abound had some even breaking into tuck-shops and making out with a few dollars and sweets. At the very least, Innocent was not surrounded by people who enjoyed spending their free time reading or doing puzzles in his neighborhood. Richie and Mabhaudhi knew this too, and that is why their invocation to Innocent was more tongue-in-cheek than anything else: they could not, in all good conscience, fault him for choosing to spend time in another neighborhood. They were, however, jealous of his newfound acquaintances.

"Why don't you come and sit with us today? We can fill you in on what has been going on around here. Did you hear about Mai Tonde and Mr. Mutasa of the grade 4D class? Haha, you are going to laugh..."

Innocent cast a glance at me as if asking for permission. I just smiled back and started walking towards the two boys. This would be fun, I thought; a nice change of pace from what I was accustomed to in MaOwnership. Having received the blessing he felt he needed from me, Innocent asked Richie what they wanted to do, and we walked over to his house just across the street from Innocent's. I listened with foreign interest to the fascinating tales they spoke about; a robbery here, a fight there, a pregnancy somewhere else. Not to say these things did not happen in MaOwnership, but they happened less frequently and, when they did, the adults did their best to keep it away from the children.

After we arrived at Richie's house and sat around the beautiful, rough-top wooden table that he had made for the family, his mother came to give him some chore instructions and bid farewell for the afternoon. Richie and Mabhaudhi watched her leave in utter silence, waiting to make sure that she was gone. In turn, I watched them watch her, wondering why they seemed so eager for her to leave. I found out soon enough. As soon as she had turned the corner, Richie reached behind the tiny wooden shed that housed a few rabbits and pulled out a slightly torn, rugged brown paper bag similar to the type Old Man Chimutondo would have used to wrap his tuck-shop bread. From the grin on Mabhaudhi's face, it was obvious that he knew and was excited for what it was. Innocent might have known too, as he threw me a glance similar to the one he had thrown earlier, except that this time he looked more panicked.

"Which one is this? Is this the bag you bought from Blah Jombo?" Mabhaudhi asked as he watched Richie pull out crushed golden-green leaves from the tattered bag.

"*Maya*[30], this stuff is better. I bought this one from Mickey Dread, the guy who fixes bicycles and radios up the road!" Richie replied in utter delight before continuing, "*Vafana,* do you know what this is?'

Innocent and I nodded yes, although only one of us was being truthful. I had my suspicions, but I had never been in such close contact with anything of the sort to know what it was or how I was supposed to react to it.

"Alright, brothers," Innocent finally spoke up, "It was good seeing you. Mavima and I need to get to MaOwnership."

"Come on *vafana*! You don't want to get a puff in? I tell you, this stuff is great, especially if you are going to be playing football or working the field. Mabhaudhi and I will be heading down to the valley to pick up some timber for sale, and nothing gets us readier for the job than a few puffs of this medicine!"

By then, Innocent was already standing up and tugging on my shirt to leave. I saw that he was shivering by now, so I got up, and we trotted out into the street with an awkward goodbye to Richie and Mabhaudhi.

Once we got into the street, Innocent began to scold me.

---

30 "No" (Slang)

"Why were you still sitting around? Did you not know what that was?" He said, all the while walking two steps in front of me, never breaking stride to look at me.

"I had an idea, but why does it even matter? We were not going to smoke it!"

"You have no clue, do you? If Richie's mother came back, or any of the parents happened to see us, the story would say that they saw the four of us smoking. No one would think to say that two boys were smoking and the other two just sitting there. Secondly, the stench is strong and unmistakable. If we had stayed any longer, it would have been all over our clothes—good luck explaining that to Gogo."

I followed him silently the rest of the way.

We arrived in MaOwnership to find that a game had started already. Innocent and I took our places on opposing teams without any mention of what we had just seen. What emotions we may have carried with us from Richie's house persisted only a short while once we got onto the field before being diluted and then washed away in the sweat and excitement of the game. We realized that you could always count on the field to be an infallible tonic, as long you cooperated with it. If you played nice and played your best, the field was bound to give you what you had come for; whether it was a victory, a memorable individual experience, or to forget about the unusual encounter you just went through and the subsequent quarrel with your friend.

The Tennis Brothers had still not come back to the field, and we were beginning to think that they had been unable to come up with a plan regarding the poles. At the risk of stirring up dormant frustrations, there seemed to be an unspoken agreement not to bring it up until they actually showed up, if they did at all. At the height of today's game, Babylon finally spoke. He had seen to them recently, and they were just stumped on where to get the wood. They had asked if we knew any such places.

"No, don't tell them!" Wellington said with a diabolical smirk on his face,

"Typical short-sightedness from this child," Babylon immediately responded with a rehearsed mean-spirited rebuttal, "so you would rather have our field stay this way than have those fellows help?"

"But if any of us know where to get the wood, then we don't need them! We can just get it ourselves",

"Except that the good logs cost a few dollars, and I don't know anyone who is willing to pay that type of money for them. It would be no problem for the brothers," I said.

"Well still, we don't know where to get the wood. Now, can we get back to the game?" Wellington snapped and kicked the ball towards the center of the field.

"Wait a minute. Inno, what were your friends saying about going down to the valley?" I asked excitedly, forgetting temporarily anything that had surrounded that earlier conversation. Innocent looked at me in defeated disbelief. Apparently, he was not willing to discuss that option. I decided to let that lead go, at least for now. No one else had caught wise to what we were talking about, so no one pushed any further. We followed Wellington's lead and went back to the game.

That evening as I walked Innocent home, he brought up the source of his discontent,

"Blaz, I just don't get you sometimes! After all we went through with Richie and Mabhaudhi today, you still want to go back over there?"

"I was suggesting that..."

"It's all trouble, I tell you! They already know you, and know that you know they smoke. You think they are just going to do business with you like that?

"Look, Inno, I don't know what you know about those guys, but you can't be angry at me. I didn't smoke with them, nor did I want to. Now, I bring up the idea that we may be able to get wood from the same valley that they do, and I am in the wrong?"

I rarely argued or raised my voice when I was irritated, so my reaction gave Innocent pause. After a few seconds, he spoke again. He was calmer this time.

"To be honest, you don't want to go down to the valley to get wood. I have overheard Richie and other boys talking about what goes on down there. It is a bunch of older boys and men smoking, drinking, fighting, all the while chopping down wood for sale. They are mean to any new faces, kids or otherwise. It took Richie more than two months before they allowed him to cut down some wood too and, even then, he was only able to gain their trust by smoking with them. That is how he got into the habit. We have no business being down there. I know you Ownership front-street people don't like The Tennis Boys much, but sending even them down there would be wrong."

I understood. It worked out well that we had continued our conversation away from everyone else. Wellington would surely have insisted that we tell them to go get wood from the valley, and the other boys would either have agreed or not spoken up against it. Babylon, eager to have his "friends" play and being too sheltered to appreciate just how much danger may have been involved, would have agreed to send them down, too.

"Okay, how about this," I finally said, regaining my composure after taking a moment to digest all Innocent had said, "I know Richie and Mabhaudhi get wood from the valley for firewood. If, however, we told them we could give them a few dollars if they brought us half a dozen long pine poles, do you think they would do it?"

He was still hesitant at the idea of doing any business with these boys. We would insist that we get our wood first before we paid them, I said. Besides, it would be The Tennis Brothers doing the haggling so, in the worst-case scenario, they would get conned out of their money, not us. Innocent was less than thrilled hearing me speak this way, and made it known. I was supposed to be the nicer, peace-making one; where was all this resentment coming from? I shrugged, but I also knew he was right. I toned down the vitriol and conceded that if The Tennis Brothers would be up for it, we would arrange a meeting with Richie and Mabhaudhi, and let them take it from there.

Selling the plan to Babylon would be easy because he did not know Richie and Mabhaudhi. An unconvinced Innocent by my side, I walked over to his fence and yelled his name out three times. Alarmed, he scurried out of the house and wore a concerned expression when he met us.

"*Kwakanaka here?*[31] What's going on?" He said, still baffled by our presence. The only people who ever came to the Pastor's house demanding any sort of audience were church people. On the rare occasion that a layman did, it most certainly would not be a child, and definitely not me. I had not considered that, having been wrapped in the excitement of the scheme at hand. I had to tell him right then— before Innocent tried to stop me, before Babylon found out who they were, and before The Tennis Brothers decided that they were not interested anymore.

"Oh, everything's fine. I just wanted to tell you that we—I— have the perfect plan to get our wooden posts for the field!"

"Really? You two felt that could not wait until the next time we played? Or, at least, until the next time I left the house? All this yelling outside will get me in trouble with my parents!"

Innocent hung his head, twice ashamed for not only being yelled at but also because he had not wanted to be there in the first place. I, on the other hand, barely heard him. I was obsessively trying to tell him about our piece of ingenuity.

"Look, this is important! Two of Innocent's fri—two of the boys from Innocent's neighborhood go down to the valley a few times a week. If we tell them what we are looking for, they may be able to get us what we need."

"Well," Babylon replied, still annoyed, "If you think that works, why don't you tell them?"

---

31 Formal way of inquiring if there is a problem

"See, you're not hearing me *blaz*. You can now pass this message on to your racquet-wielding friends. If they still want to be part of the field, tell them that we may have made their work a lot easier."

He began to come around. He had been, after all, the one pushing to have The Tennis Brothers play.

"So, what are you saying? Do you want to talk to them and just have them give you the money?"

"Well no, that's their job. We don't want to talk to either of them. The most we can do is tell the brothers where to find Richie and Mabhaudhi, but that's after you have already told them of the plan. After that, they can go up there themselves and figure it out."

Babylon's demeanor revealed an unsettled soul struggling to pin down the actual source of its discontent. Something was not sitting right with him. Nevertheless, he promised to pass the message on to The Tennis Brothers and to let us know how it went.

The entire matter took place with little or no knowledge on the part of anyone else. Babylon spoke to the brothers, and they were only ever overjoyed to be finally getting somewhere with their own plan. They still did not show up to the field. I took care to make sure Babylon and I only met to update each other when no one else was around. I passed on Richie's address and what time he was usually home, and he took word back to them.

That was the last we heard of that for another week and a half. We had almost settled back into our afternoon game routine when, one day, we were interrupted by the frantic sight of Tiberius charging towards the field with the biggest smile I had ever seen him wear.

"Men, come quickly! Fungai and I have the wood! We need some help carrying it though; it's the least you can do!" He declared in victorious glee. There was a collective uproar from the field. Nigel, Tinashe and some of the younger boys who were not engulfed in the neighborhood politics cheered for the new goalposts. Fox, Wellington, and Ta were surprised that this was happening at all. I caught glances from both Innocent and Babylon; the former was relieved while the latter was brimful of delighted gratitude. The younger boys flocked around Tiberius and barraged him with a dozen questions as they began to walk towards where the wood supposedly was. Babylon, Innocent, and I were the logical next group to go. The other three front-street boys took a few more seconds to grasp what was happening before they conceded and followed the mob with noticeably less enthusiasm than everyone else.

We arrived at the B bus station where we were met by Mabhaudhi, Richie, and Fungai. The two Area B boys had agreed to help The Tennis Brothers carry their merchandise halfway home, after which they would need to get other people to do the rest of the job.

Once Fox and Wellington saw Richie and Mabhaudhi, they began to put the pieces of what had happened together. They knew each other from around Dangamvura. Fox looked at Innocent, and then at me, and smiled wryly to himself. Nothing more needed to be said- at least not then. We grabbed the six wooden poles and began walking back home amidst excited chatter.

I had several questions myself, but I figured now was not a good time to try and get answers. I doubt I would have gotten them anyway. I would have to talk with The Tennis Brothers later when the excitement had died down and fewer people were around.

By the time we arrived back at our field, dusk was setting. We decided we would leave the poles there and erect them the next day.

17

For three years after his father passed away, Ta donned the envied blue blazer and rode the bus to his city school. His big sister had never left our Dangamvura school; she was smarter than Ta and never had any problems at school. I also suspect that having two children in the city schools would have cost too much for their means. On the other hand, their mother worried that Ta would slip into bad company and other trouble in the absence of a strong guiding hand. She worked in the city for days at a time, their uncle had since died, his sister was only a year older than him, and the slew of housemaids that worked for their family could not be trusted with ensuring that Ta stayed in line. Moving him to the city school was the best possible arrangement and, while it lasted, his grades and confidence improved.

Then one day—the day after we brought the wood to the field—we saw Ta and his mother getting off the bus as we were getting home from school, which was unusually early for him and even more so for her. I waved and called out to him, but neither he nor his mother broke stride. He waved in my direction without lifting his head. That was weird, I muttered. Nigel agreed. Hungry and excited to dig our new goalposts into the field, we did not need to dwell on it for too long; he would tell us if there was a problem when he came to the field. We went inside and sat down for ten minutes for lunch. Before the last bite was swallowed, we had dashed toward the field where The Tennis Brothers Fungai and Tiberius, eager to exercise their newly earned field privileges, were already kicking around a tennis ball.

This was the first time Nigel and I had been alone with them, away from the mediating hand of Babylon or the distancing ones of the other front-street boys.

"*Ndeip* Boys," I began with the pleasantries meant to get the ball rolling on smoothing existing tensions; a process I deemed necessary if we were going to be working and playing together.

"*Hapana apa!*[32]" They replied in brief, awkward unison without breaking away from their game.

"So, when are you guys thinking about putting the poles up?" Nigel cut right to the chase.

"Oh, we were just waiting for some of you to get here so we can help nail them together and dig them into the ground. We have, after all, fulfilled our end of the bargain," Fungai asserted, refusing to pass up an opportunity to center him and his brother in the conversation of the field.

"Well," I reacted immediately, "Let's get to work then. Nigel, grab Gogo's two little hoes. They'll be perfect for digging the holes." He dashed home, taking a shortcut through a gap between the barbed wire that separated our yard from the field. As Nigel left, Tiberius asked him to bring a hammer and nails as well. We did not have a hammer, he replied, but he could definitely grab a few nails from the toolshed.

While Nigel was away, the brothers and I walked to where the wood rested. I stood over it for what seemed like a few minutes,

---

32 "Nothing much!"

marveling and envisioning already the envy we would evoke in the boys from all the other neighborhoods. I imagined how better goalkeeping would be when you had to dive back and forth between two posts as opposed to meager rocks. Oh, and just think, if you dribble past one player, then another, then you hit a screamer from maybe eight meters out, and you stood there watching the goalkeeper jump high and scramble to get his hands on it, but he is not fast enough. The ball floats over his head and hits the crossbar before bouncing into the goal behind him. Amazing. Just like on TV.

I was awakened from my stupor by the sound of ripping cloth behind me. The seam of Nigel's shorts had caught on the barbed wire fence as he made his way back onto the field. Tiberius, Fungai and I shared a laugh. Unfazed by our delight at his expense, Nigel ran right up to us and threw one hoe to me before fishing into his pockets for the nails. He passed the nails to Tiberius, who was now wielding a large rock for some reason. Nigel and I began digging the holes.

On the side, Tiberius hammered the nails viciously into the wood with the rock. It seemed loud and tactless, and I was sure that was not the best way to assemble the goalpost. I also did not know what the best way would be, so I kept quiet. Fortunately for me and the future of our field, Wellington showed up at that very moment. He took one look at Tiberius's lousy handiwork and chuckled.

"Oh man, "he snorted "It seems we have a dream team of workers today. On one side of the field, it's Gogo's darlings and over here, hard at work destroying the poles we have all been waiting for, are The Tennis Brothers!" Nigel and I were used to his teasing, but Tiberius and Fungai did not take lightly to the comment, especially because of the unabated resentment they knew he bore for them. I watched as Fungai curled the edges of his lips in preparation to lash back, so I interjected.

"Haha, we get it Wellaz. Not all of us grew up in the bush like you did!"

Everyone, including myself, was surprised by the quip. No one, except Fox, had ever been able to come back from a Wellington wisecrack with anything of matching wit; he was speechless. The Tennis Brothers were laughing like hyenas, half because of the actual statement and half to get under Wellington's skin. It took Nigel a few seconds to get over the shock of me actually having a decent, mean retort before he joined in on the chorus. As angry as Wellington often was, he appreciated nothing more than a good joke. If clever and harmless enough, he would even applaud jokes said at his expense. He must have deemed this to be one such joke because he started laughing as well. The Tennis Brothers may have been a little sinister in their gawking, but they were on the field that he built—he was impenetrable to the vices of anyone he deemed an outsider for as long as he stood there. It was only then that I breathed easy and began to laugh as well.

"Good one, Mavima!" He said, as he walked over to me and playfully punched me on the side of my stomach. He then went on to explain to us that first we would want to dip the wood in some oil to make sure that they did not fall prey to termites. He had learned that from building fences in the rural area. Even then, you were not supposed just to start beating nails into them: what if the sides do not end up evening out?

Still eager to at least be in good graces with Wellington and everyone else, Tiberius announced that they had half a gallon of oil that had been sitting in their tool shed since their father left five years ago and, before we could ask anything about it, he was running home. While he was gone, we all gathered around Wellington and watched him work on the wooden poles with exceptional mastery. He knelt down and tapped lightly on each of the four rounded poles that would stand upright, and then the two flat ones that would go across the top. After that, he put the four up side by side as if to measure them. Two of them were a little longer than the others. From seemingly nowhere, he pulled out a saw-blade and began sawing the tops off to make sure they evened out. He tossed one of the sawed-off ends to Nigel and said,

"*Mfana*, continue digging the holes you and Shingi had started digging, and dig until you can put this piece of wood in it so that its top is level with the ground." Nigel obliged. Since there were two hoes, it would have only made sense that I went and dug the other holes too, but I doubt that Wellington was ready to be left alone with Fungai in one corner of the field.

We waited for a few minutes before Tiberius returned with the oil. While Wellington got to work rubbing the oil all over the wood, I saw Ta coming up the street. His walk was without its city school spring. He had been on my mind all afternoon since I had seen him get off the bus. I had not seen him that morose since his father passed away. I momentarily forgot about Fungai and Wellington being alone in the corner and ran up to the street to meet him.

"*Ndeip Sha?*" I inquired under my breath, lest I drew unwanted attention.

"Oh, I am goo-good, just tired" he replied with a quiver in his voice and teary eyes.

"*Aiwa ka*[33]. Ta, for how long have I known you? You don't cry."

"My mother just lost her job," he said. No stutter.

"Oh. Oh. That's tough. I am sorry." The news was more than I had bargained for. What do you say? What did that mean for his school? Did she do something to lose her job? I just stood there in front of him.

Wellington, like everyone else, had not noticed anything unusual, so he called to Ta.

"Hey, city boy! Ready to get your hands dirty? Come work this oil with me!" Ta scurried over there, grateful for the distraction.

I walked to where Nigel was and helped him dig up the last two holes, and then we walked back together to join the rest of the group. We caught everyone in light-hearted banter. There was nothing

---

33 "Come on now"

at that moment that spoke to the sworn enmity of the front and back streets, or the life-shattering news that Ta had just received.

"So Fungai," Wellington asked, "how much did the wood cost you? I thought doing business with Richie and them would be difficult!"

"Oh, it didn't cost us much at all, and they were nice, actually. We just had to cut a deal with them" Fungai answered and grinned cryptically.

Interesting, we all thought.

We hung around for a little while longer before everyone bade farewell, promising to reconvene the next day.

18

The oil gave the poles a distinguished black and brown hue. Babylon and Innocent, who had not been there the day before, gazed upon them for a while before Babylon spoke up.

"Well, what are we waiting for then? Let's put these up and get a game going."

"Wellington insisted that we wait for him before we do so. I think we should wait a bit," Nigel replied.

"Who cares if he is here or not? This is not about one person wanting to be in control; it's about the field. We can just do it ourselves now!" Fungai retorted, to Babylon and Tiberius's approving nods.

"I don't think Wellington wanting to be here for this has anything to do with control." I jumped in, trying to overturn the imminent coup. "He said he had done this before and had some good ideas on how it should be done. The grease was his idea."

"He may have said it first, but I knew that already. I was going to get the grease anyway," Tiberius said. A lie, I thought. "Now are you guys just going to stand there and wait for your friend or help us?"

Nigel started to walk over to where they were but stopped once he saw that I was not coming. Not only was I positive that we could not do a good job without Wellington, but there was also no good reason to leave him out of the final part of the project he had led thus far. I refused to be caught up in whatever dirty scheme was taking shape around me. We had been playing that way for a few weeks; why rush it now? They were surprised by my decision to stand back, as it was not consistent with neither my obsession with building the best field in the land nor my typically neutral stance in the face of conflict among friends. We walked back into our yard and watched them work from under The Avocado Tree.

They started on the job, simply putting the poles into the holes Nigel had dug the day before and then refilling the dirt. Once they were sure that all four posts were even on both sides, they tried to nail in the flat pieces that would go across the top, and then things got tricky for them. None of them were tall enough to reach the top of the poles. Stuck and trying to come up with a solution, they kept throwing inquisitive, almost pleading glances towards the Avocado Tree. I was taller than all of them and would have been able to reach the top of the posts with ease.

Having realized that I was not going to be any help, Babylon decided he would shimmy up the posts and have the other two pass him the rock, nails and flat wood. Nigel and I looked at each other in utter disbelief; it was a ludicrous idea, and it was incredible that everyone had agreed to it. No sooner had Babylon got three-quarters of the way up the greasy pole did he start slipping. He tried desperately to hold on, but the post was already shaking uncontrollably and beginning to fall. He landed on his back and hit his head on a small rock. We cringed, as did The Tennis Brothers.

Babylon stood up and initially tried to play it off. He dusted himself up and, when he reached for the back of his head, he realized he was bleeding. The pain and humiliation must have kicked in right then because that is when he started to cry and ran home. Once he was out of sight, The Tennis Brothers started laughing as they walked back home. I could hear fading portions of their conversation as they got further and further away.

"Haha, can you believe that kid? Who does he think he is, Tarzan? Nobody is going up a greasy pole like that!"

"I know brother! How about that fall! I was struggling so hard not to laugh. Then he runs off crying like a little girl! Hilarious!"

"Say, did you hear about Ta's mom?"

"No, what happened?"

"I overheard some neighborhood mothers saying she stole some money from work and got fired..."

"Wow. Doesn't she go to our church...?"

Upon seeing some of the poles already shoddily in the ground, Wellington wanted to walk away from it all. This is why he had been against working with The Tennis Brothers in the first place, he said. They were subtly yet certainly undermining each one of us in turn, and soon none of us would be playing here or with each other.

Ta, who had not been to school since his mother lost her job, joined us a few minutes later. By now, rumors were all over the neighborhood about what had happened, and Ta was unnerved and embarrassed about the whole affair. It was nothing to us. We wanted to hear what he made of the other boys going ahead and trying to put the goalposts up themselves. I was also dying to share my story about Babylon's fall, and I was not going to tell it to just Wellington: that story deserved a bigger audience, and Ta provided just that. After we all had a hearty laugh about it, the air around the field was more cheerful and thus conducive for work. We got to it.

First, we dug up what the other boys had tried to do without us. Because they had used nothing but dirt to refill the holes, the goalposts were bound to fall once a strong breeze—let alone a flying ball—hit them. Their frailty may even have had something to do with Babylon falling the way he had. We found small and medium-sized rocks to help support the posts before refilling the rest of the holes with mud. Once we had stomped them into the ground, we pushed into and threw a ball at them for two minutes before deciding they were strong enough or at least would be once the mud dried and hardened. Due to the participation of the two tallest boys in the group, Ta and I, we were able to get the crossbars nailed into the goalposts with no accidents this time.

We did not play on that day. There were too few of us to commemorate such a moment. Besides, we were exhausted. We sat down, not on Faru's bench as usual, but right in the dusty center of the field where we could gaze at the labor of our hands on all ends. Dusk was setting in, casting a glorious red curtain over the valley from where the wood had come.

The next day we played. Everyone who had built the field came out soon after lunch and, after little chatter, we broke into two teams. This time, the team captains, Babylon and Wellington, disregarded convention and just picked whoever they wanted for their teams. Babylon picked The Tennis Brothers, Innocent, and Tinashe. The rest of us went with Wellington.

We played for hours. The score tied at 4-4, and with darkness and exhaustion beckoning, Wellington—playing goalkeeper at that moment—threw the ball down to Ta who proceeded to hoof it clumsily high into the air, only to have it fatefully fall at my feet. Fungai, slow and tired, lunged at me. I merely dribbled the ball to the right and watched him slide past me. Now, I was face to face with Babylon, who was playing goalie for the other team. He had played well all afternoon, proving to be acrobatic and incredibly hard to beat for a small man.

I kicked the ball hard and high. Babylon leaped as much as he could, but his diminutive frame was no match for the shot. The ball floated past his head and hit the crossbar before bouncing into the goal behind him. Amazing.

Just like on TV.

Just as I had always imagined.

19

The weeks following the arrival of the goalposts were easily some of the best days to grace MaOwnership. The boys enjoyed playing every day, the back and front streets would both come and often play together on mixed teams, and the parents cherished the double benefit of having the children out of the house while still keeping them within the neighborhood.

Word spread about our beautiful field. Several people passed by it on their way home from school, and we would talk about it to anyone who listened. Soon, everyone was talking about the new MaOwnership field. As smooth and delightful to play on as it was, everyone was hesitant to regard it with the same esteem with which they held the riverbank field and Gwanzura fields. First, the other two had been around for a few years and thus stood the test of time. Secondly, because few, if any, of us, were any good, there was initially little talent to display on our field that people should come from other places to watch or be intrigued into play against us. Finally, we did not have a memorable name like Gwanzura or Riverbank.

There was nothing we could do about the first qualm; the only way to prove that you stood the test of time is, after all, to look back after having done it. We were able to plan solutions to the other two problems at least though. We meditated and debated on the name for a week. It came up in every conversation when we would take a break from playing or when we sat under The Guava Tree. Two names were emerging as strong runners: The Mountain, as homage to its proximity to our favorite early childhood game; and in the interest of simplicity and easy recognition, some advocated for MaOwnership field. While I preferred the second option, I was not sold on either one. Because Dangamvura, and Mutare as a whole, is mountainous, "The Eastern Highlands" they call it; it would make no sense to outsiders why a tiny field somewhere would name themselves "The" Mountain when surrounded by thousands other mountains. The second one lacked creativity. Besides, reaffirming our MaOwnership reputation was not going to attract the attention we were hoping for our field.

Debate raged. One afternoon, during a heated three on three game, the Pastor had stepped out of the house looking furious. He screamed for Babylon to come home and yelled at him about coming to the field at the expense of the household chores he had been supposed to do. Amidst our giggling at Babylon and all the yelling, we heard the Pastor say,

"Now your mom has to pick up your slack while you are busy *pashena apa?*"

My face lit up, and I fell silent. "Pashena apa" simply meant "by the dirt," an expression the Pastor was using to berate not only Babylon's truancy from his household duties but also the cloud of dust that arose during the games and the subsequent filth we would carry home every evening.

With the Pastor and Babylon now in the house, I turned to the rest of the boys and announced, "Did you hear that? The Pastor just gave us our name!"

"What do you mean? He didn't even speak to us!"

"Pashena... Boys. Pashena. We'll call the field Pashena!"

Maybe everyone was caught in a moment of glee; maybe Wellington and a few others had not forgiven Babylon's betrayal a few weeks earlier, or maybe we were all just tired of arguing about the name, but the name passed almost unanimously. The only resistance we faced later came from Babylon, who felt he had been left out of the decision and that the field's name would always be a reminder of his public shaming. Everyone heard him, but no one paid him any mind. Pashena it was.

20

In the post-independence era up until 1997 (give or take, depending on who you talk to), Zimbabwe was termed 'The Breadbasket of Southern Africa,' and justifiably so. With marvelous weather; incredible tourist attractions; one of the continent's strongest and fastest-growing economies; and a resilient and hospitable people to match, the country looked set to be a stalwart of hope and inspiration in independent Africa.

It may have been the $50,000 that the government shelled out to the liberation war veterans: every one of them, even those with only marginal proof of having been involved in the war. It may have been the haphazard land redistribution from the White large-scale commercial farmers to members of the black majority. It may even have been because the onset of AIDS in the community was eating away at our economic core: the working man and woman. The jury is still out.

What is certain, however, is that in 1997, the promise that was Zimbabwe was shattered and would continue on a downward economical and socio-political spiral for decades to come. Historians have since named the specific day that Zimbabwean stock exchange crashed, November 14, 1997, "Black Friday."

21

The first team we played from outside MaOwnership was a group of Area P boys from Babylon's church. It would be a safe first step into the rest of the world, we had reasoned. Because the Pastor would have already known the boys, he would be less apprehensive than he would otherwise be about boys from other neighborhoods. We also figured that, since the boys spent most of their time at church and their neighborhood was not as renowned for football as others were, we could actually compete with them and possibly win.

They got to Pashena promptly before the agreed upon two o'clock and met up with Babylon and me. They spoke in a cheery tone and not once uttered an insult or profanity. Interesting, I thought. We were not the most foul-mouthed boys in the land and I personally seldom cursed, but it was still remarkable to see a group of eight boys who could speak so light-heartedly without crossing into that abyss of ungodly vocabulary. By now, we were sure we could at least beat these guys. A few minutes later, Wellington and Fox arrived, which left us needing one more to get a decent game going.

Soon enough, Ta arrived as well.

Unable to return to his city school, Ta transferred back to our old school. At first, he continued to carry himself with the same aristocratic hauteur that he had obtained from wearing a blazer and riding the bus to school. He even continued wearing the blazer to school for a while, until the incessant teasing caught up with him.

"Ta! Did you miss the bus today?"

"Hey, blaz. We are struggling at home; do you reckon your mom could throw a few of the dollars she kept on the side our way?"

"Hahaha, you can wear that filthy blazer all you want; your mother is sti-sti-still a common crook, and now you are poor like the rest of us."

Soon, the blazer came off, and the head hung low again. Often, he would come back from school, head into the house and not come out. When he did come out to play, he hardly smiled and flew into an angry tantrum at any small matter.

His mother, attempting to placate him, bought him a football—a real, leather one. While the ball brought some of the spring back in his step, it was not the same type of confidence with which he used to get off the bus. It had a distinct mean streak to it. Soon, he had developed a reputation for throwing a fit and storming off with the ball whenever he got slightly hurt, his team was losing, or he had a disagreement with another player. On this day, he brought his ball and appeared in brighter spirits than he had been recently. We were not only excited to see him because we could now play, but we were happy to see him looking better.

As soon as the game began, we realized just how misguided our assumptions about the church boys had been. They were good. They may not have been as skilled and flamboyant as the MaTwo Rooms boys, but they were still easily better than us. Besides, whatever they may have lacked in talent, they made up for in positive attitude and camaraderie. They applauded each other at every touch and were quick to encourage whenever someone made a mistake.

As if on cue, our thinly veiled tensions began to unravel. Wellington and Babylon could plaster smiles and bear being around each other for as long as things were fine, but congeniality is undone in the face of trials. The most skilled players on our team on the day, they appeared to have made a silent pact not to pass the ball to each other, choosing instead to outdo each other with cheap tricks at the expense of the team. After ten minutes, we were down two goals to nothing. By then, the Tennis Brothers had also arrived and were clamoring to be substituted into the game, which only added to the discord. Babylon, assuming the role of captain, then screamed for Ta and me to take a break and let The Tennis Brothers in. I obliged. I was getting tired anyway. Ta, on the other hand, would not leave the field. He was the last one to get there, he argued. Everyone else had been playing longer than he had, and it made no sense that he should be the one to get out. Ta was right. Outwitted, Babylon turned to Ta and snarled, before turning angrily around and lunging viciously at one of the other boy's legs with the underside of his foot.

Babylon immediately realized the extent of his lunacy, as he just stood there with his left hand over his mouth while the other boy writhed in pain on the ground, too ashamed to even apologize. His rage had caused him to hurt an innocent boy; a cheerful character from church no less. The boy limped off to the side as Babylon and Fungai tried frantically to keep the game going. By the time they had convinced anyone who still cared to come back to the pitch, Ta was already into the street, ball in hand.

We lost our first game against a team from outside MaOwnership 4-0. We lost our temper. As it stood, we had failed our first real test at being taken seriously as the patrons of a reputable field. Win or lose, you at least have to be hospitable to your guests, be gracious in defeat and, most importantly, not allow people to see the cracks within your team. None of us knew where the rules came from or when we earned them first, but we all knew them. Kulu used to say the same to and about the family, and I assumed everyone's father or grandfather did the same.

We took a while to recover from the debacle of our first game. For a week after that game, neither Babylon nor Ta showed up to the field. The Tennis Brothers came once and must have picked up on the uninviting, bleak vibe that Wellington, Fox, Nigel and I still carried as we unenthusiastically kicked a ball around. They did not come back.

The crisis could not have come at a more suitable time—three weeks before the rainy season. We needed a break from each other to redress our friendships, as well as meditate on the work that had gone into making the field what it was. Before the rains began to fall, we removed our goalposts and bench and put them away for after the harvest. We kept our promise to the Pastor's family by helping them till the field. Tilling the field is always hard work, but it was especially hard this time because the ground had become rock hard from the constant running on it. We helped for a week or so before a dozen church folk showed up and took over. Our relief was only short-lived, as our release from the Pashena fieldwork meant that we now had to go and get our own fields ready for the rains.

That season, Nigel's parents and little brother Anesu came home for Christmas and to help with the fieldwork from the rural school where his father taught. My other uncle who taught at another rural school, Sekuru Gerry also came. Together with Gogo and Kulu and our occasional help, they made light work of the sowing. The rains were generous too that year, which made for a magnificent crop. The family would be well-fed for the better part of next year, with some feed potentially left over for the livestock. If all went well, we might even have a sack or two to sell.

If the promise of the harvest was the spectacle of the season for Kulu, for Gogo it was the Christmas holiday. All her children and grandchildren would be in town from either the rural areas or Harare. With my two uncles and the rest of Nigel's immediate family already there, it was only a matter of time before the city part of the family showed up. Gogo, with the help of Mai Nigel and my aunt Paula would prepare food for days to come, and stock up the cabinets with all manner of sweets and biscuits. The house looked impeccable a week before everyone arrived, and we would be under strict orders to keep it that way. The night before their arrival, Gogo barely slept, waking up even earlier than usual and sweeping the yard before the roosters crowed. When everyone finally arrived, she would always break into tears. Always. Every year, once or twice a year. She left nothing to argue about whence most of her pride and joy stemmed.

With the exception of my mother, my relationship with the part of our family that lived in Harare was ambivalent. I enjoyed visiting them in the big city and playing with their bottomless pit of toys. Maiguru, my mother's older sister and mother to my three cousins, was, to this day I believe, the best baker in all of the land. On the other hand, I detested the very thought of having my cousins around Dangamvura. When they were in town, time froze for the entire family (and many in the community), and all attention shifted to catering to them. They would swagger into our home with their big city English and music and, for a moment, Nigel and I were relegated to the margins of the household. My young mind concluded that Gogo and my aunts liked them better: their every need was catered to, their slightest achievement applauded, and every joke was the funniest thing ever told. It did not hurt their cause that my girl cousins were fair-skinned and beautiful, and the boys were objectively hilarious. Even all my friends loved them. I hated it and would express my dissent with little passive aggressive behaviors like leaving for Innocent's house and only coming back just before dusk—often bringing Nigel with me because, well, one person's act of defiance is mere craziness; it is the second that makes it a rebellion. My cousins struggled to reconcile the quiet and cheerful Shingi that would come to visit them in Harare, and the begrudging, distant one they found in Dangamvura.

They also didn't play or care much about football or any of the *rokesheni* traditions. To make matters worse, my Dangamvura friends tended to get insecure when talking to the cousins and would embarrass themselves by speaking in affected English and pretending not to care much about *museve*[34] music, *mauyu*, and catching locusts.

Gogo's Christmas feast was always elaborate, and this year's feast was no different. It would always include an insurmountable amount of rice garnished with delightful Mediterranean herbs that my aunt Paula, who had just recently started attending culinary school, was fond of using. No sadza on the day. Some of the chicken was fried and crumbed, and the other cooked in rich gravy. We would often have two types of salad; Gogo's preferred cabbage coleslaw, and aunt Paula's potato salad. For Kulu and the men, it was mandatory that they have beef. That was the one dish that the men usually cooked themselves, mixing the oxtail with green vegetables and hot peppers. To top it all, we kept Old Man Chimutondo busy all week with several runs to buy drinks at his shop. After we had indulged in the excess, we gathered around the television and watched reruns of *Mukadota*[35].

It was always a feast reminiscent of biblical kings.

On Boxing Day, I rose before any of the other children and stepped outside into the street to be away from the madding crowd and hopefully catch one of my friends hanging around. Ta was already out, kicking his ball around with his younger friends, Faru and Tinashe. We hadn't seen those two much at the end of the last season, and we hoped we would see more of them once the harvest was done; especially Tinashe. From the little they said on the matter, I was able to piece together that the tension between some of the older boys had scared them away.

---

34 Literally meaning 'arrow', museve music is a Traditional Zimbabwean genre with notable guitar and drum influences, named so because the high pitched guitar sound- for better or worse- pierces through the sound barrier!

35 Zimbabwe's most celebrated comedian

I joined them for a light-hearted session of pass-and-run. A few minutes later, Nigel joined us. When everyone else at the house finally woke up, Gogo sent my two oldest cousins to find us. As soon as I saw them coming down the street, my heart sank; they had either come to call us home or, even worse, ask to play. It was both.

The problem is, they were both terrible at football and could not be bothered to try. Because Ta and everyone else found them funny, he was excited that they were joining us. Despite my reservations, I was not going to storm off and look unreasonable to both my friends and the cousins. We continued to kick around, and my friends soon had tears rolling down their cheeks from watching the cousins clumsily blunder all over the street, struggling to at least place their foot on the ball. Fadzi, the oldest of my cousins by at least six years (16 or 17 at the time), then placed the ball dead center of the street as if to take a penalty kick; exactly where Fox had run into the dog. He ran up and hoofed it with what appeared to be no other purpose but to send it as high and far away as possible. He would have achieved his purpose too had the ball not struck the barbed wire on top of Tinashe's gate and exploded upon impact, sending pieces of leather and rubber flying in every direction.

Just as the ball had burst wide open the moment it hit the wire, Ta burst into tears the moment the first piece of leather hit the pavement. I had seen him cry on occasion even in recent times, but I had not had him wail like that since we were in crèche. He ran in place like little boys do before turning around and dashing home. Fadzi, who famously never showed neither fear nor timidity, shrunk into his shell.

I waited diabolically for what would happen next. I looked over to Nigel, who was doing his best to stifle laughter. We knew we had just witnessed something we would be talking about for years to come. Maiguru, the best baker in the land and Fadzi's mother, made a cake that evening and sent a humbled and apologetic Fadzi to deliver the cake to Ta's house the next morning.

Far be it from me to take delight in the misfortune of others, but that incident was the funniest, most memorable moment of the holidays. Fadzi's subdued demeanor as he carried the cake to Ta's door was a sight for sore eyes.

Besides, Ta had developed an unbecoming sense of entitlement since he got the ball. It was, for both of them and the rest of us, for the best that the ball had been destroyed.

A week into the New Year everyone, with the exception of Mai Nigel and Anesu, returned to their big city and rural homes. For all my qualms with my extended family, I missed them when they were gone. On the bright side, my friends and I could go back to catching locusts and eating *mauyu*. With the harvest and clearing only a few weeks away now, we could also go back to Pashena.

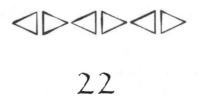

22

"Ane! Anesu!" Nigel called out to his brother, "Ane, throw us the ball."

Anesu, who was playing with the dogs and his back to
Pashena, turned around to find that the ball had rolled under the
barbed fence. He threw the ball back to us and went back to playing
with the dogs. The older of the two dogs, Spot, had since died, and
Kulu had replaced him with a black and white puppy that he wanted
to name Danger. Anesu, for some reason, obsessed over the name
Spooky, and that is the name that stuck.

At the end of crop season, the church folk returned to clear
the Pastor's (and our) field. This time, we were more than willing to
help. The more hands we had working the field, the faster we could
get back to playing. Nigel, Ta, and I showed up for the two days of
work and assisted with moving bundles of twigs and what menial labor
befitted a child at the time. Babylon was obviously there, and so were
some of the boys from the church team against whom we had played.

From my part of the field, I saw them chatting and laughing with Babylon in a manner that only people who had buried the hatchet would. I walked over there and gave my regards.

"Ndeipi. So that last game didn't go too well huh? Maybe you guys can come again this season, and we can make things right?" I inquired, hoping to capitalize on the prevailing good mood.

Babylon, reveling in how both he and the other boys had avoided any awkwardness by not mentioning the ill-fated game, cringed. The other boys pretended not to hear me and went back into their work. Ultimately, the one boy who had been kicked by Babylon spoke up;

"Well, we will be busy helping several church families with their field clearing. But who knows? Maybe we will stop by when the autumn kicks in!" He spoke with the conviction of someone who had always been taught to say the right thing, even if to a fault. He probably wished he could have said no or, at least, lied in saying yes. As it were, his principles mandated that he, at some point, explore the option of stopping by.

When the church folk were gone, and the work shifted gears from the clearing of the summer crops to the clearing for the football field, Ta joined us for the final touches. We had stored the goalposts and bench at their house, so we brought those back and re-planted them in the ground.

With the memories of how the last Pashena season ended still fresh in the mind of the conscious cynic, I found my excitement compromised by the realistic concern that we would all return to the same ugly place at which we had departed. The Tennis Brothers were notably absent from both sessions of field clearing, and Faru and Tinashe were still not showing face around the work, so my fears were proving more and more justified. If anyone else felt the same way, they did not say anything. Instead, the rest of the afternoon was cheerful, and the work went fast. We finished an hour before dusk and walked over to The Mountain as in the days of old to sit back and bask in what was left of the day's late summer sun. We figured it would be best to have our first game of the New Year the next day, seeing as it would be Saturday and more people were likely to come.

Maybe the New Year had renewed spirits and friendship. Maybe the season's rains had washed away uncertainty and resentment. Maybe it was the excitement that, after four long years, the World Cup would be back in the winter. Or maybe we were all just delighted to get back to the game we loved the most. Whatever the reason may have been, I was surprised to see that everyone had turned up that Saturday morning. Tiberius and Fungai in their tiny white tennis shorts, Fox and Wellington with humorous stories of their Christmas in the rural area, Babylon and the enthusiasm for life that had earned him the "monkey" nickname, Tinashe, Faru, and Nigel with a determined excitement that had been apparently hidden behind their infancy all last year. Innocent also joined us, as did another boy from a lesser-known section of MaOwnership. I cannot remember what his name was; just that he was chubby and dark-skinned, and we all called him Buddha. For all but that eternal moment, we were in love with everything that was MaOwnership, football and us.

We played all day that day. We took unintentional turns to go home and eat when the stomach snakes began to bite and sat under the peach tree when the sun-scorched harshly upon us. We spoke to each other unlike we had done before. We learned about how Fungai and Tiberius's father had been a successful businessman and high-ranking official in the political opposition when they were younger. Then one night five years ago, some men had taken him away. They stormed into their house and beat him mercilessly with knobkerries and whips while the boys stood in the corner with their mother trying futilely to cover their eyes. He had wailed, and their mother had screamed. The neighbors had caught wind of who the aggressors may have been but would dare not speak or do anything. That was the last time they had seen or heard from him. Rumors abound said that he was locked up in prison, while some more morbid folk assumed the worst. Stories of people found in shallow graves were not unheard of. For the first time, Ta, Fox, and Wellington felt some sense of kinship with The Tennis Brothers, having lost their fathers as well. While the rest of us listened with wide-eyed fascination, they had their heads fixed to the ground, only occasionally shaking them in empathic pain. Fungai had been so entranced in telling the story that he did not see his little brother begin to cry behind him. Fox's big brother instincts kicking in, he took two inconspicuous side steps until he was standing next to Tiberius and then put his arm around his shoulders while Fungai told the rest of the story. When he was done, no one knew what to say. Babylon stood up and kicked the ball towards the goal.

"How about we switch up the teams this time?" He said, scrambling to change the subject. We did.

One team had Fox, Tiberius, Ta, Nigel, Faru, and Innocent, while I was on the other with Fungai, Wellington, Babylon, Buddha, and Tinashe.

That night, after supper, every single one of us met up again to go locust catching.

*****

The first few weeks of the year went so well both on and off the field that we forgot the tribulations of the previous year. Innocent, Ta, Fungai and I were in Grade Six now while Fox and Babylon were in Grade Seven. We were delighted to be seniors in primary school. I had since found my stride in school and was arguably the smartest person in my grade of about 250 students—the smartest boy. It had been that way since Grade Four. There had been two or three other contenders to that title, but they had since transferred to city schools. Now, my only competition was three girls whose genius I would be disingenuous to deny. While we swapped places at the top from term to term, I was content with being a king among a host of queens. That year, they also introduced a chess club at school. Naturally, Innocent and I were the first two there on opening day and were later joined by a few other students including the chess master's two sons. The club met once a week during lunchtime. Innocent immediately distinguished himself as the unmatched champion of the school. I am confident he would have been the primary school champion in all of Dangamvura, but the other schools did not have chess clubs at the time.

Things in MaOwnership were also looking as positive as they had ever been. By now, many of the adults who had been sick had since died, so there were fewer funerals. Mai Ta also left the jaws of the crippling unemployment idleness and joined a wave of women who had taken to traveling to South Africa and bringing back goods to sell in Zimbabwe. I often overheard Gogo and my aunts talking about how things were getting expensive and harder to find in town, and Mai Ta and the other cross-border traders were making the most of this unfortunate turn of events. The first time she came back, Gogo had bought a beautiful two-in-one blanket from her. Sincere was not as iron-fisted as she had been before with Fox and Wellington. In fact, she was hardly ever home. She now lived with her boyfriend, Fox told me, and he was going to marry her soon. He was excited for her. I barely knew her, but I was excited to see Fox be genuinely excited about something for once.

I was also happy at home. My mother was done with university and was now working full time in the big city, which meant she could visit us once a month. Nigel's mother and brother Anesu, who had moved in over Christmas break, had added some festivity to the already jovial spirit at 1043. I liked Anesu. He was only in the second grade but, having spent all his life in the rural area, had the vocabulary and savvy of a much older boy. He would not stop talking. Come to think of it; he never stopped at all. When he was not talking, he was dancing. Like Nigel, he was a fantastic dancer. When he was not dancing, he was running around the yard or climbing the Avocado Tree. Then he would sleep, only to get up with the roosters and do it all again.

Because of his age and much smaller size, he was not invited to Pashena. O, but how he yearned to join his big brothers upon that revered field! He sat intently on the other side of the barbed fence, relishing the opportunity to throw stray balls back into the field of play. The hunger in his eyes was ill-concealed. He dreamt of the day he could play with us. He spoke about it for hours. With him, it was not even about playing with friends or belonging; he dreamt of being the best thing that ever happened to Pashena. When Nigel and I got back home, we would listen to stories of his fantastic exploits and laugh.

As routines inevitably do, playing amongst ourselves soon got boring. We craved a new challenge. In all this, however, we had not forgotten the fiasco with the church boys last year. In good conscience, none of us were willing to pursue another game with them—or anyone else for that matter—until we were certain that our ugly ghosts had been safely banished into the ground. As it were, the church boy I had spoken to at the clearing began coming around Pashena. Babylon said he just wanted to play too, but I knew better. Why would he leave his idyllic group of football-playing friends, walk several kilometers to another neighborhood where their last game had been horrible? He was either a spy sent to verify that Pashena was a different animal now than it had been last time, or a diplomatic envoy invited by Babylon to bear such testimony. Either way, he must have liked what he saw as, one Wednesday afternoon, he announced to us that his friends had agreed to come back for a game that Friday. We buzzed.

We had been playing together longer now, and our tensions were undeniably lower than they had been. We were ready for it, we felt. His job probably done, the church boy did not show up that Thursday. Just as well, we thought; it would give us time to fine-tune our team play. By now, we each knew what our role in the team was. I would start in goal. I was gangly and flexible, although not as flexible as either Wellington or Babylon. My size and fearlessness in the face of flying balls and charging strikers gave me a slight advantage and, besides, those two would rather be playing in other positions. Fox played on the right side of defense. He was slow but could kick the ball far and was also callous. Ta was left-footed and big, so he naturally took over the left side. Wellington, being skillful and fast, played in the middle of the field, while the diminutive and nimble Babylon played as a striker. Innocent, who was probably better than any of us, would start as a substitute because he was not from the neighborhood. He understood and was confident enough in his skill that he did not mind the compromise. Tinashe was also excellent but young and small, so he would come on for either Babylon or Wellington whenever they needed a rest. The Tennis Brothers were both slow and not particularly skillful, but we would make sure to pair them with one of the more dependable defenders when the need arose. Everyone else would get a run-around at different points of the game.

The church boys arrived at the field at two o'clock on Friday-a full thirty minutes before the agreed start time. None of us were there yet, so they began kicking their ball around and warming up for the game. Soon, we trickled to the field. Babylon arrived first, followed by Nigel and me. Fox and Wellington followed, and soon everyone was there in exaggerated high spirits—an unspoken attempt to compensate for last year's disaster. The other team seemed to appreciate the effort, as they neither brought up the awful last game nor withheld their own pleasantries to each other and towards us.

The beginning of the game was reserved, as both teams were sizing each other up; not so much in skill as that had already been established, but rather in spirit. It was not until after a drab and goalless first ten minute that the game began to gain momentum. Because they were more confident in their talent and had been there before, the church boys scored first. Then they scored again, and nightmares of the previous thrashing began to resurface on our end. Although no words had been exchanged yet, one could never fully dismiss the volatility of Babylon and Wellington's tempers. If we were to keep it together, we needed a goal and needed it soon. The other team was still on the attack. With their two attacking players down both sides, the one on the right—the spy—galloped down the field with the ball before dribbling past a hapless Fox, then attempted to slide it through to his teammate on the left. I dove forward to intercept the diagonal pass, sprung back onto my feet and tossed it downfield to where an anticipating Wellington was waving his hands invitingly. The ball landed at his feet, and he made the easy task of scoring more fancier than it had to be on the day, rounding the goalkeeper before tapping it into the goal. The celebrations were uncontained. Babylon, who had been nearest to him and had been watching impatiently, was first to leap into his arms. Fox ran the length of the pitch to congratulate his little brother, and Ta began to chant

"*Timu Timu, ndikusortere timu!*"[36] only for the bench to join in, "*Haa tikusotere timu!*"

Little Anesu, who had joined us on the bench on the day delighted everyone with a variation of the famous *Ndombolo* dance[37]. I smiled and clapped my hands from the goalposts. The goal was exactly what we needed. We ended up losing the game 5-3, but our faces told of victory. As the game had gone on, everyone except Anesu had gotten a chance to play, albeit brief for some. The church boys were gracious in victory and vowed to come back in a few weeks.

"Maybe when you guys come back, we can play two games! If you have some more friends or younger brothers, we could divide each team into two, so everyone gets to play!"

"Sounds good." They agreed, although they were clearly tired and in no state to commit to any future plans. I, on the other hand, was well aware that the euphoria of the moment would not be enough to keep the peace at Pashena: it was inevitable that soon everyone would be clamoring to get their fair shot at playing. We could make sure everyone played, but that would undoubtedly compromise the flow of the game. It may even mean having our better players out at

---

36 "Team, team, Let me pick you a team…" a football war cry in which you shout out all the players on a team in turn.

37 A style of central African popular dance music that originated in Zaire (now DRC) and grew to fame in the mid-1990s

crucial moments. I also know that such gracious defeat as we had lived through today would not fare well in the long run; we were bound to start chasing and demanding victory in the near future. We needed to figure out a way to both appease as many of our people as possible while remaining competitive.

We waited for two weeks to hear back from our church nemeses before we figured they might not be as hungry for a rematch as we were. They had played us twice already and, despite our obvious improvements between the two games, they had beaten us both times. They were probably out seeking stiffer competition. Much like a first-time lover, we found it hard to even explore the possibility of pairing up with another. We only wanted the church boys.

As often happens with first-time lovers, it would take domineering assertion to pry our infatuated hearts from the grip that held them tight. And so, it happened.

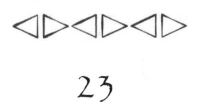

23

"Ko Fox, is it true wh-wha-what they are saying about Sincere?" Ta asked callously, "Is she really pregnant?"

It had been all the talk around MaOwnership. It was bound to happen; I overheard the women say. She was basically living with her boyfriend now. It was not the same boyfriend from a few months ago either, they said. He may not even be the same one as a few weeks ago.

The usually tacit Fox grimaced at Ta, who had been intelligent enough not to bring up the matter in front of Wellington.

"Who told you that?" Fox snarled, "has your crook mom been talking about my family again?"

Ta stood back, fists uncharacteristically clenched. Things had escalated much quicker than he or any of us would have anticipated. Fox had always been defensive of his family but was also mild-mannered in his responses, preferring to take aggressors down with wit and an unfazed smile. This was new.

The reason Ta's question had upset Fox so much was because Sincere was, indeed, pregnant. The authoritative pillar and moral compass of what was left of their household had, at 16, fallen prey to the same fate that typically only befell spoilt loose high school girls. To make matters worse, the man whose seed she now carried was not even the same one they had been introduced to last year. They did not even know this man. Fox could not bring himself to terms with it, let alone confront her. Besides, she still provided for them. Lately, she seemed to be outdoing herself: their school fees were paid on time, they had new school shoes, and often had Mazoe and biscuits in their house— treats that they never had before and were becoming a rarity in households around Dangamvura. Why bite the hand that rocks the cradle?

I jumped in, eager to de-escalate the quarrel.

"Ta, are you crazy? You can't just ask people that!" I said, choosing to hold the slightly more stable of two unhinged people accountable. Ta looked up at me, ready to ask why I was not scolding Fox for what he had said but decided against it when he saw the stern but understanding look in my eyes.

"Forget the game today," Fox said and stormed into his house. As Ta and I made our way to Pashena, I admonished him gently.

"Some things are better unsaid, you know? We will know soon enough. You cannot wrap in cloth that which has tusks," I said smugly. I was impressed with myself for having been able to regurgitate almost word for word that wisdom I had overheard Gogo dish out to my aunts the night before on the same matter. Ta was still reeling from the swipe Fox had taken at his mother, but he half understood the source of his ire; the other half was consoled by not having to see his antagonizer for the rest of the afternoon. Wellington came home from school, had his lunch, and came out to the field.

"Does anyone know what happened to Strive?" he asked. "He was just sitting there and said he did not feel like playing today." We had no idea, we lied. I figured if Fox had not told him, then there was no reason for us to do so. Soon, everyone else joined us.

Because MaOwnership was halfway between our school and neighborhoods like Area 3 and Ma P, Pashena soon caught the attention of several of our schoolmates as the reputation grew and our games became more intense. It wasn't long until one of my classmates who lived in Area 3 came up to me and suggested a game. We did not know much about Area 3, but with the church boys being reticent, we were thirsting for a game with an outside team, any outside team.

The following Thursday afternoon, the Area 3 boys visited Pashena. Our team was unchanged from our last game, with the exception of Fox who had still not returned from his self-imposed exile. Innocent took over on the right side of defense in his absence. We played an inspired game that day and, for once, felt the sweet fruit of victory within our licking range. Even Ta, who usually played conservatively and stuck to the left corner of the field, ventured into opposition territory a few times and scored a left-footed beauty. If my memory serves me well, we narrowly lost that game 3-4.

Despite that incredible result, one thing was becoming increasingly apparent; we needed to find a way to get everyone to play without compromising the quality of the team.

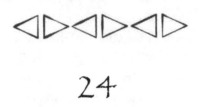

24

Another perk to being in grade six and seven was that you were now eligible for the school's football team. If you were a phenomenal talent, you could get into the team in Grade five and, in some rare cases, even Grade four. That was a matter that we, as Pashena boys, did not need to be concerned with much, as we stood no chance of making the school teams anyway. Most of us were not good enough. Wellington and Babylon were probably as good as the average school team player, but the institution of team selection had fallen victim to the ugly practice of nepotism, and thus the teams were almost always entirely composed of boys from Area B, Area C, and MaTwo Rooms. Diego, one of the boys from the lesser-known part of MaOwnership, was our sole representative in the school team. However, or therefore, he deemed himself above playing with the Pashena crowd. Not only was he too good and stood to benefit little from playing against us commoners, he could not risk an injury at the hands of Ta or Fox's barely skilled yet rock-hard limbs. We understood.

The benefit to us was that as more people tried to harness their skill and develop a reputation in time for the school football season, more and more neighborhood teams were willing, if not desperate, to play a game. While they may not necessarily be thrilled with the level of competition we promised, Pashena was as good a field as any to prepare for the games to come.

Our accidental bait soon began to work. An acquaintance of mine from MaTwo Rooms, Simba, whose grandmother happened to be in the same church group as Gogo, initially started coming to kick around with us much in the same way that Innocent did. Because so many people lived in MaTwo Rooms and they had all been raised on football, there were many players who were on the fringes of the school team or who stood no chance that were still looking to play. Besides, with their rocky, unpaved streets and no backyards, it was hard to get a good game going in their neighborhood and, although they were pretty close to Beit, the field would have been packed this time of year. He figured that he could practice on and with us alone so when he went back to his neighborhood, he would be better. He soon found the games insufferable. It was not necessarily that we were not up to his standard of play (a few of us were pretty competitive by now), but that his style of play was fundamentally different from ours.

"Ko boys, I see you have been playing among yourselves for a while. How about I bring some of my boys for a quick game soon?"

My friends winced. Once Simba started playing with us, we anticipated that the conversation would take that turn soon. Still, we had hoped he would be content with the status quo, and we could avoid the entire conversation. I had met Simba's friends and, because Area B bordered MaTwo Rooms, Innocent knew most of them well. For the horrible reputation their neighborhood received, they were not as notorious as one might have been led to believe; at least not the boys our age.

Even with Innocent and I throwing our weight behind the idea of playing against Simba and friends, the other boys and, by extension, their parents needed convincing. Simba, blessed with the guile one could only get from growing up in a neighborhood like MaTwo Rooms, knew exactly how to sell it to them. First, he volunteered to act as messenger for Gogo and his grandmother's church group, knowing very well that the aging ladies would lean heavily on him to deliver notices of meetings to truant members and other news. He did such a good job that he was soon being sent even to women outside the church group to deliver owed monies and messages about funerals and such. In no time, he had become a darling to the MaOwnership community and beyond.

Simba had learned early one of the most fundamental lessons of communal living: if you can earn the trust and partiality of the old women, you get everyone to like you. The only qualms that the Pashena boys ever had against playing a team were based on how the rest of the neighborhood would feel. Now that Simba was fine by MaOwnership, nothing stood in the way of him and his friends coming to play with us.

If any of us had been skeptical, the next words out of Simba's mouth sealed it.

"Maybe we can have two games? Everyone Grade Four and under can play in a juniors' game, and everyone else can play for the seniors!"

Although he made it seem an afterthought, the suggestion was nothing short of an excellent conclusion to Simba's well-conceived plan. During the time he had played with us, he silently picked up on our concern that not all of us got to play when we played other teams. He heard us debate on, even in the unlikely event that guest teams would bring enough people for two teams, how we could possibly divide our team. He could have said it then, but he did not; saving it for this poignant moment.

For him, it was more than just a ploy to convince us though. Because the houses in MaTwo Rooms were so confined and small, all the boys there grew up physically and emotionally close to each other.

MaOwnership boys felt a proud and growing loyalty to each other, but even we knew that it paled in comparison to that of MaTwo Rooms. They went everywhere together; so much that we should have known there was an ulterior long-run motive to Simba playing with us by himself.

Thus, when we finally agreed to play against them, Simba knew he would not be able to convince only six or seven of his friends to come and leave half the battalion behind. He also knew that Nigel, Tinashe, and some of the younger boys got to play the least in our team, so dividing the team by age would appease them while preserving the strength and pride of the older boys' team.

We agreed to have the game in two weeks, which would give us enough time to both practice and ensure that we had enough players for the two teams. Our senior team was tried and tested, but our juniors needed work. We had Nigel, Tinashe, Faru and Tiberius already; we needed at least one, preferably two more people to be able to field a team. We were not concerned much with how well they would do against the MaTwo Rooms juniors. Based on experience and anticipated skill level alone, we expected our little brothers to get annihilated. I doubt that many of the seniors cared at all; they were just happy not to have the pesky fourth graders insisting on being brought on as substitutes at the height of action.

25

"Do you guys know Diego?"

Fungai asked the Monday before our big double game. Ta, Innocent and I looked at each other and smiled. We had had this conversation a few times before. It had almost taken the importance of a rite of a passage into full Pashena membership: you would play for a while and, although you enjoy it and often see glimpses of talent, realize that we need at least one exceptional player to push us to be better and to show off to other teams. Then you would hear the legend of Diego. If you were lucky enough, you may get to see him play at Beit. He was MaOwnership's best, nay, sole representative on the fields that mattered most. Inevitably, you would ask why he didn't play with us; a question that would be proudly answered by whoever it was that had received the explanation last.

This would be Innocent's turn, but Fungai stopped him as soon as he began to venture into the finer details.

"Oh no! I was not suggesting that we get Diego to play with us. Ha! Can you imagine that?" Fungai retorted. His propensity to condescend often meant he would mock even the groups to which he belonged.

"I think he has a younger brother, Donald. If he is any bit as good as Diego and looking to practice for the school team this year or later, then he will be perfect for our juniors."

I hated to admit it, but that was actually a brilliant idea. Up until now, Donald would have been going to other neighborhoods to play with Diego's friends and their younger brothers. He would be relieved to be playing closer to home and on our redoubtable field, no less. We still had to approach him carefully though. Diego and others would probably try to dissuade him from playing with us and encourage him to try out for at least the school's B team. Although he was only in fourth grade like Nigel and the others, he was one of those protégés known around Dangamvura for being able to hold their own on the field against much older boys. Admittedly, almost all the renowned 'protégés' bore the dubious distinction of being the younger brothers of beloved players as well. Regardless of what bias there may have been, they still had to be good enough to at least warrant the good name that had been thrust upon them.

We placed upon Ta and Tinashe with the enviable task of roping Donald into our juniors' team. The latter would serve to show that there was some talent to be found among the younger crop while the former's exceptional ability to connect with younger people would come in handy.

Our delegation ambushed Donald when they got out of school for the day. Although he lived in MaOwnership, his house was so far down the street that he would typically walk with a group of classmates who lived in Area 3; that way, he could have some company all the way home while they still had each other to go the rest of the way. This time, Ta and Tinashe got to him first. Anticipating some resistance, Ta had tactfully brought with him some sweets that his mother had brought from South Africa as bait. Donald bit. They walked with him until part of MaOwnership and down the street to his, all the time hinting at their mission. Just before they arrived, Ta finally blurted out,

"We are starting a juniors' team for Pashena, for everyone Grade Four and below. You sho-should come and play with us!"

"That sounds good, and maybe I will stop by some time. I just don't have much time though. I play with some Area 3 boys, and Diego thinks I could maybe try for the school team!"

"But look," Tinashe chimed in with his rehearsed part of the pitch, "you may be good enough to be considered for the team, but practicing with us will only get you better."

"We'll see," Donald replied without conviction. He was not interested, and his reticence annoyed Ta.

"Okay, ma-an. Just know that, if you go and try out for the team as you are now, the fact that you are Diego's brother is not going to be enough to get you in."

Donald's eyes opened wide. How dare he? He took pride in his skill and hated both the Diego comparisons and the assumption that he was only worth talking about as a football player because of their relationship.

"What did you say? What are you talking about? I am better than all of you guys and better than half those fools playing for the school right now!"

Tinashe, realizing that Ta's tactless comment had left their mission on the hinges, thought on his feet and replied.

"Oh, we don't doubt that at all. Ta was merely saying what he heard some boys from MaTwo Rooms say about you."

"Who?" Donald snarled.

"I don't know," Tinashe continued, "some of the younger boys who have agreed to play us in our first juniors' game on..."

That was all Donald needed to hear. Nobody was going to discredit him as a player. He would be there Saturday morning to prove them wrong, even if it meant playing on a shoddily assembled team of inexperienced juniors.

Mission completed, Tinashe and Ta bade farewell and began the long walk up the street. Ta knew that he had almost botched it and was not keen on apologizing or thanking his younger friend for rescuing their efforts. He instead put his arm around Tinashe's shoulders, and they walked that way for a few meters. Tinashe understood and smiled at his older friend. They had added a quality player to the team and could return to the tribe with their chests inflated after a successful hunt.

That Saturday morning, the air over Pashena was more festive than we had ever felt. The two outside teams we had played against already were both decent, but playing the MaTwo Rooms boys was the pinnacle of Dangamvura dirt field teams. They were born playing football; thus their ways and words about the game were gospel. They were playing money games before they even started school. They had vast collections of footballer stickers from around the world and attended the big games at Sakubva stadium[38]. Games against MaTwo Rooms represented more than just two teams facing each other: it was validation of your team and your field.

Most of us arrived at the field as early at ten am, a full two hours before the agreed start time. We kicked around and waited for our friends to get there. Wellington was helping Sincere with some chores but would be there just before the game started, and some of the younger boys came around 11. There was still no sign of Donald though. I began to feel, and I suspect I was not the only one, that Ta and Tinashe had lied about their encounter with him. There was no way he would have agreed to play at Pashena. Besides, it was not beyond Ta to pull a stunt like that, and Tinashe would have had no choice but to participate in the ruse. I hesitated to say anything, lest they had

---

38 The city's main stadium

actually done as they had said. We were getting nervous with each passing minute though.

With ten minutes to go before the game, we saw the MaTwo Rooms boys descending down the street like a renegade army. There were about 15 of them, complete with two or three toddler siblings who were coming to support their big brothers, a cunning way to combine babysitting duties and playtime. All the boys wore replica jerseys of professional European teams. Some of the jerseys were nicer, and some of them looked like they had been passed on for generations. That alone instilled fear in us. None of us owned any shirt that bore the name of a famed footballer. The closest thing we had was my 1994 World Cup mascot shirt, which counted for nothing in this scenario.

I said none of us owned such a shirt? I lied.

While all eyes were fixed on the army coming down from ahead, a lone warrior had silently made his way onto Pashena from the other direction. It was Donald, looking as menacing as any of our adversaries and draped in an Argentine blue and white jersey with the name "Batistuta" on the back. It only made sense that he, as the little brother to Diego (named after Argentina's greatest player of yesteryear Diego Maradona), would adopt the moniker of the present day Argentine sensation, Gabriel Batistuta.

MaTwo Rooms boys' arrival only intensified the festive ambiance. While the likes of Wellington and I had spent enough time outside MaOwnership not to be surprised, everyone else seemed overwhelmed by the group's filthy comportment and crude vocabulary to match. Even more mystifying was how comfortable they were in their skin. When we were dirty, or our clothes were worn out, we knew it and knew something had to be done about it. In moments when the grimness of such filth was lost on us, the adults made sure to remind us either with a gentle word or the wrath of a peach tree switch. It was a sight to see.

We greeted each other and arranged the logistics of the games. There would be two games as planned, with the juniors going first as is customary in the sport world. "Curtain Raisers' I learned they were called from Simba. We agreed that, since we had exactly five players and no substitutes for the juniors, they would only play for twenty minutes- ten minutes per half.

The game started with Tiberius as goalkeeper, Nigel and Faru as defenders, and Donald and Tinashe upfront. Tiberius and Faru were in their positions by default as the other players had picked the rest. If this had been previously unknown to MaTwo Rooms boys, it became apparent once the game started. One of the bigger boys on the team hoofed a seemingly aimless ball from halfway down the field and Tiberius stumbled around and caught it briefly before it seeped through his hands for a goal. MaTwo Rooms seniors cheered with their little brothers, while we groaned from the bench. Immediately after, a small boy- could not have been more than eight years old—blazed past a hapless Faru on the left side of the field before dribbling cheekily past Tiberius for a second goal. Our young boys looked well on course for a demoralizing rout. Things only got worse when Faru, the joint-weak link in our fledgling team, went in for a nasty clash with the big fellow who had scored the first goal. In all honesty, it was not too horrible a challenge, but apparently, Faru had had enough of the game. He fell on the ground and rolled around as if he were being stung by bees, all the while screaming at the top of his lungs. Fearing the worst, Ta and I ran onto the field and whisked him off, but not before he stopped crying and winked at us to show that he was okay. He must have been so ashamed of his performance that he did not want to play anymore.

I dropped him callously next to The Mountain. Ta chuckled. I didn't. How selfish was he? It is one thing to weasel your way out of a game when there are other players to replace you. He knew, however, that the game's five-versus-five parity rested entirely on having all our players stay on the field. His decision to leave mid-game was rude and inconsiderate, I felt. I knew the rest of the boys would feel the same if they found out that he had pretended to be injured, so I decided to keep that act of treachery between Ta, Faru and myself.

I jogged over to the bench where Simba and the other boys were standing around, concerned more for the fate of the lopsided game than the frail deposed player.

"What's the plan now, Shingi? Are we just going to leave the game here?" Simba asked in disappointed disbelief.

"Looks that way, sha. These young ones can't carry the entire field playing four on four. They were barely managing the five on five!"

"*Aiwa ka,* but we have brought our boys here across Dangamvura only to have them play five minutes? This is pathetic!" He fumed to a chorus of approval from the other boys.

The integrity of Pashena was at stake. The only reason MaTwo Rooms boys should ever leave your field disappointed is because you beat them. I cast a desperate glance at Faru from across the field, silently imploring him to get back on the field. He flashed a disguised smile at me, before clinching his leg and moaning again. I turned back to the crowd, struggling to maintain my composure. Innocent detected my frustration and pulled me away from the meddling congregation.

"Anesu!" He whispered to me with the excitement of someone who held the secret key that everyone was currently searching for.

"What do you mean, Anesu?"

"He has wanted to play for a while now, and he has been watching the game from behind the fence. Just call him and let him play!"

"That's ridiculous," I snapped and got ready to turn back, "If he was not ready to play when it was just us, why would he be ready now?

"Aah, but look brother. We just need someone to finish the game. The boys are already losing, and that doesn't look likely to change. Anesu will allow us to play out the rest of the game. Besides, it will appease his fantasies and, hopefully, if the game continues to go as horribly as it has been, he will never want to play again!" he rounded off his speech with a victory snicker. I walked back over to everyone and considered discussing it further with them but decided against it.

I looked over the fence, under The Avocado Tree where Anesu sat, and yelled out to him, "Ane! Ane! You want to pl—"

He had heard enough. He had been watching the game intently as he always did and must have been praying for someone to notice him sitting there. Before I was done with my invitation, he was crawling between the barbed wire like his brother always did, and onto Pashena.

The MaTwo Rooms juniors jeered at the sight of little Anesu scampering into the field and looked at us as Goliath would have looked upon the Children of Israel as they sent David into battle. How dare we let a mere infant play against them? Even Ta and my other teammates doubted the wisdom of the decision. They, however, realized that I stood to lose much more than they did from the gamble, and I would not have taken it if it was not the only option available.

Like a coach, I gathered the shape-shifted junior team around to discuss strategy.

"Alright look. This is unfortunately how things are. Now, Anesu is too small to play defense, so what..."

"How about Tiberius plays defense and I go in as goalie? I like goalie!" Anesu again interrupted me in excitement. His idea was not bad. Nigel and Tiberius were as big as the biggest player on the other team and, while I had never seen Anesu play, having him in goals would be enough to last us the rest of the game.

"Okay, good. Tiberius, take over on the left where Faru was. Everyone else in the same place. Let's go!"

In the same condescending fashion that had started the game, the big boy from MaTwo Rooms hoofed the ball downfield towards our goal. He had beaten Tiberius with ease that way earlier, and the much smaller and raw Anesu would be no task at all. We shamefully shared the sentiment.

We watched with hopeless intent as the ball veered to Anesu's slight right. With his chubby legs wobbling for nerves, Anesu sprung up and dove to the right and, beyond our wildest expectations, parried the ball out. He had saved it. He had actually saved it.

I screamed and charged onto the field like we had just won the game. Nigel and Babylon were right behind me, and we hoisted my little cousin into the air while everyone else cheered. Faru, forgetting about his supposed injury, jumped up from the Mountain and ran to celebrate with the rest of the bench. Even MaTwo Rooms seniors applauded and laughed a little. It was the stuff of dreams! It did not matter what else happened in that game; it had already been an outcome we would be talking about for years.

Anesu's save was enough to re-instill a spring in our juniors' step. Our boys lost the game 2-5, but not before two or three more exceptional saves from our debutant goalkeeper and a well-crafted team goal which Donald finished with the finesse that made the hustle that led to his joining the team worthwhile.

The seniors' game that followed only serves as a footnote in the story of the incredible juniors' game. To be honest, I do not remember what the final score was—none of us do. We competed well but still lost. It did not matter. That Saturday was the Saturday that the juniors played their first game; the day that Donald introduced himself to our part of MaOwnership; the day that Faru feigned an injury and forgot after a few minutes; the day that Anesu dove slight right into Pashena folklore. As it turned out, the raising of the curtains became the show.

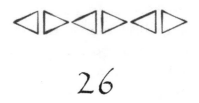

26

The aftermath of MaTwo Rooms game brought about the publicity for which we had always yearned. Word of Pashena adopted a new tone as it made its rounds around Dangamvura. Instead of a pretty field put together by the MaOwnership boys, it became a fierce battleground where some of Dangamvura's finest would meet to play. By now, we had overtaken the riverbank field in popularity and were neck and neck with Gwanzura, and even that was just because of its proximity to the Beit Field. We were still particular about who we played against though, sticking to the three neighborhoods we had already played against. While the field earned a reputation faster than the team that called it home, we soon began to be recognized among the Dangamvura teams as well. We gained notoriety not so much for our skills on the field, although we were indeed much better than when we had started. People liked to play against us because we had become organized and punctual, and we always compensated for what we may have lacked in talent with fervent performance. We left everything we had on the field of play every time.

One of those upon whose ears had fallen news of Pashena was my second cousin Gandanga, Priscilla, the librarian's little brother. They lived in an area of Dangamvura called the Village, which had been built for soldiers and war veterans after Independence. Their father was a dignified yet feared veteran of the Chimurenga War and now served in the Zimbabwean army. The name *Gandanga* means guerrilla fighter or warrior, and my cousin was so called because of his father's reputation. I spent much of my infancy there, as it was close to the crèche and Gogo was well acquainted with their mother. I had not been there since then. I stayed the truant second cousin for years until one afternoon Gogo sent Nigel and me to deliver a bundle of homegrown vegetables to Mai Priscilla. We groaned in unison. The Village was at least 45 minutes each way, which meant the trip and the subsequent obligatory chitchat and almost certain meal disqualified us from any Pashena activity that day. I had also not seen Priscilla since my expulsion from the library and had hoped to avoid the ghost of that humiliation until we had both forgotten about it.

Our dejected departure was helped in no way by the sight of all our friends, Anesu included, beginning to get into the stride of the game as we walked past.

"*Kwakanaka here?*" Babylon yelled out, surprised that we would even be doing anything else during sacred Pashena time. We yelled back that we had an errand to run for Gogo. The silence that followed our response bore testimony to the all-trumping sanctity of the commands of the elders, regardless of how they might make us feel.

We arrived at Mai Priscilla's house in predicted somber spirits and, despite her exaggerated attempts at being hospitable; we made it no secret that we were keen to leave.

"*Yuwi yuwi*[39]" You have finally decided to visit us! Aaaah! Sit right here. Priscilla! Gandanga! Bring *vana Sekuru*[40] some Mazowe! Ah. I am sorry you had to walk all this way!"

"Aaah *nhai*," I said, speaking with as much formality as I could summon in the instance, "we are full, *Mainini*[41], don't even bother! In fact, we have to get goi..."

"Ah! So, you can say Mai Priscilla did not feed us! No, no, eat something. Priscilla! Gandanga! Where are these people? Gandanga, bring some biscuits as well!"

Nigel and I looked at each other and resigned to our fate as Mai Priscilla's lunchtime hostages. Priscilla must not have been around then, as it was Gandanga who walked in with an annoyed look that we knew well; it was the same one we had worn at the beginning of our trip. His changed as soon as he saw us though, turning into the genuine smile which long-lost friends around the world exchange at the point of meeting again. Abandoning all guest-host protocol, I jumped to my feet and embraced my estranged cousin.

"Hey, you! What has it been? Five, six years? You would think one of us lives in Harare!"

"*Nhai*[42] Gandanga," his mother interrupted our moment, "What was taking you so long! What were you doing back there?"

"Sorry mother, I was watching *Hard Target* Again!"

Our ears perked up. *Hard Target* was my favorite Van Damme movie of all time. I am not sure it was Nigel's favorite too. While Van Damme tended to be my action hero of choice, Nigel fancied himself a Schwarzenegger man. An action movie was an action movie nonetheless, and Gandanga's words had unwittingly stolen our

---

39 "Hear, Hear!"
40 "Grand-uncles"
41 Customary greeting for maternal adult relatives younger than your mother. Literally means 'little/deputy mother'
42 "Say"

attention. We forgot that we had been trying to rush back home to catch what was left of the game and sunk deep into Mai Priscilla's sofas.

"So, Gandanga, how do you like that *Hard Target?* Pretty good huh?" I said, easing into the conversation.

"It's crazy!" he responded gleefully. "I personally prefer *Kickboxer*, but maybe because I have watched *Hard Target* too many times already."

"You have *Kickboxer,* too?" Nigel asked, eyes barely remaining in his head.

"Of course, I do, sekuru! It is all part of this big box of tapes that Father brought back from the DRC."

In 1996, Laurent Kabila's rebel troops had overthrown Mobutu Sese Seko's regime in Zaire after years of tyranny and promptly changed the name to the Democratic Republic of Congo. Gandanga's father was sent there as part of a large army contingent to back the new government. Often, the soldiers did not make it back home alive. Those who did, however, always came back with a bag full of presents for their families. Gandanga's father was no different. He had sacks upon sacks of clothes and shoes for Mai Priscilla and Gandanga's five sisters upon his return. Being the only boy, Gandanga undeniably reaped the finest crop from his father's wartime escapades: toys; movies—football jerseys—anything that his heart desired, he received when his father returned. The big box of Van Damme, Rambo and Schwarzenegger's tapes was the most recent delivery.

As fate would have had it from the moment we found out of Gandanga's cinematic wealth, we ended up staying there until the early onset of dusk when we begrudgingly pulled away from *Kickboxer 2* and vowed to be back soon. Although we were certain to find Pashena deserted for the day, our excursion to the Village had been worth it. We ran home, buzzing from the adrenaline inspired by Van Damme's round-kicks and the absolute need to be home before it got too dark. We passed Sincere on the way and could not help but notice how big her belly had grown since the last time we saw her: it had only been a month! We greeted her, and she grunted back at us. She had always been mean and aloof, but she seemed particularly miserable and unpleasant lately. I remembered Gogo mentioning a thing called "pregnancy brain" earlier—how women with child often have mood swings and act uncharacteristically from time to time. I figured it was that from which she was suffering. Because, however, we were not accustomed to her niceties, her brashness did not bother us much. We had to get home.

We arrived just as Mai Nigel was beginning to dish out that evening's sadza. She had a chagrined look and tongue-lashing prepared for us when we walked into the house.

"What time is it?" She yelled at us in the kitchen, struggling to curtail her voice so that Kulu and Gogo did not hear the conversation from the dining room.

"I said what time is this to be coming in? You were supposed to deliver the veggies and come right back, not go over to your friends' houses!"

We tried to explain that we had been at Mai Priscilla's house the entire time but, based on our earlier reluctance to even go, she was not buying that story. After about five minutes of scolding on her part and adamant denial of guilt on ours, we finally sat down at the table, said grace, and began to eat. Kulu and Gogo must have been baffled by the solemn silence that prevailed during supper. We were usually talkative during meals, often to their annoyance. They had not caught wise as to when we returned or our subsequent squabble with Mai Nigel.

"*Nhai Mai Nigel. Maitana sei nevakomana*[43]? What is the matter?" Gogo inquired, her voice reverberating with empathy. Mai Nigel began to explain but was interrupted by the ringing telephone. Gogo answered it and spoke with rhythmic gratitude and pleasantness for two minutes before bidding farewell with similar gusto.

---

43 "Mai Nigel, what's happened between you and your boys?"

"That was Mai Priscilla. She said thanks for the veggies and wanted to just thank the boys again for their visit this afternoon. She said to tell you guys to feel free to come back anytime!"

I smiled victoriously, and then glanced across the table in time to see Nigel break into an identical smile. Gogo must have realized that the visit to Mai Priscilla's had been the source of our supper time discontent, or she had just seen us begin to smile; either way, she decided not to interrogate any further. Mai Nigel, never one to shy away from a good laugh even at her own expense, magnanimously explained the misunderstanding to Gogo amidst our vindicated grins, Kulu's half-hearted attention and Gogo's compassionate smile at the foolery of youth, and Mai Nigel's own guilty giggles.

27

Since Mai Priscilla's phone call had tipped the scales of justice back in our favor, we were able to visit their home anytime without either permission from our end or an invitation on theirs. The arrangement was perfect for us. We spent four or five afternoons each week with our friends at Pashena and, on the days we felt we needed a change in scenery and company; we would go over to Mai Priscilla's and rummage through Gandanga's action movie box. Despite the lazy and repeated plotlines of the movies—a small, peaceful, and/or unconfident man is going through the paces of daily life, an aggressor hurts a loved one or threatens the well-being of his people, the first man trains rigorously under an unlikely mentor and ends up defeating the aggressor—we never got tired of them. At the end of each movie day, we would select two more that we would watch the next time we visited. More exciting than the experience of watching the movies were the conversations to be had back in MaOwnership and at school the next morning. Whether it was by The Mountain, The Guava Tree, or basking in the early morning sun with a dozen classmates before school started, one could always count on the undivided and lustful attention of his peers when he had a Van Damme or Rambo story to tell. These were the proving grounds upon which we all sharpened our narration skills. We would gather around to hear each other relay with great animation and aplomb the tales of how our heroes had defeated yet another cold-hearted opponent. The feverish excitement tripled when the movie had been watched by several people, in which the story-telling would then turn into a beautifully choreographed dance that left the listener feeling like they had watched the movie, too—which was not that hard to do. The movies' similarities and predictability usually meant if you had seen one, you had seen them all! Ta and some of the younger boys had always gathered to watch the movies at Tinashe's house and would come out buzzing with detailed and gleeful descriptions of fight scenes and explosions. Because I was banned from Tinashe's after the peanut-shelling scandal, Nigel and I had been left out in the wilderness until now. Although Gandanga had the infuriating habit of watching the pre-selected movies before we got there so he could 'predict' what was going to happen next, we were just delighted to finally be able to command some early morning spotlight among our sun-basking friends.

Our fraternization with Gandanga eventually took the inevitable turn after two weeks of over-indulgence in exaggerated explosions and nick-of-time knockout punches. He had been coy about it thus far, but he too was curious about the legend of Pashena; all his friends were. Although they had grown up together, they had, like us, only recently mobilized into a neighborhood team. We started by talking about football in general. Mutare's local team "The Buffaloes" had been playing some amazing games lately and looked set to be promoted into the Premier League in the next two years. We also speculated about the World Cup due to begin that June. Like most people around us, we were sure that Brazil was going to win again as they had in 1994. The Germans and Italians were always good too, so it would be interesting to see how that went. As the conversation progressed, he began to inquire more about our specifics: who we had on our team, how often we played, and whom we had played against. The line of questioning was different from that to which I had become accustomed in that it focused less on the field and more on our team, and this turned out to be with good reason. As a novice team on the growing and increasingly competitive Dangamvura pre-teen neighborhood team map, they were sizing up the competition. While they had indeed heard Pashena flatteries, they were more interested in our team because reputation had it that we would be an easy first game. So foregone was the notion that talent eluded us that Gandanga felt at ease explaining the condescending train of thought that had led him and his friends to this conclusion. I spoke about how we had improved and, although we still had not won a game, the teams we had played recently would testify that we were worth their time in competition. He just jeered and claimed that the very people we spoke about had told him how bad we were. I tensed up and prepared to argue a storm and drag the names of the libelous boys out of him, but I caught Nigel's disapproving look in the corner of my eye. He knew my short, defensive fuse when it came to things with which I identified and had learned all the foreboding signs: the double-head nod, the vein popping on the left side of my head, and the right clenched fist. He also wanted to keep the door to Mai Priscilla's open until we had at least gone through the entire box.

Quickly processing what stood to be lost, he interjected into our rapidly heating conversation, "Well, why measure the snake with bark when it is right here[44]? No need to argue; let us set up the game then" he said, voice raspy with lack of conviction.

Gandanga smiled, and I let out the heavy breath I had been withholding in bubbling ire. Nigel's dubious expression turned into

---

44 Literal translation of a Shona proverb, meaning "why argue on what could be when we can know for sure?"

that of triumph at the sight of our reactions. He rarely ever spoke up when my peers or I discussed anything and, when he did, his contributions were often laughed off or ignored. We had listened.

As we walked home later that evening, I replayed the encounter with Gandanga and Nigel in my mind. Were people really saying that about our team? Why had every game this year seemed to end so well and respectfully then if the other boys looked down upon us? Was Gandanga just trying to get a rise out of me? I would not put it past him. Anyway, Nigel did a good job stopping that downward spiral of a conversation. How he has grown over the years.

Gandanga's patronizing had made it remarkably easy to rally our already game-hungry troops into battle. They were relieved to have us come back from Gandanga's and talk excitedly about something other than a movie. We shared the angering remarks with the same fervor and roused a thrill out of the boys, not unlike that commanded by the epic tales of Van Damme.

Because Gandanga lived close to the high school, it was decided that the game would be held there. The school had a handball field which was only slightly bigger than Pashena and boasted real metal goals that were smaller than those at Beit but, again, bigger than those at Pashena. While we would have been more comfortable playing at Pashena, we agreed to meet Gandanga and his friends at the handball field for a number of reasons. The field was well kept, and we did not often have a chance to play on such. The handball coach was an uncle to one of Gandanga's friends, and would occasionally let them in on Sundays if they asked ahead of time. More importantly to us, we wanted to play them on a field of their picking in utter defiance; we would play them in their home and beat them there. It was an incredibly confident mood for a team that had still not won a game. We set the game to be in three weeks' time.

The following weeks were devoid of much excitement. On the field, Anesu continued to impress with his infantile agility and game awareness. In addition to Donald, there was, for the first time, serious talk of a few Pashena folks possibly making it into their school team at some point in the future. Definitely not this year though. Fox and Babylon, our Grade Sevens, stood no chance; the former was neither good nor passionate enough, while the latter's skills were done a great disservice by his diminutive size and the fact that he was little known away from Pashena and the church. Innocent was in a good place to try for the team, but he never sounded like that is where his heart was. O, what we would have done to have his skill and Area B connections when it came time to try out for the team. He was, nevertheless, adamant that he did not want to play alongside his wayward neighbors, let alone depend on his relationship with them for a place on the team. I did not understand his lack of appreciation for these favorable odds, but I also knew Innocent was not one to be impulsive or petty; all his decisions were well thought out and probably tinged with a dose of elder sibling advice. I was getting rather dependable as goalkeeper, and had an outside chance for the next year. My fate was going to come down to pandering to the boys from the other neighborhoods though. We had no doubt that Wellington and Tinashe would make it in a year or two, provided they kept disciplined.

Wellington was struggling to stay out of trouble. His behavior at school was growing increasingly worrisome. At Pashena, he comported himself much more pleasantly than he had in past days but, away from us, he was getting into fights and spending time with crowds that the average MaOwnership boy would have had nothing to do with. His mindset only deteriorated when Sincere fell pregnant and became the chief subject of the communal rumor mill. Although she had only recently begun to show, there was talk that her pregnancy was not going well. Against convention, she seemed to be losing weight the longer her pregnancy went, with the obvious exception of expanding belly. This oddity only fueled the gossipmongers' incessant chatter, which forced Wellington to spend his time away from Pashena in neighborhoods where his family's affairs were either unknown or insignificant. Fox felt the same pressure, but he withdrew into the house instead, stepping out occasionally to join us Pashena. With all that our families had been through, we had learned not to bring up anything that was unsettling beyond what we had watched on TV or which team we would play next.

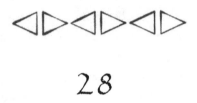

28

Baba Nigel happened to be in town the weekend that we would play Gandanga's team. He was a funny man and storyteller par excellence; each weekend he was in town from the rural school was one for the memories. This time, he had strolled in unexpectedly on Thursday evening, much to everyone's delight. After we had exchanged greetings and eaten the evening's sadza, he took the customary walk to the Tavern with his brother, my uncle Sekuru Gerry. They stumbled back home just before midnight, pungent smell of home-brewed beer heavy on their breath. Objectively, the stench of the fermented grains was insufferable but, because we grew up associating it with visits from funny out-of-town relatives and the protective powers of the household, it was an endearing smell of home to us.

Exhausted, Sekuru Gerry went straight to bed when they arrived but Baba Nigel, having found me still awake with the witching hour beckoning on a school night, came into the sitting room where I was.

179

"Hey there Shingson! *Ndeipi?* You are still awake?"

"*Hapana apa* sekuru. I was just watching *Walker, Texas Ranger* and getting ready to go to bed."

"Well, this is pretty late for someone your age to still be up. Was your show almost over?"

"Yes, Sekuru; just five more minutes."

"Well, finish up and go to sleep. I am going outside for some air. Stop by and say goodnight before you go."

I walked out of the house a few minutes later and found him leaning against the chicken shed, puffing on a cigarette.

"Ah ah. Your show is already done?" he said while battling a smoke-induced cough.

"Ehe. I told you it was almost done."

"Good. How is school going?" he asked, his drunken conscious drifting away from the pressing matter of me needing to be in bed.

"It is going well. We don't have any exams this term, so that is good" I replied, delighted to be getting away with a few more minutes before sleep.

"Oh right. No exams in the first term. So, what do you boys do these days?"

I went on to tell him about our days at Pashena and the time we had been spending at Mai Priscilla's house. Mention of his old friend, Gandanga's father the soldier, made his eyes light up.

"We actually have a game with Gandanga and his friends this weekend!" I said with a grin before I noticed that my uncle was already in a distant world of thought.

"Ah yes. Those are our people. I am happy you are spending time with them. We grew up together, his father and I, first at the rural home and then here in Dangamvura. Good man. There are not too many of those around here. There are not many of those anywhere, really," he said, gazing at the stars.

"It has always been that way. This is why it saddens me to come back from the school to hear all these stories about people dying here.

Both Baba Ta and his brother, and Strive's uncle, these were all good friends of mine. Now they are gone. And who knows who is next? This creature's appetite is insatiable." He said stoically as if resigning himself to the inevitable fate of people he knew to this "creature."

"What is this creature everyone talks about Sekuru?" I asked, seizing the opportunity to probe an adult on an issue that I was sure I knew about but was still being treated as taboo by the adults.

"This creature. It is, it's just life mwanangu. Most times, we say it to mean the disease, but nowadays, the creature can be anything."

The euphemism had seeped into the community's colloquium, and it needed no further explaining. Baba Nigel, still gazing into space, figured from my silence that I had not been able to read beyond his mystical explanation of the creature, so he proceeded:

"The disease is one thing. But as you have heard Gogo say, or maybe you have seen this for yourself, things have been getting more expensive and harder to find in stores. Your school fees are up. This has been since they gave all the War Veterans $50,000 each. Many of the people who got that money did not even fight the war. Sure, many of them were affected but, guess what? Gogo and Kulu were many a day helping people and having to stay underground due to the war—I don't see them getting any money. They would not claim it anyway. But you get some people whose involvement in the war was giving up a goat to the guerrillas when they stormed past their village, and now they are claiming $50,000! It was a bush war, a war for independence; is that not the prize? How are you going to fight to get your people free, then hold them hostage like so? Now they are starting to take away the farms from the whites. It smells like trouble! It's all one thing."

"But Sekuru, what does that have to do with all the people dying? And, why shouldn't the *povo*[45] get the land from the Whites? Isn't that

---

45 The general populace (slang term from the Portuguese for poor people, with the same roots as 'poverty')

what the war was about in the first place? I hear they own almost three-quarters of all the good farming land in the country!" I asked, fascinated but struggling to hold on to the nuggets of wisdom and knowledge tumbling from his beer-drenched breath.

"Yes and no." He chuckled as he answered with the ambiguous response that I had noticed a lot of adults used. "The land is ours by right, but the White Man has made an empire out of his commercial farming. Tobacco, flowers, grain, cotton; he has excelled in these. He has been perfecting this art for over 100 years now, and that is why he is good. Meanwhile, we have either been living in the townships or working as the lowest level of farm help, and now we want to just come in and seize the farms? What do we know about farming on that big a scale? If there were any reason in this world, we would slowly transition large pieces of the white-owned land to black farmers who have proven themselves capable of working on that level. Besides, is that not what reconciliation is all about? This idea of *Museyamwas*[46]s going in with sticks and machetes to seize the land is not only going to make us poorer, but it will also make the rest of the world hate us. But of course, the White Man is so comfortable in his empire and would keep it that way if he could. What else could Museyamwa do? I don't have the answers. Someone out there does."

If he did not have the answers, my fatigued young mind barely understood his words.

"The people dying though, *sekuru*..."

"Aah yes. Like I said, it's all one thing. The disease has people sick. Young adults mainly. If they are sick and dying, they cannot work. The economy suffers. The powers that be make some poor decisions in government and the economy suffers some more. Now we cannot support our sick because the hospitals and other things are not getting enough funding. So, more people die. And if more people are poor, then they become more desperate for a means to live. Many of them

---

46 Local tribe, often used to mean "ordinary Joes"

might start sleeping around for money. They catch the disease. And so it goes..."

Gogo had, at that moment, woken up to make a late cup of tea in the kitchen and saw us through the window—much to her annoyance.

"Nhai Baba Nigel, this is no time for the boy to still be awake. You know he has school tomorrow!"

"Haha, it's okay *Mhai*[47], we got distracted and lost track of time..."

"Shingi, you know better! Go to bed at once!" I shuffled into the house and went to bed reeling from the contentment of having been in an adult conversation. I had hoped to talk to him some more about football, but this was good too. I could always talk to him about that the next day.

---

47 Variation of "mother"

◁▷◁▷◁▷

29

After our late night socio-political lesson, Baba Nigel had apparently received a gentle but stern chastising from Gogo. It was not uncommon for Gogo to share such words with her children and, often, grandchildren, I would have never known or thought an extra moment on it had it not been for my uncle's unusually meek demeanor the following afternoon. Nigel and I came back from school and found him sitting under The Avocado Tree smoking his customary cigarette. He asked us how school was; a gesture more ceremonial than heartfelt. We responded with an equally underwhelming "fine" and shuffled into the house where our lunch awaited. He was obviously not in the highest spirits, so we thought it best to leave him alone until he returned to his lively self. Besides, we had to head over to the field for our final preparation before the game on Saturday.

We tore through lunch with the unapologetic haste of vultures that have landed upon an absent-minded eagle's half-eaten prey. We thanked Mai Nigel and dashed out towards Pashena without bothering to wash our hands. We tried to scamper past Baba Nigel unnoticed and were unsuccessful. Still in his mellow mood, he called out to us. We walked towards him slowly, maybe even cautiously. We were not nervous or scared; we always felt safe with him. Because, however, he was rarely ever like this, we did not know what to expect.

"Shingi, did you say you boys would be playing against Gandanga's team this weekend?"

He had heard me.

"Yes! Yes, we are!"

"Good people. His father is a good friend of mine," he said, repeating almost verbatim his words from the previous night with the same erstwhile look. My eyes rolled to the back of my head in dreaded incredulity: he must have forgotten that he told me all this last night and was about to hold us hostage for the next half an hour! Oh, how I would have given it all to have him speak to me for that long last night and now I stood, willing to give as much to be free to get to Pashena.

"But I already told you all that last night!" he said, snapping out of his daydream and much to my relief.

"I just wanted to give you this," he said as he stretched his clenched fist towards us. Nigel, always eager for treats, lunged at his father's arm. His father smiled and unclenched his fist to release a $10 note. We stood there slack-jawed. Even as the price of things was gradually creeping upwards around us, $10 was still a lot of money! Most of the students at our school would get between $1 and $2 to buy a freezit and *maputi* for lunch, often with some change left over for a fruit or snack of our liking. Awe must have been Baba Nigel's intended response from us because we could feel his melancholy lift as he spoke to us with the slight wink in his right eye that we all so loved.

"I just thought this would help spice up tomorrow's game. Tell Gandanga that I put $10 on the game. Whichever team wins walks away with ten dollars."

Nigel stood still with his mouth wide open, but I had heard enough. I could see my friends already congregated at the field beyond the barbed wire fence, and I felt the urge to share in this joy with them come over me. I pried open Nigel's entranced hand, snatched the note, and sprinted toward the field all the while yelling out inaudible but evidently joyous proclamations. When I finally explained to them what had me so animated, nearly everyone shared in my excitement. Nearly.

Innocent waited for the elation to die down before he pulled me to the side.

"Shingi, I know your uncle meant well with this money. Do you think it is a good idea though? In my neighborhood, they play these "money games," and they almost always end in fights. This is why people are so scared to play against some of these teams. I mean, the best-case scenario is we win the game; that handball field is bigger than Pashena, so I think we will need at least six or seven to play at a time. If we throw in the subs, then we have a group of ten or eleven. Can you imagine splitting that money between all of us? Let's do the math; do we want to risk the fights among each other and with the other team over what could be less than a dollar each? And I know Gandanga is your brother, but the rest of us do not know him, and his friends do not know any of us. They will have no qualms fighting us if it came to it. I don't like this idea at all."

"There you go again, Inno!" I yelled tactlessly for everyone to hear. "You worry too much. Remember you said the same thing about the goalposts, and look how that worked out. You need to calm down. This neighborhood is not like your neighborhood—people are civilized here!" I said with a chuckle and looked around for the approving laughter of my peers. Not one person thought it was funny. I looked over at my friend and saw him hanging his head in embarrassment, trying his losing best to look unfazed.

"Well," he started to speak to the crowd, his voice breaking, "I guess we have a game to get ready for tomorrow. Shall we play?"

It was a poorly disguised attempt to get the attention away from him, which everyone understood and respected. As people took up their positions, I felt the judgmental sting of piercing eyes. There had been absolutely no need to talk to Innocent like that, especially since I was the friend for which he traveled across the neighborhoods. Even the Tennis Brothers looked apologetically at him.

The rest of that day's play progressed without the joy with which it had started, or any at all, for that matter. We went through our paces, briefly discussed how our team would look the next day. Because the handball field was bigger and would require that we play with at least seven people at a time, we decided we would bring Donald and Tinashe up to play with the seniors. After that somber discussion, we called it a day and agreed to meet at Pashena the next morning so we could walk over to the high school together. Innocent managed to sneak away while I was talking to some of the other boys. He never walked home without me. He was also not the one to make it known publicly that he was upset; this was his way of telling me.

As Nigel, Anesu and I walked home, my little cousins would not stop looking up to me in confusion. As far as they were concerned, I was the paragon of civility when it came to interacting with peers. I was supposed to bring people together and stay out of conflict. I also always spoke highly of Innocent; why would I humiliate him in this way? And for what? Tacitly giving his opinion? My cousins said none of this, but they thought it. Their eyes haunted me.

Or maybe they thought nothing of it. Perhaps the gravity of my public show of callousness had been lost on them. Probably not. Either way, it haunted me. I could not recall a time in the past when I had felt this way.

The next morning, we won our first game.

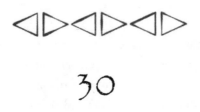

30

Unable to sleep due to unchained excitement and a guilt-ridden conscience, I got out of bed upon the roosters' first crow and wandered outside. The early sun was sitting atop the foggy valley hills like a blazing crown sent to govern the landscape. I grabbed the bucket of leftovers from the night before and took them to the dogs. After that, I went back inside and watched cartoons as I waited for Mai Nigel to wake up and prepare the morning porridge. Nigel woke up two hours after me and joined me on the sofas for an episode of "My Pet Monster." By his jovial mood, I figured the vile cloud that hung over us the previous evening had lifted. Or maybe it never had been at all. The morning bliss only increased when Gogo woke up and got to work on her customary farmhouse breakfast; complete with the crispy bacon, Sunny-side-up eggs with a side of onions and tomatoes, toast and English tea. This was a treat reserved for when Gogo had a little extra to spare in both money and time; which was usually once or twice a month. We indulged in the feast with the fervor deserving of such a cherished occasion. We finished before anyone else had cleared half their plates and impatiently excused ourselves from the table under Anesu's envious eye. The boys had decided that, despite having earned his worth as the juniors' goalkeeper, the trip to the high school was still too much for him. He was distraught, but Ta and Nigel calmed him down by pointing out how far he had already come and promising that he would be going to games with us before he knew it. That had placated him the night before but was not enough to stop the sting of seeing us leave that morning.

By the time we jumped over the barbed fence onto Pashena, everyone, except The Tennis Brothers and Innocent, had already gathered. The brothers arrived ten minutes later, laughing and mucking around, seemingly unbothered that they had kept everyone waiting. Fortunately for them, we were more concerned with Innocent's tardiness or, worse still, absence from the group. Not only was he one of our better players, but he was also not one to not show up without letting us know. Everyone took turns to throw inquisitive and accusatory glances at me; the former because he was my friend and I ought to know, and the latter in light of our fallout. Not a word was uttered about it all, which only made the situation more awkward. Unable to bear the tension any longer, I announced that he was probably not going to come if he had not already, and we were better off getting started on our trip lest we be late. Everyone agreed, albeit begrudgingly. The walk to the high school continued in much the same spirit, with no one particularly talking to each other or making a public show of their excitement. No one who saw us then would have believed that we were in the middle of a dream come true; the culmination of our efforts and camaraderie over the past few years. Suddenly, the dream that had kept us up many a night did not taste as sweet as we had imagined it would. The sight of a big, obviously ailing Sincere seated outside the high school did little to alleviate the group's spirits. Wellington and Fox ran up to greet their sister, then rejoined the group without a word.

What we lacked in enthusiasm, our opponents on the day more than made up for with unprecedented fervor. From the moment we arrived, Gandanga and friends greeted us with the high-strung hospitality with which Gogo would receive the cousins from the big city. They discussed briefly with us that they wanted to warm up a little more, gave us one of their two balls and told us we could use half of the field to get ready as well. I pulled Gandanga to the pitch side to tell him about Baba Nigel's donated stakes on the game. It was a futile exercise in subtlety, as he failed to contain himself in the slightest.

"Ten dollars? Ten of them? Let me see!" he yelled indiscriminately, "*Yohwe*[48]! Boys! Boys! They are putting ten dollars on the game? Haha!" He laughed joyfully as he hustled toward the rest of his teammates. I followed behind him with a grin and explained to the group that we were not, in fact, 'putting up ten dollars' as Gandanga had stated and that it was money donated by my uncle on both teams' behalf. It was important that everyone understood that, as that would shape both the nature of the game and our reputation. If people believed that we had traveled across Dangamvura to voluntarily defend our own money while the other team brought nothing to the table, it would make us look desperate and unwise; especially if we ended up losing the game.

I was in the middle of explaining this when I noticed a lone figure sitting on the terraces at the edge of the field. I had spotted it earlier but had discarded it as probably some high school student basking in the sun. Now that I looked closer, he looked familiar. He started walking towards the group, and I immediately saw it was Innocent. Because the rest of the group had their eyes on me, they did not see him just yet, so I took that opportunity to rush through my explanation about the money before he arrived. The last thing we needed was to meet again under the very same conversation that had brought about the bad blood between us. When everyone else finally

---

48 Gleeful expression, much like "Good Lord!"

saw him, their jubilation was uninhibited. They ran up, embraced him like a long-lost brother, and then inundated him with a dozen questions and salutations.

"When did you get here?"

"We thought you weren't coming!"

"I'm excited. Are you excited? Let's talk team strategy!"

He just smiled meekly. He blandly explained that he knew a shorter way from his house to the high school, so he had just decided to take that instead of meeting up with us for the trip. It was a fair excuse to the naked ear, but I, together with Fox, Wellington, and Ta knew Dangamvura well enough to know that this was a lie and that the fastest way for him to get to the High School would have been past MaOwnership. We looked around to each other to make sense of it. He had just not wanted to walk with us that morning. When he finally caught my gaze, his meek smile faded instantly, and a lingering pained look stood in its place. I walked up and hugged him as I would often do, and he hugged back as he would. Nothing had either been forgiven or forgotten; it just meant the game could go on.

That game is, ironically, one of the few moments of our Pashena days of which I have little recollection. Maybe it was the altercation with my friend or the ten dollars that hung over our heads that clouds my memory, but only one or two glimpses of the game I can actually remember. I remember that, with the score at 3-2 in favor of Gandanga's team, Innocent replaced me as goalkeeper and, with my first touch on the field, I scored! It was less skill on my part than it was fortune; Innocent threw the ball from our goal area, and I had awkwardly swung my leg towards it. It landed generously on my lap and bounced off my leg and over the other team's goalkeeper. I remember running the length of the field to embrace Innocent. I remember Donald scoring the first and last goal of the game. I remember winning our first game.

(The rest of the game's details are fortunately immortalized on two sides of a laminated piece of paper. I arrived home that evening and wrote, in true sports journalist style, an account of the game. While I had just done it for the love of writing, it found its way into Gogo's hands and ultimately to my mother who held on to it and only recently, on occasion of my 26th birthday, presented the laminated copy to me as a birthday present.)

We had won our first game. Away from home, no less! We bid our gracious opponents farewell and began the long trek back to MaOwnership amidst hugs and handshakes. It was a far more jovial atmosphere than earlier. Nobody mentioned the prize money until we were almost home. As it turned out, nine people had played the game, which left us with the awkward mathematical dilemma that Innocent had predicted. I had not thought about how the money would actually be divided, so I found myself still with the $10 note in hand.

"Okay well, it was good doing battle with you warriors," Fungai said sarcastically, "but my brother and I would like the spoils of war now. How much is it again? A dollar each?"

I pointed out that the money still needed to be broken down into smaller divisible notes and coins. Fungai snickered and shook his head.

"Well, what did you think was going to happen? You should have done that before the game! So stupid"

That stung. I was about to chide him for his ingratitude; the money had been a gift from my uncle. Besides, he and his brother should not, if talent and contribution to the team mattered anything, be the first to demand your share. Also, there had been nothing said to suggest that the money would not be divided. In the few split seconds that my brain carefully constructed my well-reasoned diatribe and readied to spew it, my train of thought was interrupted by a concert of groans and statements siding with Fungai. I was stunned. All my friends, except Nigel and Innocent, were up in arms against me.

"You know Sincere has not been feeling well. Between Wellington's share and mine, we were hoping to buy a loaf of bread for the house." Fox said in a well-acted, pathos-inducing tone that I am sure was only partly based on the truth.

"But wait. Why are we all getting the same?" Donald, who was usually silent, said, "I played the whole game and scored two goals. That warrants more than Tiberius, who played only a few minutes!"

"Hah!" Tiberius retorted, "Who cares? We said the money would be divided equally among everyone! Nobody said anything about how much anyone had played and that other nonsense!"

"Shut up kid!" Wellington spoke up for the first time. "You are terrible players, you and your brother. We did not win because of you. If anything, we won in spite of you. And you guys have all the money in the world."

"Well, it's not my fault that your sister is sick. Why don't you get one of her boyfriends to buy you bread?"

O, sweet woes of victory!

Fox and Wellington both lunged at the Tennis brothers, but Babylon and Ta jumped in the middle.

Amidst the fracas, Innocent finally spoke up, "Wait! I have an idea. How many of us are here?" He mouthed a quick count, "Nine, okay, that is good. I will take the $10. We will go down and buy nine Freez-its for each player. On top of that, we each get 50 cents to take home."

He spoke so uncompromisingly that, even with the flaring tensions, nobody dared contradict him. Besides, no one was in any state to do the math to see if that was a fair deal. It came naturally to Innocent. Freez-its now cost 60 cents each, which meant nine would have cost $5.40, and 50 cents each would have been $4.50. It was a total of $9.90—as close to a fair division of $10 as we could have hoped for.

He reached his hand out to me and signaled for me to hand over the money, which I did without hesitation. It needed not be said, but his look said both "I warned you," and "You are welcome."

The best of men become monsters when money is involved, and the strongest of friendships are often ill-equipped to handle the cynicism surrounding the division of wealth. This, I learned on that day.

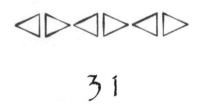

31

Because Gandanga's team had not witnessed the madness that surrounded the prize money, our reputation received a boost in the aftermath of the game. As the story would be told, we had won away from home, and done so gracefully. What it meant, then, was that we had neither time nor space to wallow in the misery of our fallout; we had to keep playing and do so like nothing had ever happened. This was, of course, easier said than done. I cannot say with any certainty that I took it worse than anyone else, but I was shaken up by the mutiny of the troops. The gesture had been one of goodwill, and I had never given them a reason not to trust me. If I had not intended to share the money, I would have never told of it in the first place.

So consumed was I by my own meditations that I overlooked the impact that the incident had had on my other friends and the team as a unit. I never revisited that Innocent had walked over to the game himself and, despite being publicly humiliated just the previous evening, ended up quietly resolving our crisis. Fungai's insults to Fox and Wellington were some of the harshest, rudest words we had ever heard uttered. Beyond reigniting the long-buried backstreet and front-street rift, they were the type of words that my mother had always warned against using: words so heavy that, no matter how we may try, we can never take back and whose damage was irreparable. Nigel and the other younger boys had just seen their big brothers at their most uncouth and probably wondered what basis our claims of being morally and behaviorally superior to our peers from surrounding neighborhoods had.

For the first time since Pashena's inception, there was not one person on the field the following Monday. The only times the field had been empty since we started had either been when it was in use for crops, when we were all in school, or had all decided that we would be watching a show on TV. Otherwise, there would at least be one or two people there. On this day, we had all decided, without any consultation, that we did not want to play. The next day was the same, and so was the one after that. The parents of MaOwnership must have been worried sick, but dared not ask why. Besides, the neighborhood's drying laundry would benefit from a few dust-free days, they figured.

It was not until that Thursday morning that Simba approached me at school about bringing his juniors for another game on Saturday. Sure, the seniors would have a game as well, but he knew that I was especially eager to keep the younger boys playing and it would be hard for me to refuse such an offer. We agreed on Saturday at noon again.

The juniors, having either been absent for the fallout or not active in it, were easier to round up for the game. That afternoon Nigel, with the self-importance of city council radio license inspectors, took on the honorable task of going house to house to alert the other younger boys of the game. Because it was already Thursday afternoon, they would just meet and practice on Friday afternoon. Perhaps some of us older boys would join them.

They could not wait until Friday.

As soon as Nigel left their door, they followed behind him and all, except Tiberius, were at the field that very afternoon. I had hoped that some of my friends would be ready to come around by now, but I had no such luck. Nevertheless, we had a spirited game for about an hour, and the younger boys agreed to meet again the next day.

The kids were all right, I thought to myself; possibly even better than us as friends and teammates. Maybe it was just as well that we were all approaching the end of our primary school careers; we could go off to high schools around Mutare and the country then they could restore some prepubescent sanity to MaOwnership.

For all their passion, organizing and training with the juniors was still a consuming task. For all my passion, it was a task that I had neither the patience nor the skill to handle by myself. I had naturally become the 'coach' for the juniors simply because of my role in getting the team going. When all the older boys were there, the coach title meant little; we all just played and instructed the younger boys as needed. At this time, however, I was stranded. The older boys had not been to Pashena all week, and I had no reason to believe that they would be there on Friday either.

The following morning, Friday morning, I knew I had my work cut out. Gogo was up early and preparing for Nigel and me a conservative version of her farmhouse breakfast. She brought it to the table—toast, beans, and bacon—and said a quick morning prayer with us. She then got up to make our lunch sandwiches. While she was doing that, I stuffed two slices of bacon into a small plastic bag I had been carrying in my uniform pocket. Nigel stared at me with a bewildered look on his face, and I winked back. Over the years, he had either grown to trust my judgment or conceded that there was no curtailing my foolery, so he knew just to watch and wait for what absurd explanation I had.

Once at school, I walked in and greeted Innocent more affectedly than I had all week. I had, indeed, wanted to talk to him like everything was normal every day but my shame and guilt consumed me, so I waited in the hope that he would open up first. Now, I found myself with my back to the ropes. I needed help with the juniors, and Innocent was the best person to fill the role. Not only did we usually have a good work dynamic, but he also had the silent respect among the younger boys that people typically reserve for elders or foreigners. Also, he was the best player on the team and, because he lived close to MaTwo Rooms, knew the opposition well.

After we exchanged exaggerated civilities, I walked over to my group and sat down. Over the years, he had steadily worked his way up to Group Two and, even though I never told him, I was proud of him. Throughout that morning, I kept throwing glances at him to see if he was feeling any more cheerful since the beginning of the week. I was learning how nerve-wrecking and frustrating it is when you and a loved one are leaving it to the wind to carry the messages of your mind and heart to each other. I could not wait until break time so that I could actually talk to him.

As soon as the bell rang at ten, I ran to the door and waited for his group to get there. When he got closer, he pretended to be engrossed in the conversation he was having and acted like he had not seen me. It stung, but I was also under no illusion about the task that lay before me. I walked over to where he was walking with some other people from his group and just followed behind them like a calf headed to the dip. Eventually, the other people went to their break time corner, and Innocent was left with no option but to talk to me.

"So, how are things back in MaOwnership?" Any good games lately? "He asked, looking around at everything but me.

"Ha. Oh, we haven't played since the game against Gandanga. Nobody has been by the field since." I said, overlooking the juniors' practice yesterday, as it would have taken away from the pathetic picture I wished to paint.

"I'm not surprised. Money is, as the adults say, the root of all evil. Plus, you people seem to...Well, what's up? Did you need something?" he asked, trying to escape from the clutches of this uncomfortable conversation. I had many questions for him, but I realized that this tiny window he had given me would not be open for long, so I hurried to explain to him about the juniors' game against Simba's boys and how I needed his help.

Hearing me basically plead for his help must have struck a chord with either the friend or the quintessential philanthropist that he was. He only thought about it for a few seconds before agreeing to come over to Pashena that afternoon to work with the young boys in preparation for the next day. I thanked him and handed him a small token of appreciation in the form of the two bacon strips I had stolen from the breakfast table. He nodded his head incredulously and thanked me, before reiterating his promise.

As I walked away, the joys of my successful diplomatic mission were short-lived. Innocent had meant to say something earlier. "You people seem to..." What was it? Why did he stop? I understand he was upset with me, but I had never thought he had a problem with 'us people'? Or did I just never notice? He was always quiet and shy, and I was often too occupied with the game and the business of Pashena to observe anything else. Also, what was that incredulous look when I gave him the bacon? I had seen him be grateful before; this was not it. I hope he did not see that as me trying to buy his favors. That would be insulting, and that is why I waited to give it to him until after he agreed. The bell rang for us to return to class and derailed my train of thought. I thought about it a few more times during class but decided to let it go for now; the important thing is he had agreed to come over and, for now, that is all I could have hoped for.

True to his word, Innocent showed up at Pashena that afternoon; much to the delight of the gathered juniors. The reception was not unlike it had been when we saw him at the game against Gandanga's team the previous weekend. Again, I wondered if this affection towards my old friend was a new phenomenon or if I had never noticed. One thing was for sure; there was something in his gentle mysticism that my other friends seemed taken by lately. I was rather jealous of both the attention he was receiving and everyone else's claim to my friend. We, nevertheless, had work to do.

After two hours of spirited football by the young boys and us, Innocent summoned the boys to the center of the field, a ritual usually reserved for me. At this point, I knew he was in a far superior position to inspire them than I was, so I kept mum. First, he cracked a few jokes about MaTwo Rooms boys and had everyone in a relaxed mood. Then he reminded them that they had given those other boys a good run on their first ever game and now, with increased confidence and team understanding, there was no reason why they should lose. Then he called it a day and told them to be there early the next day for the noon game.

After the juniors left, I walked Innocent home.

"Sha, thanks again for coming out today. I think the training was good, but your words at the end sealed it. They will be ready for tomorrow."

He let slip a wry smile before shaking his head.

"No, I'm not sure. They are definitely better off after today, but I don't think they will be ready."

I was taken aback. He had just given that rousing speech and, by all appearances, the hearts of the young troops had been touched; yet he, the very orator, was not convinced?

He must have seen the puzzlement on my face and continued, "They look okay now, but they are without their greatest source of drive. Have you ever wondered why we play? And why they would want to play? Why was Anesu dying to join the Pashena group? It is only half about the game. If the game we played here were cricket or volleyball, the younger boys would still want to join us. What does that tell you?" He looked at me expecting an answer. At that moment, Richie and Mabhaudhi passed by where we stood and cracked a few crude jokes before cheekily asking how Pashena was doing. It was as if every word they spoke reeked of mischief and condescension.

Paying them no mind and realizing that I had failed to follow his thought, Innocent picked our conversation back up and explained:

"They only play because their big brothers play. They want to be like you. When you guys are fighting and being stubborn about playing, they see no reason to cherish the game. This week has been terrible, and a speech from the great Farbisch would still not be enough to bring this team into the right spirit for tomorrow." He spoke with the dignified authority of a spirit medium foretelling the fortunes of a damned people. I listened close, like a messenger sent to receive the remedy.

"What they need from you is a sign of confidence in them. Tomorrow, have all the seniors there before they play their own game and cheer for the juniors. Also, if you can, bring a small token to show that you are proud of the younger boys for stepping up when the older ones were truant."

I understood. I dared not tell him that I was not sure that we would even have a senior game tomorrow. As we parted ways, we saw Tiberius and Fungai conspicuously shuffling on the other side of the street. It was most weird, seeing them in this part of Dangamvura, especially at this time of day. I waved, but they seemed so focused on rushing home that they must not have seen us.

I paid no further mind to the odd sight.

I did, however, meditate on Innocent's reference to a 'small token' and wondered what I could get that would both be sentimental and obtainable overnight.

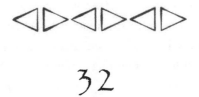

32

The next morning found me as excited for a game as I often was. We went through our Saturday breakfast ritual at the house and dashed to Pashena, where Innocent was already waiting with a few of the juniors. Although he was happy to see Nigel and Anesu, he was still puzzled.

"Where is everyone? I thought we would have a seniors' game!" he asked. I could not figure out if he was being unreasonably optimistic about our ability to get over our recent hostilities or if he was just in denial that it all happened.

"I...I don't think they're coming man," I explained unconvincingly. No sooner had I spoken these words did I see Simba and his team— seniors and juniors—coming down towards Pashena.

"Well, that's pathetic" Innocent said, his tone dripping disappointment, "did you at least think about what I said yesterday?"

I had meditated on it all night but had come up with nothing. Everything I could have thought of, like sweets or toys, would have cost money I did not have. By now, Simba and friends were almost to the field. As I looked at their miserly demeanor and tattered clothes, I had an idea.

"Yes. Yes, I did! Hold on." I said as a grin spread across my face. I turned around and ran home. Innocent yelled after me, but I was already over the fence. He walked over and greeted a baffled Simba, who had just noticed that there were no seniors around.

"Ko, where are Ta and those boys?" Simba asked with the assured smile of someone anticipating a positive response. Innocent bit his lips and shook his head, scrambling for an explanation. He was silently furious with me for putting him in a situation where he had to account for our team's shortcomings; he wasn't even from here! Before he said anything, I emerged triumphantly with an old sports bag over my shoulder. Everyone stopped still and looked at me and the old bag curiously. I stood at one end of the field and summoned all the juniors. They come running, Innocent following with dignified pace behind them. Before each had come to a complete stop, I tossed them a token of my appreciation: a shirt out of my own wardrobe.

Over the years, I had accumulated more than a dozen white t-shirts in gifts from my mother and other relatives. They would usually tear or permanently stain early from rough play, or I would chew on the collars until they had holes in them. Nobody at home would even notice they were gone. They were, for the most part, still in decent condition though; better than those worn by MaTwo Rooms boys, at any rate. For all our attempts to stand out among Dangamvura's fields and teams, why had none of us ever suggested getting team uniforms? No other neighborhood team had uniforms. Our juniors would be pioneers! The shirts were the perfect token that Innocent had described.

The juniors were initially confused by it all but were soon thrilled as they dug through the shirts and exchanged them with each other based on size and preference. MaTwo Rooms boys watched from across the field in humble envy. The reaction from both parties is what

I had hoped for, so I was pleased. I walked over to where Innocent stood with Simba and his boys, smug smile across my face, and explained that many of the seniors were busy that morning so we would only be able to have the juniors' game. They let out a collective groan and smirk. Simba spoke on their behalf in an animated fashion.

"What, what do you mean? You know the senior game is what it's all about! The juniors play to build up to that. I can't believe you made us walk the way across the township for this. I shouldn't be surprised; you MaOwnership people only think about yourselves. You, my friend, only think about yourself."

That stung. They were understandably upset, but that tirade was mean and unjustified. I bit my lower lip and clenched my fists in anger. Realizing the anger was directed at nobody in particular, I slowly unclenched them, and my eyes began to water. I looked over at Innocent to see if he agreed with Simba's savage character attack. He looked down. Keen to ensure that the other boys did not notice my mild emotional breakdown, I gathered my wits and responded to Simba with a calm that even I was surprised by.

"I am sorry sha. I can walk door to door and call the younger boys to the field, but I can't do that with Fox and the others! When they say they are busy or don't want to play, there is no budging them; you know that. Now, are the juniors going to play or are we going to keep talking?" I said, making sure to avoid the point about our general, and my particular egocentricity. Soon, the game was underway.

I do not remember watching that game. This time, it is not just my memory failing me like it does when I try to recollect the game against Gandanga's team. In this case, my mind was not present for the game. After wading through the pre-game near confrontation, I walked over and sat pensively on the bench. My mind was plagued.

Did Simba mean all that? I know that MaOwnership has had that reputation in the past, but I thought we had done well with Pashena and the team to reach out to other neighborhoods. We were not as sheltered as we had been, say, five years ago. Had we gone overboard with Pashena? Had we gone full circle and ended up alienating people through the field that had been supposed to bring them closer? By now, the field was easily the best of its kind in Dangamvura. They were just jealous. The shirts. If they were already jealous of us, then the stunt with the shirts had sent them over the edge. Was I wrong though? We needed something to re-instill pride in our boys, Innocent had said. Why was he not saying anything?

Ta wandered onto the field a few minutes later and came to sit by Innocent and me on the bench. He acted like he had not been away one day, and joined Innocent in barking orders to our young players. This was just as well, seeing as my thoughts were somewhere else. I sank back into my contemplations.

The next thing I remember was a sharp pinch to the ear that snuck up from behind me. Before I could turn around, I heard Mai Nigel shriek, and my heart sank.

"What is all this? You think we buy shirts for the neighborhood? Are we that rich? Who is going to wash all those shirts when your little friends are done?" She yelled, her long nails digging into my right ear. She had been coming from the store and, from a distance, noticed one of the boys wearing what was distinctly my shirt. Coincidence, she must have initially thought. Then she saw another, and then two more. Furious, she crept up undetected from behind the bench and pinched my ear. Now, she was dragging me home, accompanied by a chorus of jeers from everyone on the field. I remember hearing Simba and the rest of MaTwo Rooms boys bellowing louder than everyone else. Ta, who lived for the pain and humiliation of others, was in tears laughing. I looked back to see our juniors, draped in my culpable garments, looking puzzled. They wanted to laugh at this objectively hilarious sight but felt constricted by their own role in my public shaming. Half of them had already removed the shirts.

That stands apart as the most embarrassing day of my childhood. The morning had already been heavy to bear with the older boys not coming out, Simba's harangue and Innocent's disapproval. The nail had been in the coffin, and Mai Nigel had just thrown the last of the soil atop the grave. Kulu caught wind of my shenanigans, and I received a rare but painful beating that evening.

The story goes that our juniors won that game 4-2. They decided to play on in my shirts after all.

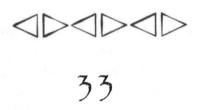

33

Nobody ever saw Sincere anymore. None of us had the courage to bring it up with Fox or Wellington. Once or twice a week, a nurse or some people from their church would stop by their house, and her brothers were spending more and more time inside, so we knew she was there.

The weeks following my beating and the juniors' victory saw a return to the drabness of old. With my humiliation and Fox and Wellington's home responsibilities, the older boys were struggling to come out of the $10 slump. The juniors, however, were rampant after their win. They had appropriated the field in our absence and were now there every afternoon. Often, one or two of the seniors would join in, but it was clear that the guest and host had swapped roles.

The Easter season soon descended upon us and did nothing to raise the monotonous cloud that rested over Pashena and the neighborhood in general. With the holidays here, I left for Harare to spend a few weeks with my mother. Just as well. Everyone else traveled to visit other family in the big city or the rural areas. Fox and Wellington took the ailing Sincere back to Birchenough. I had seen her twice just before she left. Her skin now clung desperately to her bones and, with each step, her life-holding belly seemed on the verge of toppling her over. It was reminiscent of how Ta's uncle had walked in his last days, only this time, the pregnancy made it worse. It was better for her to give birth around other family, the neighborhood whispers said.

The restart of school brought no such rejuvenation, as we had grown accustomed to over the years. If anything, everyone came back and picked up from the same dreary place where he had ended the last term. The winter looked set to be a bitter one that year, and that thought alone was beginning to keep many people indoors. Also, the school football season was beginning so many of our opponents and friends from other neighborhoods would now be occupied with trying to stake their place in their respective teams. From our group, only Donald and Babylon tried out for their school teams, with the former doing so successfully. For all his talent, Babylon was deemed too small and inconspicuous for the big stage. Had their hearts been set on it, Wellington and Innocent would have been serious candidates for our school team. Wellington was, however, spending every weekend and, oftentimes, missing school to travel to Birchenough to be with his sister. Innocent was still uninterested in the politics of making the team, deciding instead to invest his efforts to the school's newly founded volleyball team. The World Cup would be starting in a month and a half, and therein lay the main source of anticipation amidst a sea of drudgery for the rest of us.

I have gone on to see a few more World Cups since 1998; some of which were, all things considered, grander and more intense. None, however, have stuck in my memory like that one has. It was held in France, and I remember my fascination with the radio profiles of the country and its culture. I remember all five African teams starting the tournament with flare only to be eliminated unceremoniously as the tournament progressed—a pattern which I have since learned to be recurrent at every World Cup thus far. Nigeria went as far as the last sixteen but was beaten convincingly by Denmark. I also remember, at eleven, learning about countries that I had never before heard of: Croatia, Chile, Saudi Arabia and a few others. I remember Croatia doing exceptionally well and only losing to France in the semi-finals. Ronaldo, Zidane, Kluivert, Sunday Oliseh, Laudrup, Suker...What odd names, I thought at first, yet I soon felt like I knew these men personally.

I remember the morning we found out that Sincere had died. As her condition had worsened in her rural home, they decided it was best to send her back to Mutare for medical attention. Upon her return, Gogo and the other elderly MaOwnership women took turns in going over to their house with fruits and different brewed drinks. Soon, she was not walking at all, and I heard she had to wear diapers. None of us, with the obvious exception of her brothers, were allowed to see her through it all. We were, however, invited to their house for what I now realize was one last farewell. She lay there, her sunken eyes and cracked lips an unrecognizable form of the stern yet beautiful big sister we had grown begrudgingly fond of, under a two-in-one blanket that Mai Ta had given her as a gift from South Africa.

The next morning, the morning of July 12, 1998. I remember it so because it was the morning of the World Cup final between Brazil and France.

Word has it that she died giving birth in their house. She held her baby in her arms, and they shared a tear—his first and her last—before she convulsed one last time and stopped breathing. The baby died within the hour.

Word has it that Brazilian star Ronaldo was under the weather going into the World Cup final and had been warned by doctors not to play. He insisted, and soon found himself on the floor and unable to continue. France won that final 3-0.

That was July 12, 1998.

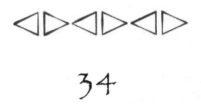

34

The somber ghost of Sincere's passing overshadowed the excitement for the game that should have been born out of the World Cup, at least at Pashena. We had seen other people die before, but none as young and vivacious as Sincere. Fox and Wellington were seldom seen. Once a week or so, we would see them catching a break basking in the miserly winter sun. Fox was without his humor and Wellington was leaden. Their grief-induced languor was not without an effect on us. We had already been away from the field after the debacle against Gandanga's team and the subsequent World Cup; the solemn cloud that hung over us only served to remove what interest we, the older boys, may have had to get back on to the pitch. Nigel and the other younger boys were far less fazed, but fazed nonetheless. They continued to play, albeit less frequently and without the intensity you would expect from game-hungry boys who had recently won their first game and watched the world's biggest football spectacle.

Fox and Wellington faced yet another obstacle. Although they had had to grow up faster and in ways that the rest of us had not, they were still in no position—at least financially—to sustain themselves and the house. To help with this need, a family that had just moved to Mutare began renting out the room that had been their sister's. Born out of desperation, there was no easing the hurt of being forced to compromise the memory of their sister so soon or the discomfort of having a strange mother and her three children come in to share their tiny space.

The August school holidays brought in some color by virtue of spritely spring flowers and a much-needed respite from the ambiguous winter. The two older boys, grade five and six that had moved into Sincere's room were instantly enchanted with Pashena. They had lived in a series of apartments all their life, and living this close to a football field that was readily accessible was something of which they had only dreamt. They did not understand why only the younger boys ever played on the magnificent field across from their new home. Fox and Wellington were in no place to retell the meandering path that had led us to where we stood. Ta and I attempted to pick up that hospitable task but soon realized that the boys had moved from Bulawayo and thus spoke Ndebele and not Shona. Even if we spoke the same language, the intricacies of our reasoning would have been lost on them.

Unmoved by the traumatic stories we failed to tell, they wandered over to the field and began kicking around. Soon the younger boys joined them. We watched them from under The Guava Tree across the street, early nostalgia already setting in. Gandanga, having gone through his big box of action movies and with his father back on duty in the DRC, also started visiting us. He, like the new boys, had no inhibitions towards taking to Pashena. Next to rejoin the Pashena party were the back-street boys. Fungai and Tiberius were done with tennis season, Babylon was bored, and neither of them liked the sight of the younger boys and outsiders feasting on the fruits of their labor in their absence.

The rest of us stayed aloof for a while, occasionally watching the strange games from under The Guava Tree. With time, we found our attention gravitating towards the old dirt field upon which we had done much of our growing in the past few years. First, we reminisced about the early days and previous games. Then, we berated how these little ones were not half the team we had been. Soon Ta and I were yelling instructions from under The Guava Tree, much to the annoyance of the playing boys.

"If you know the game so much, come over and play then! Don't just talk and talk!" They yelled back in both Ndebele and Shona. We chuckled back. Although no one would say it, we were starting to feel the ancient itch that had brought the field to us in the first place

One day, the ball rolled across the street towards Fox's house. Anesu began to pursue but had to give way to a passing car. Wellington grabbed the ball, felt and stared at it like an infant looking at a toy for the first time, and then shook his head in facetious disappointment.

"These kids!" He smirked and turned his head toward the council of us elders that sat under the esteemed guava tree. "This is a terrible ball! Can you believe it?" We snickered. The ball was not bad by any means, but it was pleasant to see Wellington laugh again. Besides, what proud patron does not delight in the light-hearted deriding of those younger than or different from him?

"Hey, guys! Your ball is terrible!" he yelled across the field, before breaking into the sinister cackles that we had not heard in months. The boys on the field yelled back with friendly defensive insults and demands for the ball. Instead of throwing it out or waiting for Anesu to get it from him, he hoofed it skywards and toward the field, yelled out 'muhondo!'[49] as he chased after it. The rest of us looked

---

49 "Into battle!" A war-cry

at each other once, jumped to our feet, and charged towards the field like buffalo to a river.

Soon, the routine of old gradually re-established itself in the neighborhood. Everyone was paying regular visits to Pashena again, and some laughter had returned to our presence. It was even pleasant to hear Wellington whisper ill nothings about the boys from the backstreet again. If one had left us earlier in the year and returned then, they would have assumed that nothing had changed. The return to normalcy was almost the stuff of fantasy.

Feeling like our chemistry was back to its vintage heights, and that the neighborhood games were growing stale, we started thinking about challenging other teams again. All the old foes were brought up. The church boys were all busy preparing for their end of year exams; after my humiliation at the last juniors' game and knowing how brutal their teasing could be, I was not ready to play against Simba and his MaTwo Rooms friends yet. Gandanga's friends would only be available in a month or so and, while that was fine for later, our game-thirsty limbs were seeking instant gratification. We mulled over the possibilities for a few afternoons. Through it all, Tiberius and Fungai had sat by The Mountain in unorthodox silence. Nobody had been concerned; we were all happy to be granted a break from their incessant bragging and disdain.

"So, Gandanga, you said you and your friends could only play us in a few weeks?"

Gandanga, who by now had become a fixture at Pashena, nodded his head in disappointed approval.

"Well," I continued as I looked around, "does anyone else know of other teams we could possibly play against?" As my rotating gaze passed The Tennis Brothers, I noticed they were engaged in nervous deathly stares, as if daring each other to speak. I nodded my head slightly in cautious encouragement.

"If you guys want, we have some people who are interested in a game," Tiberius began with a disconcerting lack of enthusiasm for someone who was presenting what should have been a popular idea. His lackluster proposition was greeted by a chorus of anticipative questions.

"Just... just some old friends. They can be here tomorrow if you want!"

Everyone cheered without further inquiry. We had been dying for a match and, just when our hope was beginning to dwindle, we had one the next day. We scurried to practice a little more for our phantom rivals. Our team had added a few members, and we had to make sure that playing time was distributed fairly—a struggle as old as Pashena itself. Our problem for the next day was further compounded when the Tennis brothers informed us that the team we would be playing did not have juniors with them. Many of our juniors, most notably Donald and Tinashe, had grown so much physically and skillfully over the year and, in a just world, deserved to play on the seniors' team more than most of us did. There was no chance, however, of the senior boys volunteering their places on the team to younger boys, and none of us had the courage to embarrass another by telling them to give up their spot. We discussed a superficial starting team that resembled the senior team of old and then footnoted it with endless substitutions until everyone got the chance. Once we felt we had the semblance of a plan in place, we called it a day and, as per custom, agreed to reconvene the next day.

35

"They are not good people, and the game just wouldn't be fun. I am sorry," Ta said uncompromisingly, before slamming the door behind him and shuffling back inside.

I began the long walk back to Pashena. It was the same 70 or 80-meter walk I had taken every day since I could walk, and yet today, my feet were heavy. Nerves, anger, and disappointment were all battling for my attention, and I barely noticed that my heart was beating faster with each step.

Tiberius and Fungai's cryptic announcement about today's game had been greeted with an uncharacteristic and incredible lack of apprehension from a group that had been raised to be skeptical both of anyone not MaOwnership born and of any idea brought forth by the Tennis Brothers. If I had paid closer attention to my friends then, I might have noticed their unspoken disapproval. Now, I was finding out that the calm thereof had been one huge, incidental farce. Ta had, at that very moment the announcement was made the day before, decided that he was not going to play. Despite their eagerness, many of the younger boys had decided the same. Fox and Wellington had been suspicious but decided to see how it would go the following day.

I had deliberately avoided looking at Innocent when the announcement was made. I could picture his condemning eyes and the follow-up mellow castigation. I did not want any of it, and Pashena definitely did not need it; not now.

The following afternoon, I arrived at the field soon after lunch. The Tennis Brothers who, for glory-seekers who had organized a much-needed game, were in an oddly somber and quiet mood greeted me. Innocent also looked bemused, for reasons I assumed to be different. Babylon seemed as perplexed as I was by their behavior, and felt compelled to raise the spirits of everyone else by running around and other antics that had earned him the monkey nickname when he first arrived. Although Wellington was there, Fox had ultimately decided that he did not want to play and was instead watching from The Guava Tree.

Any attempts to draw the identity of our mystery opponents out of The Tennis Brothers were proving unreasonably impossible, so we waited.

An hour later, and half an hour after the game ought to have started, our questions were answered. From the moment they turned onto our street and started coming down the hill, our stomachs tightened. The boys were, to the man, bigger than all of us: half of them easily in high school—or at least supposed to be. As they drew closer, I noticed that two of them cut a familiar figure. Any doubts I had were confirmed by Innocent's loud groan,

"No way. Ha ha. Is this a joke?" he said and looked at me incredulously. He cast a disgusted look at the Tennis brothers, then back to me. "I am not playing against that team!" he declared, and then spit at the ground.

"It's just a game man," Tiberius said, his tone lost in between reasoning and pleading, "Let's just play."

Innocent did not even look at him. Instead, he stared right at me for a few seconds as if holding me responsible for this turn of events, and then looked at everyone else and said, "It has been good playing here with you. I won't be back."

He looked at me one more time and, behind his disappointed anger, I saw overwhelming sadness. Then just like that, he turned around and walked up the street towards home.

It was Richie, Mabhaudhi, and their friends. As they walked onto the field, I now cast the deathly look Innocent had left me with towards Tiberius and Fungai. Wellington did the same. Organizing a game against their better judgment and public consensus sounded like something that the brothers would do and enjoy. Their reaction was, however, again somber and almost apologetic. I dwelt on it for a brief moment and, failing to make any sense of it, drifted back to the matter at hand: we had a game to play and nowhere near enough players.

"Hey, *vafana!*" Richie cackled. His eyes, like most of his friends, were bloodshot. The group's collective pubescent stench suggested they had not showered in days.

"So, this is your little field huh?" He continued, wrinkling his face as he walked over to the goalposts. "Mabhaudhi, remember selling them these?" His friend walked over to him and began shaking the goalpost like a madman. We feared he was going to uproot or knock it over, but were even more afraid to confront him, so we just cringed and waited.

"Well, what are you fools waiting for? Where is everyone?"

"They... they are coming. Let me go call..." I stammered, and then ran towards home, seeking more a solitary moment to grasp what was going on than to find other players. Other than Ta, there was nobody else I could call right now. Even then, I had also grown to know that his stubbornness was no light matter and so when I tried to convince him, and he refused I was disappointed but not surprised.

As I took the seventy to eighty-meter solemn trek back to Pashena, innumerable thoughts raced in my mind until they all blurred together, and the next thing I remember I was in goals, playing on the least enthusiastic, nervous team that I have, to this day, ever played on. The only people on our team who had any heart in the game were Gandanga and the older of Wellington's Ndebele housemates, and even they soon were infected by our contagious listless spirit. Richie's team was, in all fairnesss, good, but seemed more concerned with imposing themselves physically and embarrassing us. They pushed, kicked, and scratched their way through the match. After a while, I stopped keeping track of the score. We were all silently waiting for the game to end so we can talk about how we got here and how to make sure we never find ourselves there again. There was nothing about this game that represented the true spirit of Pashena, and the sooner they left, the better.

Our unspoken passive aggressive exit strategy was going well until Wellington's housemate suffered the brute force of Mabhaudhi's malevolent tackle. There was a loud crunching noise as their legs collided, and Wellington's housemate fell to the ground, writhing in pain.

Maybe Wellington was still in an emotionally unstable place after the year they had had. Maybe he was scared for his housemate's sake and the possible ire of his housemate's mother. Or maybe he was just furious beyond reason at Mabhaudhi, Richie, and the accursed game. He knelt over our fallen comrade still writhing, let out a blood-curdling scream, and then stood next to him with tears in his eyes. Everyone stood still. For their sadism, even Richie and the other boy stopped their snickering. In all but that moment, everyone stood statuesque, waiting for someone who knew better to make the next move. Then, like a freedom fighter reckless after being condemned to death, Wellington charged at Mabhaudhi, twice his size, and leaped to punch him under the chin. His fist met Mabhaudhi's face with such impact that the bigger boy went down like a tree rotten at the roots, probably from a combination of shame, shock and force. Upon seeing his friend buckle to the ground, Richie lunged and grabbed Wellington by the throat. I still did not move. Nigel picked up a rock with both his hands and threw it at Richie's head. It missed him by centimeters, but that was enough to distract him. By the time he realized from whence the rock had come, Nigel was shimmying under the barbed wires and dashing home.

Wellington took the opportunity to escape, but as he broke into full stride towards home, one of Richie's friends tripped him. Fox, who had been watching the game from across the street with a vigilant eye, hurtled onto the field, wielding and waving a wooden hunting stick. There was something so comically dignified in his demeanor that I almost chuckled. He looked like a bewildered old man, and none of us believed that he would actually hit anyone with the stick. He approached Richie in a ferocious and unintelligible tirade. Richie seemed unperturbed and, if anything, grinned. Like us, he knew Fox was merely mimicking the hunters of old. Against our assumptions and without further warning, Fox swung the mighty stick across Richie's face, and blood splattered from his face as he fell to the ground next to where Mabhaudhi was now sitting. Another one of their friends charged at Fox from behind, but Wellington grabbed a rock, the same rock Nigel had thrown earlier and heaved towards this new aggressor. This time, it hit him on the side of the head, and he began to wail and run in place. By now Fox was swinging his hunting stick in blind fury, daring the rest of the boys to approach him.

That was all Richie and friends could take. They ran off, throwing a slew of obscenities and threats at us as they did.

We laughed, jumped around the field, and even hurled back some insults. As we huddled in the center of the field to celebrate our ugly and unorthodox victory, an inexplicable gloom came over us. Our field was the object of parochial envy. We had improved as players, and both our juniors and seniors had now won a game. People we barely knew wanted to play at Pashena. We had even won today's fight, and it was guaranteed that people would soon hear of the "Pashena

Savages." This was all beyond what our wildest dreams had been when the idea of the field first was born.

We had it all and more now. We did not have Ta or Innocent. We had lost, for the neighborhood and us, Pashena's pristine image. We would walk past Richie's house on our way to school and be afraid anytime someone whistled to a friend. When word gets around, the teams we had played in the beginning would probably be reluctant to play here now.

That night, Nigel and I sat and watched some races on TV. Maria "The Maputo Express" Mutola, the famed Mozambican 800-meter superstar, was competing somewhere in Europe. Naturally, we were cheering for her. To this day, that race remains one of the most incredible I have ever seen. Maria, in her prime, was tipped to win. There was one other European woman that was also highly favored. She ran on Maria's left. Throughout the race, they battled it out. Maria kept her eyes firmly on her. In the last 100 meters, Maria broke into her famous sprint and ended up beating her rival—into second place.

While Maria had been fixed on her natural opponent to her left, an unknown girl overtook both of them to her right and ended up winning it all.

Poor Maria. She had fought the wrong war as hard as she could. She won it. In her victory, she had lost the actual race.

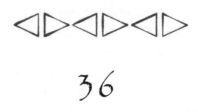

36

Only one other game was played at Pashena before the rains came.

The bloody post-war camaraderie of the last game was short-lived. Fox was furious with Wellington for even playing in that farce of a game. The woman living with them blamed them for injuring her son and, against their attempts at peace and an explanation, she would not talk to them. Innocent and I were as strangers, keeping our distance like the other had Ebola-infested breath. We were all angry and perplexed by The Tennis Brothers' choice of opponents and awkward behavior around the whole affair. Fox pointed to their earlier odd dealings with Richie regarding the wooden posts as evidence of how they had been in cahoots the entire time.

"But you know how Tiberius and Fungai are. They have no qualms about parading their selfishness or trouble-mongering. Why were they quiet and nervous throughout this whole affair? They did not seem to enjoy it at all." I wondered out loud.

Nobody ventured an answer. So engrossed was everyone in their frustrations that I doubt anyone had even looked that deeply into it. I meditated on it.

The backstreet and front-street rift that had taken years to bury had, with one ill-fated game, returned.

As had been promised weeks before, Gandanga's team did visit Pashena. Had it not been for their eagerness and our pride, the game ought to have been cancelled. Pashena and all it stood for was finished; at least until after the rainy season. Nevertheless, the game happened. I was not there to see it. None of the older boys, except Babylon, were. From what I later heard, the team had been a miserable patchwork of Pashena remnants and others; Babylon, the injured housemate who had barely recovered, and Nigel. Gandanga, embarrassed on our behalf, volunteered to play on the MaOwnership team. The other team was beginning to walk away when a boy about my age and size walked by the field and asked if he could play to even out the numbers. As it turned out, this mild-mannered stranger had just moved into MaOwnership.

That was Pashena's last game of the season. I was not there to see it, and neither were most of my friends. Two weeks later, the Pastor's men began preparing the field for planting. I was not there to see it, and neither were most of my friends.

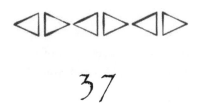

37

*W*hen you grow up in a household full of health workers, you inevitably develop mild to severe hypochondria for your own sake and those around you. For Gogo, it was always the latter and almost never the former. Any sniffle from us warranted bed rest and warm milk. On the other hand, she would be in her garden at the break of dawn even at the height of ailment. Thus when, at the beginning of rainy season, she announced that she was not feeling well and had to lie down, we were troubled. While Kulu soldiered on with the work, my aunts followed her to the house and waited on her. That bout of sickness lasted for three days before she declared herself well enough to return to the field. Although she took to that season with her vintage rigor, she would get tired earlier than in the past and often had to go home. Age was catching up with her, I imagined.

With Gogo having to scale down her involvement with the field preparation and planting, Nigel and I found ourselves thrust onto the field next to Kulu. We worked for hours at length until our tiny limbs buckled under the heat and from hunger and, always in perfect time, Mai Nigel would call us for sadza. The blistering sun had only started to relent one evening when, exhausted, I gazed into the distance. I saw a boy, about my age and size, strolling down the street. I had never seen him before, I thought. I knelt back down and began plucking away on some weeds. I looked up again and saw him now standing behind the fence, watching me. I wondered if he recognized me from school.

"Shingi?" he said with a broad smile of familiarity spreading across his face. I could pick that smile out of a crowd on any day.

It was Antony, my old friend from the house with the big radio.

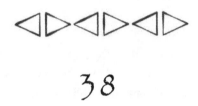

38

The toll of an ailing and dying young population, a government corruption, and absurd socio-economic policy was sinking its teeth deep into the neck of our fledgling country. By now, the reckless redistribution of commercial farms had caused widespread panic among even uninterrupted farmers, and they had begun fleeing to neighboring countries. The AIDS scourge was wreaking havoc, and everyone knew at least a handful of people who had died or were dying of the disease. They say one in every four people was HIV positive. The war in the DRC was still raging on, and the soldiers were gone for months—even years—at a time. Poverty and strife beget poverty and strife. Like my uncle, Baba Nigel, had tried to explain the other night, each of the plagues inflicted upon Zimbabwe heightened the pinch of the next. Because the economy was in the doldrums, young people were resorting to unscrupulous ways of earning an income—prostitution included. As AIDS took over due to promiscuity, the economy lost its workers. Children in the community ran wild because their fathers were away at war. The women left behind grew lonely. So it went.

Succumbing to the weight that had befallen our beautiful nation, Antony's parents had decided, after seven years in the suburbs, to move back to their humble MaOwnership home.

I gazed at him frozen in awe for what seemed an eternity until he interrupted my stupor.

"Shingi! It is me, Antony! You don't remember me, old friend?" He said, without breaking his smile.

Getting my wits back, I dropped my hoe and, with my dirty legs still shaking, ran and hopped over the fence to where he stood and embraced him. For a full minute, we allowed ourselves to be silent and lost in the warmth of rediscovered friendship. He had been gone so long and, more importantly, gone during a time in which we had done the most growing than we would ever do. We had changed so much that there was no guarantee that we would be able to recapture the magic of our infancy or even get along well. Seeing and embracing Antony, however, meant something beyond friendship. Here was someone who remembered MaOwnership as it ought to be remembered and had been untainted by the finer and lesser moments that had come in his absence.

After the brief but emotional salutation, I returned to finish tilling my portion of the field. We agreed to meet the next afternoon to reminisce, catch up, and play.

He had been in MaOwnership for about two weeks now, he said. He told wonderful stories of the suburbs, days spent at the video game arcade, libraries with more books than our two local libraries put together, and neighborhoods where every single person had his or her own bicycle. He danced around the question of why he had returned, explaining that his father's new job mandated that he come back. Since his arrival, he had not seen anyone from the old days. Except Ta and me, he would not have known any of the current crop. The other day, he explained, he had been so overcome with boredom that he walked up to the old Mountain. Upon getting there, he had been delighted to see a group of boys our age and younger playing and hoped he could recognize someone. Although he did not, the boys there needed an extra player, so he ended up playing with them.

"It's wonderful what they have done with that field!" He said innocently, much to my chagrin.

"Antony, old friend. The dead have seen nothing[50]! You have no idea the stories that come with that..."

Before I could finish, a pair of hands sneaking up from behind the curb that Antony sat and wrapping around his face to playfully blindfold interrupted me. Antony smiled and crinkled his nose pensively.

"Who is it?"

"Hahaha, I be-be-bet he forgo-got all about us!"

"Ta. Is that you? Come over here, you old baboon you!"

Ta lifted his hands from our old friend's face, sat down next to him and embraced him. For the first time since our days in crèche, we were reunited. We took turns in moving to the verge of tears, neither of us ever crossing into the watery abyss.

The rest of the afternoon was spent with Ta and I bringing Antony up to speed with all that had transpired since he left: the relocations, the deaths, the fights, and Pashena. Although our tale was long, detailed and laborious, Antony listened with evident interest throughout, letting slip a smile in all the better parts and cringing in the lesser. By the end, he could not stop shaking his head in sad disappointment. He sat there in silence for a full minute before he stood up. Although he was only two years older than us, he spoke slowly in his recently broken voice and with the acquired accent of the big city dialect, thereby creating the dignified sensation similar to that commanded by the rural chiefs.

---

50 Shona proverb akin to "You don't know the half of it!"

"This is sad indeed. Sad," he began, alternating between gazing into space and at us with varying levels of intensity.

"When I was away, the sun never went down without me thinking about MaOwnership. Although most of my memories are of infancy and we had very few photos to go by, my parents and siblings would always tell stories of our "good old days." I missed them. I missed The Mountain and the army truck. I missed church and school here. I missed you, boys. Sure, my friends in the city had more toys, but we were always one conversation away from someone bragging about how much money they had and how they had better toys. Having lived in the *rokesheni*, I often caught the brunt of their insults. Besides, most of them were not allowed to play outside anyway. Each night I dreamt we had moved back. As these things happen, my father told me one morning that we would be moving back to Dangamvura. There is no describing my delight! When we left, I did not even bid my friends there farewell; all I cared about what was coming here.

I arrive here and, at first, it looks like nothing has changed. The old army truck is rustier, and The Mountain is not as big and intimidating as I remember, but most of it is still the same. I was excited to see that there was a football field right in our neighborhood as I, too, had fallen in love with the beautiful game over the years."

He lifted his head up and narrowed his eyes at us.

"Now you are telling me the story of everything that has happened. It appears that, for the most part, the journey has been worthwhile. It is unfortunate that people have to die and leave, but there is nothing we can do about that." Ta and I nodded in agreement, hoping that he had been building up to this point of clemency. He was not done.

"The past few weeks have been full of foolery on our part, and most are at fault. The boys from the backstreet, Fungai and his brother, should have never planned that game with the Area B boys. But clearly, there is something else going on there, and I am disappointed that nobody has thought to ask them further. Ta, don't those two go to

Methodist, our church? What would our mothers say if they heard we were fighting like this? Shingi my friend, that friend of yours, what is his name again? Innocent? Seems like a good person and good friend. I know you feel that way, too, because I could tell you got really sad when you spoke about him. On several occasions, you should have listened to him. Several. It is no surprise to me that he does not come around anymore. You had all done a job to be proud of with the field and now look, it is already planting season, and we don't have another chance to set things straight until the new year. I bet I know exactly what Innocent was going to say back then when you said he stopped himself mid-sentence. He was going to tell you that we, all MaOwnership boys, walk around feeling important and better than everyone else and yet do little to justify it. The fights among ourselves and with other people, the little clandestine plans to sneak shirts out of the house and plan games against people we don't know or trust—all are pathetic and as ill-mannered as anything that some of the boys we claim to be better than would do."

He stopped short and shook his head vigorously as if awakening from slumber, and then smiled like he had forgotten the intensity of what he was talking about.

"Wow, look at that. It is almost dusk already! I have to help my mother cook. How about we get together tomorrow morning? Maybe you two can show me around the neighborhood and introduce me to some new friends." He winked at us and dashed homeward.

Ta and I looked at each other, mesmerized by our long-lost friend. After a while, all I could muster was

"Antony huh. It is good to have him back, not so?"

"It sure is."

"Well, see you tomorrow then?"

"See you tomorrow, Shingi."

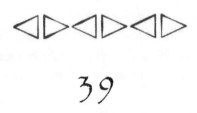

39

"I don't understand them, and I don't like them," Tiberius said, biting his lower lip as he did, "And I understand they have been through a lot in their life, but that cannot be your excuse for walking around looking like you are about to fight someone or tease them to tears every time." His brother nodded in agreement

The next morning, Ta and I had headed over to Antony's house as promised.

"Aah boys dzangu," he said with a grin, "How are you? I am glad to see you: Mother was just about to send me with these mealies to some of our church friends. Unfortunately, I am not too sure where they live just yet. Would you walk with me?"

It was not until we had turned into the backstreet that we figured that the 'church friends' he had alluded to were Tiberius and Fungai's family. Ta and I locked stares, but by then, we had no dignified reason to excuse ourselves. After all, Antony had not been dishonest with us; woe was on us for not inquiring further about where exactly he was going. Besides, if we had spent the past few years building Pashena with them, we could last the minute or two it would take Antony to drop off the mealies.

Antony, of course, had other ideas. After Mai Fungai had received the mealies with ululation and a dance, she invited all of us in for some Mazoe. Reluctant as we may have been, we were not going to risk the scolding that awaited us if word got back home that we had refused this traditional gesture of goodwill. It was a hot day anyway, and I struggle to think of many things better than Mazoe on a hot day. We gulped our cupfuls and readied to take our leave when Antony spoke up again with the unassuming charisma that we were learning to identify with him:

"Say, Fungai and Tibby, what are you guys doing this morning? I haven't spent time with too many people from the neighborhood. The sun is out, and I see you have that big, shady avocado tree in your backyard. Do you want to sit and talk for a while?" He then turned to where we stood, mortified at the prospect of spending another voluntary moment here.

"Do you two have somewhere to be?"

We did not and, although we had been able to fashion a few lies between us over the years, we came up with nothing in this instance. Instead, we threw an inquisitive glance towards the brothers, and they threw back an unsettled one. The interaction was not lost on Antony, who just smiled wryly, and summoned all of us to follow him outside.

"Some year this has been huh?" Antony began once we were all seated uncomfortably under the tree. "People dying, people moving out of the area and moving in, good and bad games! Sometimes I wish I had been here for all this!" He said, his smile fading again and turning into a distant stare.

"Hah!" Ta scoffed, throwing an accusatory glance at the brothers, "You were better off where you were. There is nothing to see here."

Sensing a potential for the complete dilapidation of his diplomacy, Antony wasted no further time on courtesies and dove right into the matter that weighed on his heart.

"So, brothers, you may not know me as much as Ta and Shingi do; and even they only know me from our days as toddlers. I do not want to speak about things I know nothing about. I have been excited about moving back to MaOwnership. You are all my friends by virtue of living here and, although I just met you two, we are bound even closer by church ties." He stopped and looked around at us to see if we still followed his meaning.

"That said, I am saddened and puzzled by what I have heard about Pashena rece—"

"Of course. You are just like them," Fungai interrupted and, turning to his brother, continued, "He is just like them. He has been here for a few days, and the front-street is already in his ear about us!" Both brothers shook their heads but stayed put, which was all the impetus Antony needed to continue.

"Not at all, friends. I was told the whole story, in which I found a lot of wrong done by almost everyone. I am not pointing fingers. I just felt that nobody had asked to hear your side of the story or even attempted to understand it." The brothers fidgeted with the discomfort of people being charmed into submission.

"So, what happened? How did you two, some of the finer boys we have in MaOwnership end up agreeing to a game with those hooligans from Area B? And say all you want about Shingi and Ta, but they have been as puzzled as I am all this time."

"Let it be done with. The game already happened. It is over. We are sorry. Who cares?" Fungai snapped.

"It is not about the game, friends. You may say it is over, but is it? Richie and them may still come back, and Pashena may never rise again. We can act like the backstreet and front-street divide is the way things were always meant to be, but you cannot tell me it was not more fun when everyone was getting along. And don't forget too, that Nigel,

Wellington, and others fought that fight against your friends from B—"

"They are not our friends!" Tiberius, who had been quiet the entire time, lashed into a near-teary tirade. "They are not our friends, and shame on you for even saying that! If only you knew what we have been through, and all because we just wanted to get the poles so we could play with everyone else!"

Antony, realizing that he now walked the fragile line between striking the nerve necessary for conversation and that which could end up deepening existent wounds, interjected, "Sorry, sorry my friends. I have not been here for almost ten years, and these things are lost on me. Do tell me then what it is you went through that I or the others don't know."

The brothers looked at each other—the younger shaking with nerves, the older in rage. They then told the story that shamed Ta and me and would have done the same to our other friends had they been there in rational mind. When the brothers had initially gone to buy the poles, they had been greeted by a man claiming to be Richie's uncle and in charge of the business. He told them the poles were a dollar each—which was much higher than they had anticipated. They paid him with all the money that had taken them weeks to save up, and he told them to come back the next day. Upon their return, they met with Richie and Mabhaudhi who both denied knowledge of the man, Richie going as far as declaring that he did not even have an uncle. They could, however, sell them poles for 50 cents each. When the brothers tried to plead their case for already having spent their last cent, Richie and his cronies ran them out of their neighborhood with sticks and rocks. Desperate, the brothers went without lunch for a few more days, saving until they had enough. When they came back, Richie told them that the price had increased, and the poles were back to one dollar each. The brothers had begun to walk away in defeated tears when Richie yelled for them to come back. He had a proposal.

"We will let you kids have the poles for the money you have if you agree to let us play on the field whenever we want." He had said with a diabolical snare.

Antony, Ta, and I sat entranced, curious eyes wide open. Tiberius read our eyes and picked up from where his brother had left.

"Of course we agreed. We had spent ten dollars buying these poles for a sport we were not even sure we liked! We had been in that neighborhood one too many times to walk away empty-handed. Also, I doubt they were going to let us leave just like that, especially since they already knew we had money on us. Had we said no, they would have beaten us up and still taken it. What were we to do? What would you have done?"

"Wh-wh-why did you not tell us all this before?"

"Hah. What were you going to do, except maybe laugh at our stupidity? Besides, Pashena was just an idea at the time and, on my father's grave, I would have never imagined that it would become the field at which those kinds of people would want to play!"

"And after that, did you hear from them again?" I asked, my interest peaking.

"Oh, that was just the beginning. For the first few months to a year, we did not hear from them. We would see Richie or Mabhaudhi now and then, and each time they would make a snide remark or just look at us in condescending menace. Then two months ago, it started."

We dared not ask what it is that had started. Fungai took over again.

"We were coming back from tennis practice when they saw us. Mabhaudhi came up to me and asked to see my racquet and, before I could answer, snatched it from my hand. He then picked up a rock the size of a tennis ball and hit it so hard that it broke two of my racquet strings. My mother has put all her earnings into buying us these things. I tried to protest and found my voice stifled by withheld tears. The next day, they waited for us in the same place and this time took my brother's pocket money. When I spoke up, Mabhaudhi slapped me and told me to shut up unless I wanted my money taken as well. We stopped using that path back home, but they found out where we lived and were soon harassing us just outside our gate. They derived the most devilish of pleasures from just taking our lunches and beating us. Things got worse each time we told them they could not come to Pashena. Part of us genuinely did not want them to play, and the other part was too ashamed to bring them around to the rest of you."

"Why did you not tell your mother?" I asked again, now gravely concerned.

"Are you crazy? With all my family has been through? Telling her that there are rogue boys waiting for us outside the house and threatening to beat us would have been akin to giving her poisoned food. The old woman's blood pressure would have shot through the roof!"

"Eventually," Tiberius succeeded his brother, "it became too much. We figured if we just let the game happen, they would leave us alone. To add insult to already bitter injury, Richie's 'uncle' who he had vehemently denied was one of the hooligans on the team—the one that Wellington hit with the rock."

We sat silently, pensively, for a few minutes. Their story was easily the most incredible ordeal that any of my friends had been through at the hands of people our age. I tried to bite my lip in anger of solidarity, yet I found myself just shivering in guilt and fear. We thought we knew The Tennis Brothers.

We still had many questions: had they seen any of those boys since then? Was Pashena worth doing again after the crop season? How would we get everyone else to hear this side of the story?

We decided to leave them for another day; we had been through enough already. Ta finally broke the silence:

"So, Wellington hit him pretty good with that rock huh?"

Everyone laughed.

40

The rainy season came and went as it did faithfully each year. With the exception of Gogo spending fewer days out on the field than she had in the past, everything else went customarily well. Antony spent the school holidays familiarizing himself with everyone. His charm was unmistakable, and people immediately took a liking to him. Fox and Wellington were in Birchenough the entire season, and rumors had it that they may not come back.

My mother and other family from Harare came again, and again amidst much aplomb. The grandparents had been led to believe that nobody would be coming from Harare that holiday season, much to their disappointment. It was, however, part of a grand plan to surprise them. Everyone arrived one afternoon, a week before Christmas, while both Gogo and Kulu were at work. With them, they had brought magnificent purple sheets, blankets and curtains. My mother and Mainini Paula took the lead in redecorating the grandparents' bedroom, transforming it into a lair not unlike we often saw on TV as meant for medieval European aristocracy. The shades hung in alternating shades of lilac and deep purple, and the bed was covered in a floral purple silk blanket. Afterwards, we all cramped into the bedroom and waited for them to get home. We did not have to wait long. Ten minutes later, Gogo opened the door unsuspectingly to a dozen yells of 'surprise' and an eternity of hugs.

Gogo would not stop crying. As the family was growing larger and people moved further away and some out of the country, she knew that seeing all her children and grandchildren in one place had become increasingly rare and only the wind knew when, if at all, we would be all together again.

Spurred by Antony and the enthusiasm of the juniors, Pashena rose again after all the crops had been harvested. The field was unrecognizable to its earlier incarnations. Innocent was long gone, Fox and Babylon were now in high school, and the rest of us were still reeling from the previous year's aftermath.

Antony's silver tongue soon made sure that the tale of Tiberius and Fungai's plight at the hands of Richie and his goons spread tactfully and without malice. Nobody mentioned it, and the brothers would surely have been pleasantly surprised by the forgiven and benevolent reaction they received from all who had seemed on the verge of crucifying them at the end of the last year.

Soon, Pashena was back to its lively presence and, although it struggled to capture the magic of years gone by, we were happy to be back. Wellington even made an occasional appearance and, although he appeared as if his heart carried a heavier boulder of hurt and worry each time, it was always good to see him. Against all things natural, and with Fox spending more and more time at school, Wellington and Antony had grown to be rather good friends. If anyone knew what was on Wellington's mind, we figured he did. We never asked though.

Unlike Fox and Babylon, Antony still played with us despite being in his first term of high school. There, he had found and fallen in love with the game of table tennis. He came back to us and would not stop talking about it, in total disregard of the obvious lack of interest on our part. Together with basketball and baseball, table tennis was one of the games that were introduced that year to help keep occupied what weird boys in Dangamvura that may not have been interested in football. Oddly enough, their popularity seemed to be increasing by the day.

Maybe it is because it was my last year of primary school and I was not sure that I would stay in Dangamvura, or even Mutare for high school. Maybe the neighborhood had, for all its good intentions, genuinely changed. Maybe, when life's seasons have run their course, the spirits have a way of announcing it to us simple beings. Either way, the air was ominously heavy that year, even when the going was finer.

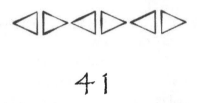

41

"This is it, boys. We leave in three months," a morose Wellington announced to us. We were all shocked, except Antony, who probably already knew.

"Why? What happened?" someone finally asked.

The woman who had been living with them had grown dissatisfied with the reality of raising her sons in what she described as a "dubious neighborhood" and had decided to move out of the house. Although she had expressed the sentiment before, it had never been with any practical devotion. Then the week before, all of a sudden, she told them she would be leaving at the end of the following month. With Fox now in high school, the little money that Sincere left had since dried up, and they were entirely dependent on the income from the lodger woman for sustenance. Her leaving meant the inevitable; they would have to move back to Birchenough and attend the rural schools under the care of family there.

We stood in stunned silence. We had friends who had left before, but it had been with their families and almost always to the suburbs or other better neighborhoods: this was the first time life had conspired against our own and threatened to send them into the abyss.

"Can you at least finish primary school here?" I said, grasping for life's loopholes. Everyone looked at me with condemning eyes.

"That's almost two more years! Will Gogo take us in, huh?" he snapped angrily. I sank back into the crowd.

Antony left with the distraught Wellington.

Tiberius broke the silence.

"Crazy that is. Unfortunate about old Fox and Wellington," He lamented. We all agreed. The awkward silence that followed was broken by the sound of Gogo calling for Nigel and me.

"*Nhai vakomana!*[51]Would you please come here for a short while?" We ran towards her, relieved to be away from all the tension.

"I had planned to go to Boka's grocery store to buy some bread, but'm not feeling too well. Would you please go? Here, there are a few extra cents for sweets, too." She spoke softly, her vintage smile garnishing her bronzed face. She looked like she had been sweating.

Eager to get away from the field as well and hoping to score some sweets, Ta joined us on our errand. We passed the Beit fields on our way. With the advent of the array of other sports, the city council had built a basketball court next to the football field, and there happened to be a lively game going on at the moment. Passing closer, we saw a boy about our size—but much smaller than anyone else who was playing—dribbling and doing tricks before throwing the basketball into the air. We watched it sail flawlessly, only to descend through the hoop with the grace of a feather. The much bigger boys cheered and hoisted the smaller boy over their shoulders. Ta, Nigel and I grinned

---

[51] "Hey, boys!"

in vicarious glory, and could hardly believe ourselves when we looked up and finally saw who the boy was: Innocent!

As we walked away, I could not erase the image of Innocent being lifted in celebration by those much older boys. When had he started playing basketball? I had not spoken to him in any depth since we had fallen out last year, although we had started chatting a little again at school. Even then, he had not mentioned basketball at all and, for all the furor surrounding the new game, I had not heard anybody else talk about him playing. It was vintage Innocent though, not letting the entire world in on his business. I was just hurt that I had descended from being friend above all others to being counted as one of the "entire world."

Ta, on the other hand, was mesmerized.

"Wow, that I-I-Innocent huh? Wha-what was that? Is that basketball? I didn't know he played! Di-did you? He is good! He moves this way, that way and goaaaal! I thought the old guys would be angry with him, bu-but no! They loved it! Can we watch this afternoon? Can we?" I agreed, partly in fascination with the game and partly to shut him up.

True to our word, we returned that afternoon. I especially came to ascertain just how good Innocent was, and just how entranced by the whole affair Ta had been: I had underestimated both. For a smaller boy who had only started playing, Innocent moved around the basketball court with the grace of a seasoned player. More significantly, it seemed the older and bigger players took him as seriously as a player as they did everyone else. Upon noticing that he had an audience, Innocent began showboating and seemed to get better with each move.

Ta watched it all with captive interest. I had initially thought his intrigue lay purely in seeing an old friend in his moment. After an hour of him watching in utter fascination, I concluded it was bigger than just Innocent. Besides, Ta and Innocent had never been so close that Ta would be engaged in the game purely for his sake.

When the game was done, Innocent came over to us and greeted us with a smile that I had not seen in months now. Although it was probably just the euphoria of a game well played, I was delighted that he had embraced us.

"Wow, Inno! Great game!" was all I was able to get in before Ta took over again with a barrage of questions about the game. Feeling embarrassed for him, I subtly tugged on his shirt. He did not notice, and Innocent did not seem to mind. Their conversation ended with Ta asking if he could play sometime. Innocent looked at me incredulously, then shrugged at Ta in concession and said, "why not? Join us on Monday."

I embraced him again, and we headed back home. I did not want to celebrate having my friend back prematurely, but I vowed there and then that, as long as time and distance allowed, I would attend every game he played. It would be funny to see old Ta, clumsy as ever, taking his honest shot at the game. Besides, Easter was pending, and there was little else going on. As soon as the second term started, people would either be trying out for the school football teams or busy watching them. Gandanga's big box of action movies would not be replaced until his father returned in August or September. Wellington had left with Antony and we hardly ever saw them.

I had time to watch some basketball, I figured. So, I did.

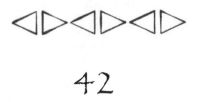

42

Across the country, the Easter holidays mark the beginning of another age-old tradition: high school applications. Grade Seven students across the land refine their mail writing skills and send a dozen letters to various high schools in the hopes of getting a form one place at their preferred choice. While everyone eventually goes to high school, it is these letters- dreaded by many—that determine the quality and reputation of the school you end up attending. The high schools fall into three broad categories; the mission schools, the private schools, and the local government schools. Among the vast majority of Grade Sevens across the country, the mission schools are the ultimate prize. These are almost always boarding schools located on the outskirts of the major towns and are renowned for their impeccable disciplinary records and equally impressive exam results. The local schools are, for better or worse, the local schools: institutions that represent the cross-section of the community in which they are located and, although often lacking in national or even regional renown, often battle for academic and athletic bragging rights with other schools in the vicinity. The private schools were, for the most part, a creature unknown to children in Dangamvura and other rokeshenis. All we knew was they wore fancy blazers, often battled for top honors with the mission schools on the High School's Quiz show, were absurdly expensive, and all the white children went there. The last two were the same thing.[52] In an attempt to spruce up the growingly unpopular 'elitist, Rhodesian[53] relic' image, private schools had recently started scouring the *rokesheni* in search of children with exceptional talents in their extra-curricular of choice: tennis, cricket, table tennis, playing an instrument and such.

That Easter, with some help from my aunts, I crafted a few letters and sent them around the country. I applied to the rural school at which Baba Nigel taught. There was never a chance that Gogo or my mother would let me go to the school, but the thought of towering over the common rural children with my city stories and comparatively dominant command of English was intriguing. I applied to Marist Brothers, the mission school that my cousin Fadzi attended. It was the most reputable school in our province and, as its patrons often argue, in the country. Upon my mother's encouragement, I applied to St. George's College, a private school in Harare. I, as said earlier, knew nothing about the school except that its all-White quiz team was a fixture of the Schools' Quiz top three and one of Gogo's favorites. I had never met nor heard of anyone who had been to that school or any like it.

Applications done and mailed, we returned to watching Innocent play basketball and bracing ourselves for the beginning of the second term and all that came with it.

---

52 The categories are, of course, not ironclad. Several private and mission schools also perform miserably, and as many local government schools churn out excellent students. There are also other school groups (rural schools etc.,) that were just not on our application radar.

53 Zimbabwe's British Colonial Name

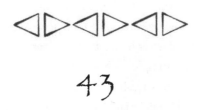

43

That winter, the winter of 1999, was exceptionally cold and harsh, thus provided a most appropriate backdrop to the times as they would unfold.

The mornings were especially bitter. We would wake up while it was still dark, and make our way to school under cover of fog, only to return at the early onset of dusk. Pashena now stood a beautiful relic whose memories were kept alive by Nigel and the other juniors, with the occasional appearance by one of us older boys.

The high school boys were either too busy or felt they had risen above the dirt field. We hardly ever saw them, except Antony, who would often meet with us after his games of table tennis. Eager to keep his young friend from drowning in melancholy, he had been able to convince Wellington to start playing with him. They spent two or three hours every day at Beit Hall, hunched over the table and viciously channeling angst and dreams into the tiny ball being sent back and forth between them.

In addition to the anxious wait for the high schools' responses and the exaggerated preparation for our ultimate primary school exams, the Grade Seven boys had assumed different pastimes at school and beyond. I went back to chess. It was not as enjoyable as when Innocent had been there, but the reverence it excited in the other students made it worthwhile.

Ta had now joined Innocent on the local basketball team. While Innocent continued to shine, Ta was, as I had imagined, clumsy and would only be allowed to play for a few minutes at a time. The problem with Ta had never been a lack of talent or natural dispositions; he had just always struggled with a whimsical sense of self-worth. His stutter and the ruthless teasing that persistently ensued from it had only compounded his plight and left him dependent on everything but himself for validation. Thus, as good as he may have actually been, we never saw it because the older players only allowed him to play for a short while and, in turn, that show of no confidence in him made him play conservatively most of the time.

Fungai and Tiberius went back to tennis, with the former doing so more actively than his little brother. In a fashion typical of them, Tiberius's indolence was part of their well-crafted plan. Although he was younger, he was better than Fungai by now. Word had fallen on our ears that Prince William High School, a reputable private school for boys on par with St. George's College, would be coming to Dangamvura later that month to recruit primary school students they deemed scholarship-worthy. This year, selections would be held at a large festival featuring several sports, and possibly a band as well. While the school tended to give the scholarships to Grade Seven students, it was not unheard of that they would offer a younger, exceptional student a scholarship for when they finally got to high school: Tiberius would be a perfect candidate. Because they only gave out one scholarship—if at all—per neighborhood for each sport, and Fungai would be starting high school soon, they decided to leave the spotlight in its entirety for him. In two years, when Tiberius would be in Grade Seven, he would most certainly get his due.

The self-appointed ambassador of Pashena to the other neighborhood teams, my personal reputation had suffered more than anyone else's at the height of our field's wiles. It was the plight of the proverbial sacrificial lamb, except that instead of being a blameless symbol carrying the sins of a sinful people, I was the reason for the sin and bore that burden with the heavy pride of knowing that no undeserving Pashena soul would have to suffer as well. By now, the sentence had since been served and, while the tarnished collective reputation still endured, everything had returned to its pre-hostilities normalcy. Old friends were friends again, and old strangers continued down their lethargic path.

Thus, when Simba approached me one afternoon at school to ask if I would be trying my luck at the school's football team that week, it was his sincerity and not his magnanimity that surprised me. While hatchets had been buried, there was still no way that Simba, hailing from the haven of Dangamvura football that is MaTwo Rooms, had watched me playing and deemed me worthy even of consideration for the school team. Was he being nice to a fault? Did they not have enough people? But of course, they did. When did school football ever suffer a shortage of men? Who else was playing? I could think of three or four other goalkeepers at school who were, without controversy, better than me...

As these thoughts raced through my head, I grew unaware of Simba who still stood in front of me. The excited smile he had initially worn had faded and been replaced by an incredulous stare. Who did I think I was, even taking a moment to debate this glorious offer internally? Did I not know what this meant?

The next words out of my mouth would have done little to placate him.

"I hadn't really thought about it, man. Let me sleep on it, and I will see how I feel tomorrow." I said, doing my best to contain my confused excitement.

"Well, I hope you come to your senses soon. Half a dozen goalkeepers are looking to be considered, and the sooner you decide, the better!" he replied as he walked away, his stare mocking what he had mistakenly thought was conceit on my part. Once he was out of sight, my bottled elation at the very thought unraveled. I jumped up and down in place, and then gazed into space, all the while muttering sweet musings to myself. "Mavima! Mavima! Mavima!" Everyone in the school will know me. People from other schools will know me. Girls will come in their multitudes to chant my name! MaOwnership, the part of it that belonged to Pashena, will finally get her due! Nobody had gone this far before. Donald was already in this year's school juniors' team but, while we loved and were happy for him, he was not born of Pashena. "Mavima! Mavima! Mavima!" I chanted to myself as I ran, knees knocking into each other for nerves, all the way from school to the basketball courts where Ta and Innocent were playing.

I arrived as the game was ending, just in time to see the coach give Ta his ceremonial pity five minutes to play. Undeterred by the others' chuckles at the gesture, he took to the game with the fervor of a rabid dog, screaming for the ball and jumping around the court like he was playing in the most important game of his life. Because I knew almost nothing about basketball, I looked around to the other players and spectators to see what they made of his fiendish performance. While the majority of the team looked unimpressed, the coach nodded his head appreciatively each time Ta made a nuisance of himself on the court. As the coach blew his whistle to end that session, Innocent was smiling as well. Was Ta actually better than the teasing and mockery he was prone to getting?

As we walked away, Ta and Innocent spoke non-stop about the basketball game. Ta probed Innocent about the other players, game strategy, among other things. Although slightly annoyed, Innocent smiled and answered all the questions with regal patience. I would have felt alienated by their conversation had I not been lost in my own world of dreams.

Shingi on the football team. A thing like that.

I debated on whether to tell Innocent about my conversation with Simba. On the one hand, he had been a trusted confidante for years now and, despite our recent estrangement, his opinion on matters such as these was still valuable. On the other, he was a staunch opponent of the school football culture and the heavy hand of MaTwo Rooms and other such folk in its running. That was, after all, the reason he had started playing at Pashena and ultimately chosen to play basketball over football, even though he was better than most of us. I decided not to tell him, and would not have had I not snapped out of my vision to hear Ta carelessly stutter:

"Ca-ca-can you believe it, Inno? I may even get to play at the big Prince William Festival in August! You and me, the o-only two pe-people from the Pashena bunch to play a team sport on the bigger stage!"

Feeling for me, Innocent cringed. In an effort both to put my friend at ease and defend my honor, I blurted out that I had been asked to try out for the football team. Ta chuckled dismissively. Innocent, however, knew well that I would neither lie nor joke about incredible things within the realm of possibility. He smiled at me. It took me a while to grasp the gravity of his reaction; not only had he believed me, he also seemed genuinely happy for me. I described to them the entire conversation and, by the time Ta left our company, they were both sharing in my excitement and wishing me well. Ta bid us farewell, and I walked Innocent home.

"To be honest, blaz, I wasn't sure if I should tell you about this football opportunity."

"Why wouldn't you? I thought we were moving past all that nonsense..."

"Oh no, not even that. I just know you have spoken about how you didn't like the school team and the type of people who played in it..."

"Look brother: the past few months have shown me that we end up where we should. A few months ago, I did not know what basketball was. Now, I have found something I love to do and at which I am very good. I would have never ended up here if we had never gone through what we did. Yesterday, the thought of a Pashena original, let alone you, being even considered for a school team would have been unfathomable, yet here we stand. And I know you have dreamt of this since we started playing. Sometimes, you are going to have to play with people you don't like, but that is part of life. If we avoid everything and everyone that makes us uncomfortable, then what would we ever do?"

We stood silent for a few long seconds. I struggled to wrap my head around the profundity of his words. In the end, I managed to come up with:

"Well-spoken. Say, do you have any time on Wednesdays during lunch? I thought maybe we could go to the old chess club again, see what young fools want to challenge the kings?"

He chuckled and promised to make some time the following week. We parted, and I ran home to tell Nigel and Gogo about the football news.

I arrived right as the High School's Quiz was starting. Saint George's was on against some other schools.

44

"Alright, Mavima! See you tomorrow. You need to focus out there man! Hope you do better tomorrow!"

That was Taona, the school's first choice goalkeeper. Although we were not friends going into the season, we had developed some rapport from practicing together. He also lived by the Complex and had to walk past my house on his way home, so we often walked together.

We had only been practicing for the school team for two weeks now, and once the euphoria of being invited to the team wore off, I was finding that the game was harder than I had imagined: the expectations were absurd, and the teammates were unforgiving. I barely had time to adjust, and a few mistakes during training already had some of the boys calling for the dismissal of the "spoiled MaOwnership brat." For my love of the game and excitement thereof, I was beginning to doubt whether it was worth it. We had not played against other schools, and I was already succumbing to the pressure of competition.

I was glad to have Donald, Simba and now Taona, who seemed at least not too eager to put my head on the chopping block.

That afternoon had been particularly rough, and although I had concealed them from Taona, I could feel the early onset of tears as I walked into the house. I planned to walk right up to Gogo and tell her I was quitting the team already. Unless it was something of paramount importance to her, you could always count on Gogo to validate your decisions without making you feel any lesser for making them.

When I entered the house, I instead found Gogo standing by the door, head tilted to the side and her beautiful magnanimous smile spread across her face. My football worries immediately lifted, as I noticed Mai Nigel standing behind her, smiling as well. I stared at her for a short while, before switching my attention back to Gogo, who I now noticed was holding a letter in her hands and had begun to cry.

"You have done it again my son. You have made us proud," she said, before breaking into ululation and a brief church dance, "they call it Saint George's, heh? The nation's finest! Red blazer! What am I going to do? What am I going to do?"

By now, I was lost in her embrace, and figuring out what she meant. The letter must have been my acceptance into Saint George's College! I would not have believed it had it not been for Gogo's blessed tears now running down the length of my face. What fortune! I had just applied to this school that we knew nothing about, and here we stood.

"They say there is an orientation on July 3rd. They want you to come to Harare and see the school!" She said, almost falling into her seat as she read the letter. She must have said some other things after that. I did not hear them. I found myself, again, lost in imagination.

Imagine me, all clad in a red blazer. I might even join the quiz team and end up on TV, flanked by two white boys! Gogo would be so proud! Gogo! If I move to Harare, I will miss her! Maybe I shouldn't go. I have not heard of anyone else hearing back from the schools they applied to; was I the first person at the school to be accepted? Wow.

Just like it had never been, all my worries about football were a thing of the past. I went back to practice the next day with renewed confidence. Although I did not share where my excitement lay for fear of inciting envy and her ugly cousins, it was evident to all that I was not the same player I had been the day before. For but a few months more, I was no longer of this world.

As more and more details about the festival trickled in, excitement hung over Dangamvura like rainclouds over the drought-ravaged countryside. Prince William had traditionally recruited only tennis players when they came to Dangamvura, and even that had been done in largely closed sessions and with little attention from the general community. This year, in the interest of philanthropy and greater buy-in from the community, they planned on including a variety of other sports and making a celebration out of the event. Although they were only interested in recruiting tennis and table tennis players, the four primary football teams were invited, as were the girls' netball teams. Innocent's basketball team was also slated to play against a city team. The Tennis Brothers were now playing every single day, readying Fungai for the defining moment to come. Although Antony was not eligible because he was already in high school and Wellington had made it clear he was not interested in the festival, they too were at every table tennis training session that the scholarship hopefuls attended. For his apparent lethargy towards the festival, Wellington was fast becoming one of the best players in his section. Each game he played was an expression of pent up anger, fear of an uncertain future, and the raw competitiveness he risked losing when he moved to the rural area. Every few practices, Antony would implore him to reconsider his stance against the festival, and each time he remained resolute.

Our football team was having an unremarkable season and had only won two of the six games we had played by the beginning of July.

I had cemented my place as the third choice goalkeeper, and I was content with the reality that I would probably never be called into an actual game. I was satisfied that I even sat on the same bench and donned the uniform as many of my childhood heroes; it was a dream with which I was only beginning to come to terms.

Ta had assumed the dubious role of unintended team clown at the basketball court. Intrigued by his clumsy demeanor and bumbling reputation, the other players and, soon, fans began to gather round the court and clamor for his introduction into the game. They cheered loud each time he got the ball and, in the rare instance that he scored or made a move worth noting, the place would go berserk. I would have been embarrassed and offended for my friend, but he seemed to cherish every moment. He had never been the center of any consistent attention and, if people came to see him play, it was worth all the teasing. Besides, he argued, he was getting more playing time from the coach to appease the gathered masses and, while nobody was paying any mind, he was getting better, and soon, their jeers would turn to amazement and celebration. I smiled in tacit applause of his maturity and optimism.

◁▷◁▷◁▷

45

I recall more clearly than most the day that Gogo and Kulu put me on the bus to Harare for my orientation at Saint George's. We rose earlier than usual and were at the bus stop before my friends had even bathed for school. It would be the first trip I went on by myself, and my mother would be at hand to receive me when I arrived in Harare. Although the trip was a mere four hours and I would be back in Mutare on Sunday afternoon, Gogo still cried at the sight of me boarding the blue and white luxury coach as if it were ferrying me to a foreign war.

I arrived in Harare to a lavish welcome and elaborate feast, after which my mother ironed and prepared my uniform for the next day and sent me to bed. We had to be up early tomorrow to beat the traffic, she said.

Beating traffic on your way to school? A thing like that! This really was the big city.

If I had been mesmerized by the idea and prospects of Harare, Saint George's College himself made the grand city look modest at best. I had never before seen such a magnificent sight. As we drove into the school, the seemingly endless fields—hills upon hills—of well-tended green grass immediately overwhelmed me. There was enough space for 20 football games at once! After a drive that would have been the entire length of my primary school, yet was merely the entrance to "Saints," we came upon a huge, ancient-looking and majestic castle. A castle. Like I had seen on the British TV shows that had flooded my childhood, except now it was here in front of me; at a high school, no less. My high school.

By now, the other prospective students had gathered around this spectacle as well. My awe turned into wrecked nerves when I realized that I was surrounded by White people. Many black people too, probably more black students, but a lot of white ones as well. There was no malice to my nerves; I had just never been so close to so many white people before! I had met a few doctors who worked with my grandparents, and maybe a few others in stores. I had definitely never been around any of them that were my age, let alone dozens of them!

With the exception of one other student in the group of almost 200, everyone else wore a fancy blazer—the age-old sign that they had come from a private or big city school. I would have been ashamed of my humble and objectively bland uniform and subsequent demeanor had I not been wrapped in the grandeur of the day. I was here too! I, little Shingi from Dangamvura, was here with all these children of the most powerful people in the country! One of the boys introduced himself as the son of the host of the High School's Quiz. I recognized a few last names from the news and the government. Everyone around me carried themselves like the Western kids from TV.

The rest of the day seemed to pass by in a daze; all I could think about was going back to Dangamvura and telling every one of the wonders I had seen. Nobody, not even Antony in his travels or Ta when he rode the bus to school, had seen sights as marvelous as I had.

I returned to Dangamvura riding on the saddles of my glorious sojourn to the heart of the country and, for but a brief moment, I was the object of anticipated envy and a slew of questions. What were the white kids like? Are they nice? Were the black kids just like us, or were they like the white kids too? Are you going to that high school for certain now?

The ephemeral moment soon faded as we switched back to the business of MaOwnership and Dangamvura. Over the weekend, Tiberius had made a snide remark about how Fungai was going to be the pride of MaOwnership at the festival—clearly a swipe at Ta, who was the only other person from the neighborhood likely to play on the day. Ta, as was becoming a habit for him, was unperturbed and insisted that he would just be glad to play at all. Wellington, Antony and the few others who had been there seemed more offended on his behalf, and upon hearing the story, I felt the same. Ta had the mockery and bullying coming from people he did not even know; he definitely did not need it from the neighborhood.

The weeks leading up to the festival were filled with feverish preparations on the part of everyone involved and heightened anticipation for everyone else. Even Nigel and the rest of the juniors, who had since become bored and disillusioned by Pashena, found their way back to the old dirt field and took charge of the games much like we had in the beginning.

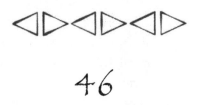

46

The Prince William Festival was held on Friday, August 5th, 1999. My birthday was on Monday, July 26th.

Much of our growing and changing in life happens over time, and we are seldom able to point to a specific time during which transformation occurs. Life, to this day, has been a series of seemingly inconsequential incidents that, when told in sequence, make for a decent story.

Except for the two weeks between my birthday and the Prince William Festival of 1999. Thus goes that story.

Because my birthday had fallen on a Monday and my mother was unable to come to Dangamvura until that weekend, she and Gogo decided it best to leave the celebrations for then. She would be in town, and Gogo would have enough time to get the cake and small party prepared. Besides, Gogo had just spent most of the weekend in bed with a headache and was in no state to host a celebration. I, for one, was not concerned about my birthday that year. Like everyone else, my life was building up to the festival. Our mid-year exams were going to be earlier in the week of the festival, but our undivided attention was on the latter, and we now found ourselves scurrying to prepare for those as well.

Thus, my birthday was not worth noting, except for the phone calls from my mother and aunts, and Gogo turning back the years and preparing a Christmas-style dinner that evening. Innocent and Ta did come up to the school football field to wish me a happy birthday before they went to the basketball court. We promised to get together for an hour that evening to study for the exams, and that we also did.

Tuesday came by and was inconspicuous as well. Some people from the city council came over by Pashena that afternoon and interrupted the juniors' game. They looked and measured around for a few minutes before going over to chat with Gogo, and then the Pastor. Apparently, the city was considering finally putting the empty space to some use other than as a playground and communal farming space. They said nothing else, and we dwelt little on it.

"*Vakomana,* I am not feeling too well tonight. How about we have some of the leftovers from last night's meal so I can go and rest early tonight?"

We needed no further convincing, as the food had been delicious. My aunts, on the other hand, were less thrilled about feasting on yesterday's delicacies and more concerned with Gogo. For her unrelenting smile, her health was definitely waning. She had, over the past few months, complained about a recurrent headache. This particular bout had gone on for three days now, the longest it had ever lasted. Her plight had put everyone, Kulu included, in unfamiliar territory. Gogo is the one who typically took care of everyone, not the other way round. We just sat around in eerie silence as she made her way to bed.

My aunts spoke no more for the rest of the evening. Nigel and I were unsure whether to lose ourselves in the birthday remnants or show our solidarity by conforming to the sudden and inexplicable somber cloud that hung over the household.

What ghost may have haunted us the night before seemed banished in the morning, as we woke up to the age-old sight of Gogo slaving over a saucepan of sizzling bacon and another of scrambled eggs.

"How did you wake up, Gogo?[54]*"* Nigel asked, with a pained sincerity that transcended our usual morning courtesies.

"I woke up just well, my boys! How did you wake up?"

We replied that we had slept well, in incredulous unison. Why did she sound like everything was well like she had not had everyone's stomach in knots last night? After preparing breakfast, she returned to bed. Nigel and I went to her bedroom when we were done to bid her farewell. She smiled.

"Have a wonderful day, vakomana. I am not going to get out of bed now. Shingi, would you please grab the two dollars from the brown bag? Make sure your cousin gets a dollar as well. I will see you both this afternoon."

As we walked away, a strong breeze rustled her purple curtains unexpectedly for that time of the year. Leaving, we felt the impending bite of cold interrupted by the slamming door and retreating into the room.

We walked in cryptic silence for a while, until we came upon Ta and some of the others. Temporarily forgetting the mysterious goings-on at home, we were once again lost in festival conversation. Rumors were spreading that Wellington may yet decide to play. The city basketball team that Innocent and Ta's team were bound to play were seasoned and were almost guaranteed to embarrass them.

When we arrived at school and went to our separate classes, I found myself again haunted by Gogo's smile, my aunts' heightened concerns the night before, and the strong breeze of earlier that

---

54 Literal translation for Shona salutation equivalent to "How are you doing this morning?"

morning. I had never felt anything like that before and could not make any sense of it. The teacher was revising topics that would be on the exam the following week, but I was in a world of my own. Goosebumps appeared all down my left arm. The breeze had followed me to school, I thought. My forehead broke into a sweat. Could not be the breeze. I think I am getting sick. Shivering.

Break time could not have come any sooner.

"Mavima! Are you okay?" Innocent called out to me as I dashed towards the boys' bathroom. He must have seen my distress during class. Who else had?

"I am fine! I will be right back."

I entered the bathroom stall and hunched over as if to vomit. The floor and toilet were filthy, so I decided against it. I stood up, walked outside, and wiped the sweat from my forehead.

"*Kwakanaka here?* You are sweating and shivering like a TB patient! You also haven't thrown your big brain around all morning; I see the teacher eyeing you each time questions go unanswered!" Innocent queried, attempting to inject some levity into the disturbing picture.

"Oh, I don't know what is going on," I answered distractedly. "Say, are you staying for chess this afternoon?"

I did not hear his response.

The rest of class went as it had gone before the break. By the time the bell rang for lunch, I was anxiously and uncontrollably tapping my foot. As soon as we were dismissed, I dashed for the door again.

"Be ready by quarter to two!" Innocent was yelling as I ran homeward. This time I heard him clearly. I did not turn around. I ran the entire way home and was soaking in fatigued and nervous sweat by the time I arrived.

There was nobody home. Maybe there was. Maybe the maid was basking under the Avocado Tree and talking to Ta's maid. Maybe we had a maid.

As I walked into the house, I felt myself going deeper and deeper into an unforgiving cold of loss and confusion. It is, to this day, the most overwhelming sensation of defeat that has ever fallen over me. By the time I arrived at Gogo's door, it was clear that something was different. Everything was different.

There she lay, a magnanimous smile permanently carved on her sleeping face.

"Gogo! Gogo! Gogo!"

Manic shaking. Frantic screaming.

"Gogo! Gogo! Gogo!"

Run to the fridge. Scrape ice from inside the freezer. Slap it unapologetically on unresponsive head and neck.

"Gogo! Gogo! Gogo!"

Darkness. Dizzy fit.

Maybe we had a maid. Maybe the maid was basking under the Avocado Tree talking to Ta's maid.

I told her Gogo would not wake up.

What do you want me to do? She said.

Fit of defeated rage.

I ran back inside and, barely able to hold on to the receiver with my sweaty palms, made furious and frantic phone calls. I called everyone whose number I knew off the top of my head. I called my aunt at the hotel where she worked. I called Kulu at the hospital. I called mother in Harare on her new cell phone.

I returned to where Gogo lay in indescribable serenity and shook her angrily for another half a minute. I realized I had started crying.

It was quarter to two.

Innocent was here.

Maybe we had a maid. I heard her tell Innocent that I was not going to make it to chess that day, as I had to help Gogo with something.

Looking out of the window to see Innocent walk away, I heard Kulu's car rattle down the street and into our driveway. A man I had never seen before was driving, and Kulu was in the passenger seat. Before the car had come to a complete stop, he had jumped out and charging towards the door with the speed and strength of a much younger man. He did not notice me, now sitting in the living room listlessly. He did not notice the maid either.

I followed him into the room. He leaned over her one time and called her by her first name. Anna. He never did that; no one did. He called her by her first name again.

Silence. He sucked his teeth in and shook his head. A woman came in through the front door, already crying and screaming in full voice. Probably my aunt Paula from the hotel.

That is all I remember from that day. I woke up the next morning to more people than I had ever seen. Every room at our house and Ta's was full to the brim. There were two tents set up outside on our front lawn, surrounded by Gogo's beloved carnations. Three bus-fulls came from Gogo's rural homestead, and a further two came from Kulu's. Cars lined the street all the way to Tiberius's house in the backstreet, and down past Donald's. People came in the hundreds from Gogo's church, then dozens of others from Ta's church, the Pastor's church, and my mother's church. My teachers came. A slew of people that Gogo and Kulu had healed and helped over the years came in full tears.   My mother and the rest of Gogo's children—and their children—came. My friends stayed until the break of dawn every day that people were gathered.

For three days and nights, MaOwnership stayed awake and mourned. The masses cried and danced. The churches engaged in unspoken battle as they tried to out-sing each other. Smoke from the giant pots of Sadza in which the women from the neighborhood were lost covered the land. A man collapsed and died in the homestead, and the police came to pick up his body. Chips the dog howled for three continuous days.

After we buried Gogo, MaOwnership was fatigued. Many stayed at the house for another week to mourn and help clean.

These things are inevitable. The human condition dictates that we lose, we grieve, and then we move on. MaOwnership struggled to move past the passing of its mother. The neighborhood lost an integral part of its soul that July 28th.

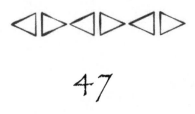

47

Chips howled for three continuous days. Then he slept for two days and, when he woke up, he would not eat. He died the morning of the festival.

48

I f the excitement that preceded the Festival had not secured its status as Dangamvura's most anticipated event, then the melancholy of the two weeks immediately before it ensured that it was the respite that we needed.

I woke up earlier than usual that Friday morning. I assume my friends did too. The sun rose with us then, for the first time since the winter began. Warmer days were upon us.

Before the last tear had fallen over Gogo's grave, Nigel and I had had to recompose ourselves for the exams on Monday. Overwhelmed by the proceedings and novelty of the funeral, we had not prepared. We had not mourned.

It was not until I was hunched over the Shona exam on Monday morning that my world caved. Poor Chips! I had known Chips since I could remember. We grew up together. We had feasted from Gogo's table since infancy and been beneficiaries of Kulu's well-placed hypochondria. Alas, my old friend had howled wolf-like for the last time. Only one voice spoke of home more than that howl did to me.

Oh, Gogo! My darling, darling Gogo! The very embodiment of life, now laying in the ground somewhere. No more farmhouse breakfasts and High School's Quiz. No more magnanimous smile and labored scolding. No more pristine white uniform to run towards and soil with our filthy embraces. All the adults keep saying that she has gone to rest and be with the Lord. Why? She was not tired—at least not until the end. Even if she was, why could she not just rest here? They also say she has gone to a better place. She loved it here. Everyone loved her here. What place was better than this, the home she had given her life up for? What was poor Kulu going to do now? Although he had not wept openly, his head had hung low since he had carried Gogo out of the house, assisted by the strange man who had driven his car when he arrived. He had never been a man of many words, but he had hardly spoken since the fateful afternoon, only speaking up in the church and at the burial.

Oh, Gogo! She was not even going to see her Shingi draped in a red blazer and catching the bus to go to school in the big city. She was not going to give me the customary wet kiss on the cheek when I finished my Grade seven exams. Exams.

Upon that thought, I awoke with a startle. I had responded to less than ten of the fifty exam questions, and my answer sheet was soaked in a mixture of tears and drool. I still had thirty minutes left, so I scrambled through the rest of the exam. I found some levity at football practice that afternoon, even if my mind was only present in half the moments. The next days were the same and, save for slightly fewer tears, so were the other two. He will never admit it to me, but word has it that Nigel had cried his way through his exams, too.

When Thursday afternoon came, and students across the land celebrated the end of mid-year exams, Nigel and I were twice relieved. I knew I had not done my vintage best, and for the first time in a while, I felt it did not matter in the slightest. I had already been accepted into one of the best high schools in the country, and the one person who had always been proud of how I did on exams was gone. Besides, there was no time to dwell on that now. The festival was the next day and, more importantly, all the participants would be selected that afternoon. Nobody went home for lunch, electing instead to stay and speculate on who would make the festival cut. I sat around and listened to the predictions of many a wiser man than myself before I felt the overwhelming sadness returning to my bones. I drifted silently towards the field.

Innocent and Ta saw me sitting alone in the middle of the field. They walked over and, saying nothing, sat down on both sides of me. I cried then. I had cried during exams, but I had tried to bury my head in the exam material and hoped everyone had been too busy to notice. This, however, was the first time I had cried in front of anyone outside of the obligatory family tears. Innocent put his arm around my shoulders. Ta looked towards the ground, battling tears of his own. We sat that way for five minutes before Innocent finally said they had to get across Dangamvura to the basketball courts. The other football players had started to walk onto the field. I wished my two friends well, and they did the same.

Across the township, Tiberius was taking his older brother through his final paces before the big day. As usual, their motivation routine was based in its entirety on citing how exceptional they were in a talent-starved community.

"Come on big man!" Tiberius chanted, "If you don't do it for MaOwnership, who is? Haha. You are our only hope!"

Fungai appreciated the flattery. He puffed his chest out and ran up and down the court with renewed vigor.

"Who else do we have? You think they'll let Shingi play? Or you think those basketball clowns stand a chance? Haha, go on my brother!" Tiberius smirked, looking around to see if anyone was actively disagreeing with him. Wellington and Antony, taking a break from table tennis and decided to watch the brothers practice, were getting increasingly annoyed with the thinly veiled condescension. They had outdone themselves in biting their tongue and would have been successful if Ta and Innocent had not arrived just in time to hear Tiberius's remarks.

Excited for the games, Ta and Innocent would have been barely scratched by the comments. We had all grown to know The Tennis Brothers and their lack of social couth too well to let their callousness bother us, especially at such a time. Wellington did as well. Antony, however, still cringed at their insults and particularly worried that, if the others heard Tiberius speaking such unpleasantries in his presence, they would think he found it funny or agreed with the sentiments.

"*Nhai mfana*! What way is that to talk?" He spoke with the affected authority of someone who would rather be quiet.

The brothers stopped, shocked by Antony's uncharacteristic assertiveness. Fungai looked at his little brother and, realizing that his more vocal partner was speechless, mumbled.

"Is it not true?"

Antony was dreading having to pursue the argument and had hoped that the brothers would give in immediately. Because they had not, he found himself pressed to respond further without neither backing down nor escalating the hostilities.

"No, it's not. I will play tomorrow. Perhaps there may be more than one pride of MaOwnership yet."

It was Wellington, not Antony who spoke. Fed up with the unrelenting arrogance of his old nemeses and irked that his mild-mannered friend had been forced into this uncomfortable conversation, he snapped and resorted to the one thing in which he had any confidence lately. They all stood slack-jawed at Wellington's unforeseen announcement.

"Wha-wha-what? I tho-tho-thought."

"I know I said I was not going to play, but who cares? What do I still have to preserve by not playing? I am losing everyone and everything, and in a month or two, I will be herding cattle in the rural area and will be nothing more than a memory to you all. I may as well do this one thing I enjoy before the devil takes me home," he said as a morbid smile spread across his face.

Innocent started to speak, but Antony smiled at him and interrupted.

"Well, we have some practicing to do then if you are going to play tomorrow," and they left for the hall. Ta and Innocent walked across the tennis court to where the basketball team had gathered. The Tennis brothers continued their practice with relative sobriety, the sting of arrogance having been taken out by Wellington's daring turn-around.

"He will lose anyway," Tiberius said after everyone had left, in a desperate attempt to motivate his brother. Neither of them believed it.

Back at the school, the coach had taken us through a rigorous warm-up routine for about an hour before separating us into four teams. Of the fifty or so players there, between twenty-five and thirty would be chosen to be part of the festival squad. As the season had gone on, two other goalkeepers had joined the team, bringing the total number to five. The coach was trying to take only three to the festival, so we had our work cut out for us. Although the thought of running onto the field to the cheers of my peers thrilled me, I also realized I had made it further than anyone, myself included, had ever envisioned. The two goalkeepers who had joined us were decent: I was better than one, although not by much, and the other was better than me, although not by much either. His name was Philip and was known more for the big mouth and ruthless wit that had landed him in many fights over the years than for his exploits on the field of play.

Innocent and Ta were going through the paces as well. Innocent's place in the basketball team to feature at the festival was all but guaranteed. Ta, on the other hand, looked set to watch the tournament from the stands. Despite the vast improvements he had made, he was still relatively young, new and the butt of many a joke among his teammates and the public. One could never fault him for not giving it his all though; each of the few minutes he was called upon to play found him leaping, running, and throwing harder and better than before. As dusk set, the team sat around the court, their sweat glistening in the orange of the sun creeping away into the horizon. Everyone was exhausted and anxious.

"Well," their coach began, "good job everyone. Great practice today, and good hustling throughout the week." He looked around at the hopeful bunch and then sighed heavily before continuing. "It is always hard selecting a team from such a spirited group, and it is even harder when you are doing so for the first ever game. I want you to know that, regardless of who is playing tomorrow, we are a team: we are the pride of Dangamvura. I expect to see everyone who is not chosen at the game, chanting and cheering loud for his teammates."

The sentiments were noble, but they fell on largely deaf ears. The boys just wanted to hear who would be playing tomorrow. The coach got the message and wasted no further time.

"Captain—Cobra. Vice-Captain—Njonjonjo.

Innocent, Tangwena and Rasputin to start the game. Shato, Clive, Buddha, and Khumbulani to be on the bench."

As the chosen nine huddled in jubilation and amidst congratulations to each other, Innocent slipped out as inconspicuously as he could. Although he wanted to celebrate as much as everyone else, he wanted to make sure not to shove his success in Ta's face. He needed not worry; for as soon as he had stepped away from the group, an ecstatic Ta jumped on him.

"Inno Inno Inno! Co-congrats my friend! Ca-can't wait to see you out there!" Innocent was surprised by Ta's gracious reaction, but did not get to probe him on it any further, as the coach had started to speak again, this time in a pragmatic tone devoid of the ceremonial inspiration often reserved for pre-big game speeches.

"Look. This is our first game against anyone—let alone a team that has been playing for a few years now. I don't expect us to win, but we should at least go out there and enjoy ourselves and give them a good runaround. Let us not embarrass ourselves."

Although genuine, the speech did not sit well with many of the players.

"Come on coach. You don't believe we can bring the heat on those city boys?"

"Oh no," the coach responded, treading with great caution the line between tactful realism and callous pessimism. "I have no doubt we will give it our best. I just don't want us to..."

"If you don't believe in us, you might as well throw in the likes of Ta to go and lose!" the vice-captain, Njonjonjo, yelled and snickered.

The coach, subdued until then, steamed at Njonjonjo's brazen disregard for a younger teammate, his authority, and the overall spirit of the team. His temper escalating unlike they had seen before, he replied.

"You know what, Njonjonjo, you are right. Ta, you will now start on the bench in Njonjonjo's place. Njonjonjo, I still expect you to be there, cheering along with everyone else. Now, is there anyone else who wants to insult my team and me?"

Nobody dared speak, not even Njonjonjo, who now sat with his head bowed and open palms touching the ground to either side of him. Ta and Innocent shared a silent smile.

Football practice had also just finished at school. I had played a decent, albeit short, game. Unlike the basketball team, the football team had played many games this season, and many of the players had returned from the previous year: the team virtually selected itself now, barring no injuries or exceptional performances, for better or worse. We gathered by the terraces to find out who the coach had deemed worthy of the festival.

An older man with grey hair and glasses, the coach spoke with a lisp and in dialect, inadvertently exaggerating his abrasiveness. He had devised a unique and stoic method to select teams before games. Once the players were all gathered, he would grab the bag of uniforms and toss the shirts out to whoever would be in the line-up the following day. In so doing, he eliminated any vocal dissent towards his decisions. We would all scratch our noses and wait patiently, hopes dwindling as the uniform bag got emptier. As the age-old tradition was repeated on this day, I felt indifferent. None of my close friends were on the team anyway, and the few people I had developed any rapport with were guaranteed their places already.

With his penultimate toss, the coach threw the revered blue goalkeeper jersey with yellow stripes going down the sleeves to Phillip, dashing what little hopes I had of being on the roster for the festival.

The coach began in his typical brash fashion. "That's it vakomana. Be early tomo—"

"*Pamusoroi*[55] sir," someone spoke up from the middle of the crowd. We were all dumbfounded. The coach's indelible frown seemed more pronounced. Nobody spoke to the coach after the team had been announced.

As he made his way to the front of the group, I saw it was Taona, the team's first choice goalkeeper.

"I know the decision is ultimately yours, sir, and I know that the third goalkeeper is almost certainly not going to play. I honestly, however, feel that Shingi has been playing much better than Phillip..."

My ears perked, and I had an abrupt moment in which I took the compliment with the gratitude it deserved. I immediately felt embarrassed and shrunk into the crowd. Why was Taona breaking revered protocol for my sake? I had not made anything of my desire to play in the festival—not enough to warrant this anyway! Now the coach was going to think I had made him say it. I looked over to Philip, who recognized the absurdity and futility of Taona's daring gesture. He just

---

[55] Excuse me!

grinned, probably creating a mental list of jokes and insults to throw my way for being left out of the team.

Before the coach could interrogate Taona further, the rest of the team ventured into a chorus of approval, much to the coach's surprise and, more spectacularly, Phillip's incredulous bewilderment. His jaw dropped, and he held the jersey tighter towards himself as if in desperate resistance.

The coach looked around, and then pensively down. There was little to choose between Phillip and me in talent and recent performance. If the team was in agreement that Shingi should play over Phillip, then there had to be a reason. He did not care to find out what it was. Besides, Taona was right, the third-choice goalkeeper—the substitute's back up—was not going to play on the day. There was no reason to mess with the team's spirit over such an inconsequential position.

"Alright. Philip, hand it over." The coach bellowed after a minute. No one—not Phillip, Taona, or I—could believe what was happening! Such was unheard of! The coach never even allowed us to speak up, let alone talk him out of decisions. Phillip reached out and handed the jersey to me in humbled surrender, all the while looking to the ground. I was so abashed by the unprecedented unfolding of events that I also looked at the ground as I received it. Everyone else made no secret of their joy for me, patting me on the back and chanting my name as we walked away. Phillip disappeared, and never returned to practice. That was the last time I saw him.

Taona and I walked together in inexplicably awkward silence and, just before I turned to go into our yard, I gathered the nerve to ask about earlier.

"*Wangu*, thank you for standing up for me earlier. It was not necessary, and I would have been fine." I said, battling to balance my excitement, embarrassment, and annoyance.

"Oh, don't mention it. You are better than him, anyway."

"No. You and I know that is not true. Why did you do it? More importantly, why did everyone else agree?"

"Let's just say you earned it more," he said with a wink. "Besides, you know how Phillip is. See you bright and early tomorrow Goalie!" He said with a snicker and clap. I had no idea what he meant, so I just laughed back and bade him farewell.

I walked into the yard and felt a mild version of the chill that I had when Gogo had died. It had only been a week, and yet the memory seemed distant. I would have usually run straight into the house to announce my good news and describe the detail. I found Nigel and Anesu sitting under the Avocado Tree, not enthused about going inside for probably the same reason as me. Nigel had been crying. I handed him a small baobab fruit I had bought on my way home, and he smashed it open in obvious anger. We ate in silence and, as we shook out the last of the powder from the fruit shell, I told them that I had made the festival team. Both congratulated me—Nigel with the listless stare of a distressed soul, and Anesu with the unbridled joy of untainted youth.

Nigel told me about Wellington's change of heart and Ta's shock inclusion in the festival team. I was happy. I wished I could find my friends right then and celebrate with them but, failed to garner enough energy to do so. I would see them the next day.

I woke up earlier than usual that Friday morning. I assume my friends did too. The sun rose with us then, for the first time since the winter had started.

Although Nigel was not playing, he was ready when I was, and we ran over to Pashena and waited for everyone else who was headed to Beit for the festival. First to join us was Wellington, dressed in a striking white t-shirt, black shorts, and white socks with two black stripes. He strutted towards Pashena with his head held higher than it would typically have been. I had never seen him dress or walk with such redoubtable confidence and swagger. He only got as far as the

Mountain and stopped. He did not want to dirty his attire before the games.

"*Ndeip* boys! Why are you up this early? Shingi, don't tell me my hundred goals past you on this old dirt field made you any better. You are not on the team, are you?" I grinned, and for a moment, he forgot about his immaculate look and rushed towards the dust and embraced me. Just then, we heard the age-old stuttering behind us.

"Ah ah. Aren't we u-u-up early? *Kwakanaka here?*"

"Shingi and I are both playing today! We should be asking you what you are doing up already?"

Ta flashed a grin identical to my earlier one. If Wellington had been surprised by my inclusion in the festival, Ta's floored him. He looked to see if I shared his amazement, and my persistent grin told him I already knew and, indeed, Ta was on the team. This time, he ran onto the street where Ta was standing and hugged him too.

"We are all here!" I said as I skipped into the street to join my friends. "Let's go!"

Ta turned around as if to head toward Beit with me, but Wellington stood still.

"Let's wait for Fungai."

"Who?"

"Fungai. He is playing today too, and he should be coming up the street in a few minutes!"

Nigel, Ta, and I looked at him, puzzled. Not only had we, in our self-indulged excitement, forgotten about Fungai, but we also would have never imagined Wellington being his advocate in a time like this! Not only had he never been fond of the backstreet and The Tennis brothers in particular, but their insults from as recently as the day before were the reason he was playing today.

Ta and I struggled to be coy with our questions, but Nigel's puerile candor blurted out on our behalf, "I thought you didn't much care for Fungai, especially after his stinging words just yesterday."

"That is true," Wellington began, again assuming a dignified tone with which we were not used to coming from him, "but think about this. When you see the Warriors running onto the field to play against Egypt or South Africa, it feels amazing for the fans and probably looks intimidating to the other team. When you see even Border Timbers at Beit, they look like heroes when they walk onto the field. Right here, when Simba and his Two Rooms friends came down the street to play us, they looked like their opponents should respect them. You think all those people like each other? The people playing for the Warriors are different races and speak different dialects and languages and, more importantly, play for enemy clubs throughout the year. Yet, on Warriors' game day, they are the Warriors..." He looked around to make sure that he still had our attention. By now, Antony and a sleepy Fox had arrived by the Mountain as well.

Wellington turned to me and continued:

"Shingi, you have—we have always said that we wanted the other Dangamvura boys to look upon us with respect—to see us as a force to compete with, right? Was that not the essence of Pashena to begin with? We may not always all like each other, and that will never change. But Strive and I will be leaving. Shingi is off to his white people school, and if all goes well today, Fungai will be off to the big city as well. Heavens know where Ta will go for high school, and I hear Babylon's family will be moving again soon to let a new pastor come in. This is the end. Today we have a chance to walk into Beit together, everyone who is playing and their friends, and show everyone that Pashena, our neighborhood, and our friendships have not been in vain."

The Tennis Brothers arrived in time for the last part of the speech. Donald, so often overlooked in conversations about Pashena and MaOwnership had shown up as well. What had started as a mere query as to why we should wait for Fungai had morphed into the rallying cry for an entire neighborhood. Fungai walked up to the front of the group and signaled for me to come and join him with a slight nod.

Soon Wellington, Ta, Donald, Fungai and I were leading the rest of the group towards Beit. Innocent joined us at the corner, our honorary MaOwnership comrade. We had been raised on absurd and deliberate shows of camaraderie and menacing in action movies and matches on T.V; it was now our turn to live out that fantasy and be the vicarious dream of our friends. We were all playing different sports and for different schools, but we were more members of the same team then than we had ever been. Such was the raw, beautiful charisma of the moment that, in the ten minutes it took us to arrive at the field, our crowd had grown to more than 30 people, all of whose excitement was now like the angry waters of a geyser in its irrepressibility.

All the racquet, bat, and individual games were to be held in the morning, while the vastly more popular netball, basketball, and football would cap the afternoon. It was an ironic, albeit logical set-up, seeing as the Prince William scouts were neither interested in neither the girls' netball nor the rudimentary basketball skills of our fledgling team, and while they would watch the football, it would be with minimum interest—seeing as football talent was ubiquitous across the country.

Wellington's table tennis game was first, and all 30 of us crowded in the tiny room, Fox and Antony standing by his side. The unprecedented deluge of fans both buoyed Wellington and panicked his opponents. One after the other, he made light work of them until there was one left; a three-year veteran of the game who had introduced the odd game to Dangamvura. As fate would have it, Antony, who had not been around long, had never heard of him, and thus had never brought him to Wellington's attention during the practice sessions. Wellington's ignorance served him well: had he known of his foe's daunting reputation, he may have been intimidated. Instead, he took to the game like he had to the earlier games and, amidst rowdy screams more reminiscent of football games than this mild-tempered sport, won. Wellington, the temper-prone, rural-bound table tennis neophyte from MaOwnership, was the first ever Prince William Festival table tennis champion.

We barely had time to pat him on the back before we had to go to Fungai's tennis game. Fox and Antony stayed with him.

After an intimate conversation in which Tiberius whispered encouragement into his ear, Fungai hopped onto the tennis court. From the first serve, it was obvious his mind was troubled. We would have noticed it earlier if all our attention had not been on Wellington. He was either bothered by the undeniable truth that he was only on the court that day due to his brother's magnanimity, or our support, which may have felt disingenuous or undeserved to him, had the opposite effect on him to what it had on Wellington. Whatever the reason, Fungai found the going tough and was eliminated from the festival after just two games. The unorthodox calm with which he accepted his defeat suggested that he had made peace with it before the games had even been played.

If the festival had already been a rollicking and massive affair, it only grew bigger after lunch. Several parents, siblings, and others in the community upon whose ears word of the festival had fallen were gathering to watch the football game. They arrived with more than an hour to go, giving the preceding basketball game an unexpected crowd. More than a hundred people, many of whom were seeing the game for the first time, gathered around to see their brothers, friends, and children try their enthusiastic hand at this new oddity.

For his harsh realism, the coach had been right about the gap in skill and experience between the Dangamvura basketball team and their city opponents. Five minutes into the game, it was obvious that, for all the heart and raw talent that Innocent and the others possessed, the other team's years in the game left them far superior. By halftime, the city team was leading by so many points that it was impossible for our team to catch up, and they were now just dribbling and showboating. There were glimpses of excellence here and there from our boys but, soon, the disillusioned fans started walking away in their dozens.

As that was happening, somebody started chanting Ta's name in certain jest. Since our team is losing, we might as well get a laugh out of it, they must have thought. Not many knew anything about Ta's skill level, but they knew Ta, and that was all they needed for a chuckle. The coach, desperate to keep the crowd, and the other players, eager for some respite for what was turning into humiliation, conceded to bring Ta on for the second half. By the time the coach turned to call him, Ta was already jumping up and down the courtside like a little boy.

"Ta! Ta! Ta!" the chants were getting louder, and to the ignorant mind, Ta was mistaking their caustic if not sadistic jeers for genuine applause. He knew better. We knew he knew better. As far as he was concerned, the chants relieved all pressure from him, allowing him to make mistakes and play the game as he wanted.

Once on the court, the crowd cheered each time he touched the ball. His initial nerves led to a few early clumsy mistakes, further fueling the jeers. Things only got worse when the other team's star, a tall light-skinned boy with curly hair unlike usually seen around Dangamvura started teasing him with the ball. He appeared to throw the ball across the court and poor Ta started to run after it, only to find that the boy still had the ball in his hand. The crowd roared in appreciation of the trickery. Poor Ta chuckled at himself and generously clapped his hands in applause to his adversary.

Soon, he was finding his stride with each touch. The coach had brought Innocent back onto the court, which turned out to be a timely boost for Ta. The crowd was less and less vocal, almost disappointed that their jester was not as pathetic as they had hoped. He even scored a few points, each shot he took better than the last. The crowd was slowly regaining their voice—only this time, it was in genuine awe of Ta and the efforts of the team.

As the game drew to a close, our boys had resigned to their heavy loss and were having some fun with the game as well now. Innocent had dribbled past two boys before passing the ball to Ta between another's legs, much to the crowd's delight. Ta founded himself face to face with his curly haired nemesis. He flashed a smile I had only ever seen once or twice before. I had seen it in crèche after he had chased off the bullies, and again when he had brought Tinashe and the others to help with the clearing of Pashena back in the day. It was a confident, menacing smile, one on whose opposite end you did not want to be. I knew the smile and so did our friends and, as soon as we saw it, we began chanting his name louder than before. The baffled crowd joined us.

What followed may be nonsensical and banal to many. It is, to this day, one of the most amazing sights I have ever seen.

Ta held the ball firmly in his hands, menacing smile on his face. He bounced it to the left and then quickly to the right. His foe was unmoved. Innocent ran down the left side of the court, screaming for Ta to pass it to him. Then he, too, stopped and smiled. By now, I was screaming my heart out from the stands, with the faith-induced glee of a child unwrapping a poorly wrapped present. Ta stepped to the left and moved as if to pass the ball to Innocent. The curly-haired boy moved towards Innocent. Except Innocent did not have the ball. He must have passed it to someone else, the boy concluded. He turned around, giving his back to Ta. Ta, who had only pretended to pass it, then bounced the ball playfully against the back of the other boy's head and, as soon as it bounced back into his hands, shot it towards the hoop. He scored.

The crowd, already in full swing, lost their senses. For all my civility, I charged onto the court to hug my friend, disregarding the still on-going game. It did not matter anyway—all my friends followed me onto the court. So did the rest of the crowd, which had since grown back to the hundreds amidst all the cheers. It was now Ta's turn to be hoisted over the heads of everyone.

There were still ten minutes left in the game. Our team was still losing 50-80. It did not matter. Poetic justice! Ta—our beloved stuttering, clumsy Ta—had just served the curly-haired, three-year veteran of the game a bitter taste of his own tricky medicine. They did not even bother to restart the game, having seen it all.

I have been proud of the people I love time and again since then, and usually for way more significant feats. I have seen my friends play football for the national team and watched my little sister graduate from University. I have seen my insufferable friend marry the prettiest woman, and my barely literate friend operate the very coffee shop in which most of this story was written. In all this, Ta's "trickery and shot" moment is the standard upon which I compare my uninhibited elation at the success of someone else. I may never sufficiently explain it, and you may never understand it. It just is.

By the time the football game came just before dusk, the festival had already outlived its billing in both fanfare and attendance. The stands around the football field were full, buzzing with the anticipation of more than a thousand people gathered to see their children do battle. The coach gathered us around and screamed a few instructions over the roar of the multitudes. His words would not have mattered anyway; the energy emanating from the crowd was all the fuel we needed. As soon as he yelled 'Go!" we charged towards the field, the team dressed in the time-honored green and white jerseys that all our local heroes had donned since we could remember: not replicas, but the very same ones. Many of those heroes now sat in the stands, watching us run onto the field. Taona wore the multi-colored "number one" jersey that the current Buffaloes goalkeeper had worn nine years earlier, and I the blue with yellow stripes that I had salivated over since grade one.

As we ran around the field doing light exercises and taking practice shots, we looked around at each other in recognition of the surrealness of the moment. The crowd's roar was deafening, and the game had not even started.

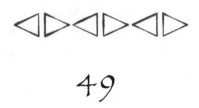

49

The day I moved to Harare was a remarkably bland day. Mother had arrived in Dangamvura earlier that December to the miserable sight of Kulu and Baba Nigel clearing the planting ground apathetically. It was not the same. We greeted her with ambiguous embraces. A week later, the cousins also descended upon the lifeless homestead. They brought with them presents and good cheer: a pathetic attempt to recapture the Christmas spirit that Gogo had embodied.

When the excitement of the festival died down, we were all forced to come to terms with the reality that faced us: nothing was ever going to be the same. Sincere was dead. Gogo was gone. Chips was gone. Soon, Wellington and Fox would be gone, as would I and possibly the other grade sevens if they would be accepted into mission schools.

It was that recognition that led to Pashena's ultimate renaissance. The August holidays were fleeting by with the vicious spring winds while we sat under Avocado and Guava Trees, captive to an unknown future. Anesu and the other younger boys were frequenting Pashena, either in an attempt to replicate the glorious times lived by their brothers or to entice said brothers back for one more run-around. We just smiled and cheered occasionally—an unceremonious passing of the torch.

Two weeks after Gogo died, Nigel and I began to fight. We had always fought here and there, but it now seemed everything the other did aggravated the other to the point of exchanging blows. Admittedly, I was the overwhelming aggressor. One day, a fight had gotten out of hand, and he hurled a glass at me. He missed, but the incident frightened and annoyed his mother so much that she had, after administering a resounding beating on both of us, banished us to play outside for the rest of the week.

Nigel came outside and saw me sitting by the rock under the Avocado Tree. Still fuming from the fight and subsequent punishment, he walked right past me and toward Pashena, where his little brother Anesu was kicking around with a few other young boys. Once they saw him, they cheered and passed him the ball and, soon, they were having a jolly time much like we had in early Pashena days.

I watched them for a while, a forlorn figure, from the lonely rock upon which I sat. Nigel was now as old as we had been when Pashena started. Anesu was now as old as Nigel was then. Maybe there was nothing apocalyptic about us leaving. We leave so others can feast from the table upon which we have indulged ourselves. We leave so we can see what other feasts others have left for us elsewhere. My eyes were, as they often were lately, brimful with tears. As I gazed wistfully, I heard Anesu calling out to me. The ball had rolled under the fence into the yard. I picked it up and prepared to throw it back to them.

I decided against it.

Without thinking any further, I found myself running towards the old field. I crawled in between the barbed wires like Nigel always did and ran towards the goalposts as I had done in early days. Nigel, my temporarily estranged cousin, smiled at me, turned around to the younger boys and yelled out, "It's Shingi from the school team, everyone! Let's see if he is any good!" The boys were flung into a frenzy, and Nigel and I chuckled. Although I never actually played in the festival, the mere sight of me running onto the field in that revered blue and yellow shirt had deified me in the eyes of the younger boys. Babylon, a peripheral figure in MaOwnership since he started high school, heard the furor from his house and peeped through the window. I saw him and gestured for him to join us and, to my surprise, he did. Ta and Fungai joined us later that afternoon and, by the weekend, Pashena was back to its vibrant self. Even Gandanga and Innocent, our adopted Pashena brothers, came back.

The new lease on life would be short-lived, but not before being immortalized in a most unexpected way.

After his heroics at the festival, Wellington enjoyed a brief moment of glory among us but soon had to come to terms with his pending relocation to the rural area. Both he and his brother loitered around the neighborhood like ghosts condemned to hell, unequivocally awaiting the dreaded day of reckoning. Even when they joined us at Pashena, we could tell they were doing their best to partake in the levity, and yet the reality of their situation always brought them back to sadness.

Then one day, the week before the third school term started and two before they were supposed to move, Wellington ran onto Pashena—where the rest of us were playing—and pounced on an unsuspecting Antony, knocking him to the ground. I hastened towards them, thinking that Wellington's intent was malicious. As I drew closer, I saw that he was laughing gleefully. He got up from his shell-shocked friend and, once they were both standing, hugged him and began to sob loudly and uttering unintelligible gratitude.

We were still trying to figure out the cause of Wellington's uncontrollable elation when Fox came onto the field holding a piece of paper in his hand, also smiling like we had not seen in years. All eyes fixed on him, he read aloud:

Prince William High School

Dear Wellington

It was our pleasure meeting you at the Prince William Festival in Dangamvura last month. In light of your exploits in the table tennis tournament, you have been selected as the recipient of our prestigious student athlete scholarship…

We did not hear anything beyond that point. Every single one of us, even the younger ones who probably knew neither what scholarship meant nor the gravity of this particular one, started jumping around in place and around Wellington as if we had received good news ourselves. We had.

"Wa-wa-wait. So, what does this mean?"

"With all the money they are talking about, I will be able to move to Harare for boarding school, with some left over for Strive to finish high school without moving to Birchenough!"

Fox, who up to now had just been overwhelmed by his brother's fortune, also began to cry. He had been left the burden of caring for his little brother and, since his sister died, had not once thought on his own fate. Now hearing his little brother declare, in certain terms, that he had seen the fear and bravado in his brother's eyes as they faced a bleak forever and that, by fate, he had stumbled on their way out of hell, was more than Fox could bear.

"No brother," he said, struggling to speak over the steady stream of tears, "This is your money. This is all you."

Wellington sucked his teeth, "What would mother and father say, hearing you talk like that, huh. What would big sister say?"

Fox said no more at the mention of their dear departed. He just cried silently and embraced his brother. After Antony, it was Fungai who came up to Wellington first and hugged him in genuine congratulations. Through the corner of my eye, I saw Fox nod his head at Antony. Antony smiled and nodded back.

The following week, the city council people who had inspected Pashena and spoken to Gogo and the Pastor the previous month came back while we were playing. They went and spoke to the Pastor again, Kulu, and the several people in the houses surrounding the field. When they came back to the field, they delivered the news that none of us had ever thought we would hear: they were going to build a house on our sacred ground. They must have known, or maybe the parents had told them, the invaluable importance of the field to us because they delivered the message stoically and curtly. They said they would be back the following week to start digging and rushed to leave.

We stood around in stunned silence. Ta, Fox, Fungai, Antony, and I walked over to The Mountain—where it had all started. We sat solemnly for a while, paying respects to the spirit of our childhood days. Finally, Fox started laughing that cynical cackle upon which we had been raised.

"Hahaha, which one of you old-timers remembers that 'King of the Mountain' game we used to play? I was always King!"

"Oh, shut up!" Fungai retorted playfully. "You front-street boys were lucky only a few of us ever came out to play."

Thus, the reminiscing began. Soon, those who had not been there, in the beginning, felt left out, until Wellington said, "How about the first time we ever met Babylon? An odd pastor's child!" and then the entire story of Pashena was retold.

The following week, men from the council descended upon our quaint neighborhood brandishing picks, hoes, and shovels. It resembled the sight of us at the creation of Pashena, except that where we had come to build and add to MaOwnership, they had come to dispossess.

From the nostalgic comfort of the shade or summits of The Guava Tree, we watched the hell-sent men dismantle our Beloved. We watched them day after day with the masochistic fascination with which folks watch car accidents and horror movies. We watched the monstrous machine pick up and crash the boulders that had been our Mountain. We saw the men's unrelenting picks make a tattered and ravaged landscape out of the dusty patch upon which he had grown up. We spoke little, our eyes fixated on our demise.

A week into the dig, the men came upon an odd find—locked boxes that resembled treasure chests from the cartoons. By the evening, they had dug up all of six boxes, each looking as if it had been there for decades. It was an incredible sight whose mystique was heightened by the workmen's childlike puzzlement. Always inquisitive, Nigel ran up to them and battered them with a million questions about what they thought it could be. Out of sheer annoyance, they promised to tell him the next day after they opened them.

None among us, except maybe Ta, would have anticipated what the verdict on the content of the boxes would have been. Because the men refused to tell us what they had found, choosing instead to go again to the parents around Pashena, we assumed that it was far more disconcerting than even they had anticipated.

They found bones in the boxes. Human skeletons.

As it turned out, Pashena stood on what had been a small burial ground at the height of the Chimurenga War in the 1960s and 70s. After independence, and as the community and bureaucracy had changed and changed again, that seemingly important detail was buried underneath paperwork and repressed memories. All that had remained for the last two decades was an unexplained directive that nobody was to build atop the old field. As the years passed, questions regarding the directive had grown louder and louder and, finally, the city council gave in and unwittingly dug up the long-sleeping bones.

The parents of MaOwnership were mortified. They had, season upon season, feasted on the fruits of the burial ground and their children plundered over it with their tiny unapologetic feet. Oh, to have desecrated the resting place of those souls! The only person seeming to get any morbid satisfaction from this ghastly affair was Ta, who had probably stumbled upon rumors of the graveyard when he was still little and had since raved about the dead people under Pashena.

"See? Re-re-remember I told you! Shingi, Fox, you were there! Who e-else? Nigel, Babylon, remember I always told you? What did you say? Ta doesn't know what he is talking about! Now look haha. Who, who sounds silly now?"

"It is a most weird thing," Fox responded, gazing into space, "that the story of Pashena should end in this way. The dirt football field upon which we have grown up was never going to be taken and converted into some miserable house without making a lasting impression, huh. We will soon be forgotten as new people move into the neighborhood and the younger boys grow, but people will always remember Pashena, the timeless field that gave life to so many while she kept safe the dead that lay beneath her."

Fungai gazed into the same space that Fox was, and remarked with careless profundity, "Death has been unusually with us this year, has it not? Odd timing, too, as if life is conspiring to cleanse MaOwnership of everything old before the year 2000 comes around."

Uninformed and puerile our theories on death may have been, but the Grim Reaper's scythe would visit Pashena once more before Christmas.

That year, Gandanga did not receive a big box of action movies or a superstar's football jersey. His father's tour of duty had been supposed to end that winter, around the same time as the festival. When he did not come back just then, everyone figured it was due to bureaucratic delays and other complexities of war that every Zimbabwean was, by now, becoming well-adjusted to. As the months had passed and whispers of atrocities occurring in the DRC started seeping into the local news and rumor-mill, we began to get worried.

With three days left before Christmas, soldiers from the barracks knocked solemnly on our door and asked to speak to Kulu. They had brought with them the sad news of Baba Gandanga's horrific death at the hands of a grenade attack on the outskirts of Kinshasa. Seven men had died in that attack. Baba Gandanga held on long enough to tell the surviving men not to tell his wife and children about his fate themselves and, instead, find my grandfather and ask him to deliver the message on their behalf.

Over the years, Kulu had only ever been honored each time he reprised his role as the revered community father upon whose shoulders such burdens often landed. For the first time, as he listened to the soldiers, I saw in him a weariness I had never before seen. He hung his head and did not make eye-contact with them as they spoke. Once they were done, he rose stoically and announced:

"Well then, we must go tell Mai Priscilla. Shingi and Nigel, come and be with your friend."

We jumped into the back of Kulu's car, not entirely sure of the purpose of our attendance. As we drove off, my mother and aunts were already beginning to stifle their tears, lest they be too loud, and the word spread before Kulu had the chance to tell the family himself.

We walked into Gandanga's yard and felt the increasingly familiar chill. We stood close to the gate while Kulu and two soldiers, who had followed us, walked up to the house. Mai Priscilla must have seen them through the window, for she dashed out of the house, her hands still wet and foamy from laundry. She must have felt the chill too, for even before Kulu said a word, she had thrown herself onto the ground and was writhing and weeping so loud that her neighbors all came out and ran to the house. Amidst the unintelligible mourning, it was obvious to everyone that the worst had happened. I saw Gandanga peeping through the window, and then he shut the curtains. He did not come outside.

That year's Christmas is the most pathetic and somber attempt at festivity I have, to this day, endured. If it had been potentially upsetting at the beginning of the holidays, the news about Gandanga's father had guaranteed the spirit of gloom a seat at our feasting table. After the burial on the morning of Christmas Eve, everyone made haste to rescue what joy may have been left in their Christmas plans. My aunts pulled together the little joy and strength they had left to prepare a decent Christmas meal and, after we had all attended a joyless mass at church, we attempted to recapture the atmosphere of the years gone by. It was an impossible feat, especially with the matriarchal chair that now sat empty at the head of the table. We all ate in silence and haste, each one desperate to leave the table. By the time I was able to escape the deathly ambiance and go outside, Nigel's father was already smoking a cigarette by the chicken shed. My other uncle was making his way up the street to the tavern. I sat under the Avocado Tree and waited for the cousins to come and bother me.

The day I left for Harare was a remarkably bland day. It was two days after Christmas and mother, both disillusioned by the listless season and in a rush to get across the country for an end-of-year church conference, decided it best to leave then.

We sat down with Kulu—Mother and I did—to bid farewell. He was weary, and thus decided to combine his annual New Year's blessing to the family and all the farewells—even though my cousins would stay a few more days.

"I have been on earth a long, long time. I have traveled and sat in the counsel of many a man. I have read the scriptures through and through and, in all that, all wisdom fails to account for the trying year we have been through. You spend your life doing right by everyone and the good that has been taught to you, yet the lots of life fall where they may. Our strength has always lain in our commitment to doing right, being generous and standing by each other as a family; never has that ancient creed been more necessary and applicable than right now. As we leave and chase what dreams our hearts may desire, let us never forget the people and values that have brought us here.

Mai Shingi, be safe on the roads. Back when we learned how to drive, the instructors would always ask, "What is the most dangerous kilometer on your journey?" and we would all be stumped. Some would say it is the last one before you get home, and some would say Pa Christmas Pass and other landmarks. The answer, we found out, was "the kilometer immediately ahead of you." Remember that as you drive, and remember that as you live.

Make sure the child comes back to see the others; visit Gogo and me once in a while. Travel well, and Mother Mary and Saint Christopher travel with you."

I leaned over and hugged my grandfather and bade him farewell, before making my quick escape to avoid the inevitable deluge of tears that had already started between my mother and aunts.

I leaned by the fence that separated us from Ta's family and called for him.

"He is not here," his sister Kuziwa said. "You know how he spends all his days at the basketball court now!"

Kuziwa.

She was all grown up now! When had this happened? I had been too busy with Pashena and hamsters to notice her or any of the other girls who had lived alongside us in MaOwnership.

I bade her farewell, turned to the other fence and yelled for Babylon.

"Alright, *wangu*. I should be leaving anytime now!"

"It has been wonderful knowing you, blaz. If I never see—"

"No don't say that, Blessing! I will be back every exeat[56] weekend and holidays."

"I know, but you know how a pastor's life is. I have a feeling that, very soon, they will be making us move again."

"Aah," I said with resigned sadness. "Well I hope to see you again sometime. MaOwnership has been good to us."

I hugged him and began to walk away. I was finding the goodbyes harder than I had anticipated, and yet I had made a commitment to share them with every one of my friends that I could reach on the day. I was painstakingly making my way towards Fox and Wellington's when my masochistic courtesy endeavor was fortunately cut short by my mother's calls. She was ready to leave, and in shameful

---

56 Long weekends that students are allocated to mark the halfway point of the school term

relief, I dashed towards her. After another tearful round of embraces with Kulu and everyone, my mother finally drove off.

"See you in Harare, blaz! And you two, see you pa exeat!" I yelled to The Guava Tree where Wellington, Fox, and Antony sat. They waved back and went back to their guavas. Fox was probably mesmerizing the others with a fantastic story again. I would definitely miss him. I wonder if I would find storytellers of his kind in Harare? Do the white boys tell stories like this too? Maybe they sit under guava trees as well. One thing is for sure though; it would be impossible to duplicate MaOwnership, Pashena, and the odd set of characters that populated both. No more street rivalries or dogs running into people, no chess club with Innocent and buying Cokes at Old Man Chimutondo's house.

I tried to look away from my friends, only for my eyes to land on the ravaged, coffin-extracted terrain that used to be Pashena, a decidedly more saddening sight.

Eager as I was to leave the misery of an elongated farewell to everything I had ever known, I had one more stop to make. My mother pulled up next to the Beit basketball courts, where Innocent and Ta were going through their paces. Sensing that this moment was probably more sentimental than the other goodbyes, she took from her bag a camera, and handed it to me.

"*Ndeipi*, Boys!" I yelled with affected enthusiasm.

"*Hapana apa.* Just preparing for the New Year's Eve tournament in the city."

"So... thi-thi-this is it, huh? Shi-Shi-Shingi is is a Harare boy now!"

We all chuckled, doing our best not to cry at the moment. I called them both to my side and attempted to take a photograph of all three of us. Upon seeing this Njonjonjo, the player who had been kicked off the festival team ran up and offered to take the picture for us.

We posed, then watched him fiddle with the camera for a few minutes before he called out, "I don't know if I am doing anything wrong, but I think the battery is dead."

I stormed over to where he stood, anxious not to keep my mother waiting and annoyed at what I thought were certain shenanigans on Njonjonjo's part. The battery was, indeed, dead.

"Aah *nhai*! We forgot to charge it last night!" I said, sad tears now compounded by the frustration of not being able to take the photograph. We stood for a few seconds and looked at each other awkwardly, before the coach barked, "Innocent! Takura! We don't have all day here!"

We shared a quick embrace, and they jogged back to join the rest of the team. I walked slowly back up the little hill to where mother had parked, swinging the disheartening camera's pouch with my hand.

"Did you see them? Let's see the picture!"

"Yes, I did, but the camera wouldn't work. The damn camera wouldn't work!" I screamed as I looked out the car window, the weight of the moment getting the better of me. My mother began to admonish me for my outburst and choice of language, but stopped herself when she saw me bury my head in shame, anger, and sadness under the flood of tears that I could no longer hold back. She let it be for a few minutes before she finally spoke in a sad yet almost prophetic tone.

"Well, maybe it is good that you were not able to take that picture. Now, you have something to look forward to when you come back."

She made no sense. I was off to Harare and, even though I would see most of my friends again, we were not going to be the same hereafter. Due to his mother's relentless cross-border enterprising, Ta would be going back to his old school—the city one with the blazers. He could not have been any prouder than he was on the day his mother gave him the acceptance letter. She had received it and hidden it from him while she bought him a new blazer. He was starting to get worried, as other students who had applied to the same school had already heard back from the school. Then one day, he returned from basketball practice to see the revered blazer hanging on his door. Baffled, he shook the blazer excitedly and out fell the letter. Still incredulous, he turned around to see his mother and sister standing behind him, smiling.

Innocent would be going to one of the local high schools and, although there was little repute to go with it, he was excited because a new basketball program was starting at the school and the coach had already spoken to him about being their first ever captain.

Maybe mother was right. The story of childhood was not meant to be captured in iconoclastic photographs. We were not meant to freeze the moments draped in sadness. Would it not be more gratifying to capture the reunions and other celebrations to come?

My uncle, Nigel's father, had finally got the urban teaching job he had long desired—at the high school Innocent would be attending! That meant Nigel, Anesu and their mother would have their own home in the city now.

Things were going to be unrecognizable when I come back. I wonder how long this basketball obsession will last. Football will still be here. Tinashe is going to be a school legend in a few years if he keeps going the way he is. He will be the first real Pashena star! Nigel might as well. I do not doubt that Anesu will go down as one of the best goalkeepers the area has seen—far better than Taona and me.

The backstreet and front-street divide was a hatchet now buried. At least, my sadness did not know the difference. The backstreet was so ingrained in the essence of my childhood that it was indistinguishable from the street on which I had grown. Babylon would surely be gone when I returned. I would miss his spirited, though often annoying, presence. The Tennis Brothers were no more; we had come to know Fungai and Tiberius for who they were as brothers and individuals. Nothing spoke to how we had grown as boys and friends than how those two had changed over the years. Fungai had not gone back to tennis after the festival—I wonder what he would get into now that he was headed to high school as well?

What shall become of my poor cousin Gandanga without his beloved father? His mother was loving and hard-working, and, if Ta's situation was anything to go by, that seemed to be essential in overcoming such loss. He will be fine once the veil of sadness and loss lifts.

I envisioned Wellington at Prince William—what a sight! Not a single one of us would have foreseen this turn of events just half a year ago. To think about it, none of us could have foreseen any of the momentous events we had witnessed mere weeks before they had happened: Antony's return, Gogo's passing, the rejuvenation of our relationship with Gandanga, and our fortunes before and after the festival. The very rise and fall of Pashena seemed the design of the supernatural.

Oh, Pashena! I thought back to the first goal that I had scored—the one that hit the crossbar before going in. A smile spread across my face. Mother must have seen it.

"What has delighted you so, *mwanangu?*"

I snapped out of my daydream. We had been on the road for almost an hour and had already left Mutare.

"Oh, I was just thinking about my friends," I said, still smiling. We still had another three hours before Harare.

"I bet you have many great memories from MaOwnership, huh?" she asked, her eyes twinkling like only a mother's can at the sight of their child in euphoria.

I smiled a while longer. Then I told her the story.

About the Author

Shingi Mavima

is a doctoral candidate in the African American and African Studies program at Michigan State University, with a dissertation focus on Pan-Africanism and Nationalism in Southern Africa. Mavima graduated from Grand Valley State University with a Bachelor of Arts in International Relations and a Master of International Affairs from Penn State.

As a native of Zimbabwe, Mavima also serves as co-founder and current director of CLUBHOUSE International, a community-based organization working with school children in Mutare, Zimbabwe through mentorship, community service, and extracurricular activities.

Mavima is a student member of the National Council for Black Studies, as well as a member of the Alumni Network of Sigma Lambda Beta International Fraternity Inc.

CPSIA information can be obtained
at www.ICGtesting.com
Printed in the USA
LVHW030405190221
679455LV00017B/747